D1249065

THE
FAST GOURMET
COOKBOOK

Poppy Cannon

AWARD BOOKS
NEW YORK

TANDEM BOOKS
LONDON

SECOND AWARD PRINTING 1969

Grateful acknowledgements and thanks to all who have shared their swift epicurean inspirations; to *Harper's Bazaar* and to *Continental Magazine* for permission to reprint material which appeared there first; and to General Features Syndicate.

AWARD BOOKS are published by
Universal Publishing and Distributing Corporation
235 East Forty-fifth Street, New York, N. Y. 10017

TANDEM BOOKS are published by
Universal-Tandem Publishing Company Limited
14 Gloucester Road, London SW7, England

Manufactured in the United States of America

CONTENTS

This book is for my editor Camille Bourgeois who inspired, encouraged and godmothered The Fast Gourmet . . . both the column syndicated by General Features and the book.

FOREWORD

NO UNICORN MEAT

In the official publication of the world-wide Wine and Food Society, published in London, Robert J. Misch writes, "How interesting it is—the truly erudite in the culinary world do not go in for long and complicated recipes or dishes of laborious preparation. Take Poppy Cannon, renowned food writer, world traveler, good friend and beautiful woman! Her tastes are uniformly simple, except for bouillabaisse. This latter confounds her. She cannot decide whether the best is at La Porquirolle on the Left Bank in Paris, served in hollowed cork vessels, at Aux Cosaques in Villefranche or in Mother Marseilles en face le chateau d'If. A puzzlement.

"Asked about her favorite foods in the world, Poppy couldn't decide . . . a tart, crisp Rome apple, picked off the ground under its own tree, stone cold and so filled with juices that it gushes all over your face; a mango in Egypt; snails no bigger than peas in Haiti; oak-smoked salmon served on an oaken plate at Shannon; a practically unborn so-new pickle, Kosher dill from a delicatessen on White Street in Danbury, Connecticut; bread and Feta cheese with purple-red Calamara olives in Greece; those yellow-brownish and wan-greenish tree-ripened olives from California; wild asparagus, barely wilted by heat at Alice Toklas's Cinquencento table, with nut brown butter and crumbs; and in that moment of truth when really hungry, a hamburger!

"Notice, no infusions of sea-nymphs and unicorn meat —no 24 hour cooking—no marinating from Christmas to Twelfth Night. The more people know the simpler it seems. Estimable as the new found interest in food may

9

be, gourmetism is becoming, to my view, a bit preten-
tious, a bit over-blown and over-done."

He adds this footnote: "Poppy Cannon's latest, *Fast
Gourmet Cookbook*, may prove a tasty and effective anti-
dote to the growing cult of too-much of a muchness.
Blithe, often erudite, sometimes unconventional, but always swift and practical, she shows the way to a simpler, happier type of gastronomical achievement."

—*Camille Bourgeois*

INTRODUCTION

HOW FAST CAN A GOURMET BE?

What do you mean fast . . . what do you mean gourmet?

It is a fair question. It is in fact two fair questions. The first shall be last to be answered.

A gourmet is—well, perhaps it would be easier to say what a gourmet is *not*. A gourmet, to our way of thinking, is *not* necessarily addicted to rich sauces, to caviar and cooking with herbs—preferably esoteric.

A gourmet is *not* necessarily nourished on hot house grapes, fruits out of season and foods with unpronounceable names from foreign lands.

A gourmet, putting it in the simplest terms, is one who does understand and enjoy the pleasures of eating. A radish, pulled from the moist dark earth on a late spring day, brushed clean of loam and munched dreamily out of hand, can be a treasured gourmet treat. So can a slice of fresh homebaked bread.

Those tiny wild strawberries of the woods flown from Paris once a year by a New York department store have not one tenth the gourmet allure—to a true gourmet, that is—as a little crock of your own fresh homemade butter churned up in 60 seconds in the blender.

True gourmets are without pretension. They judge each morsel honestly, fairly, without preconceived notions and prejudices—giving to each dish its due.

So much for the gourmet. What makes a gourmet fast?

For practical purposes in this book and in the syndicated Fast Gourmet newspaper columns we have made the stipulation that no dish should require more than half an hour to cook.

In a few instances, with apologies, we have suggested

11

periods of mellowing, marinating, chilling and occasionally rising and resting. But these instances are infrequent. Generally it is half an hour or less from start to finish.

What has surprised us in our search for such half-hour triumphs is not the difficulty of finding them, but the dazzling number and variety that fit naturally or can, with relatively slight changes, be made to conform to the thirty-minute limit.

Processed foods are, of course, the key to many of them. So are such things as pre-washed spinach and cabbage in shiny little bags all cut for slaw. The electric blender is a magic-worker, producing Mousse Chocolate, hollandaise and bearnaise, mayonnaise and maltaise sauce, almost as fast as Aladdin could rub a lamp. There is also the pressure cooker. Judiciously used, it is a wondrous tool although it suffers from a stodgy reputation.

INSTANT ELEGANCE

With the scalpel candor allowed only to a Best Friend, mine said, accusingly, " 'High priestess of the practical' that's what *Life* called you—charging off to free all woman drudges with a can opener. Now look what you've come to . . . making your own stock, churning your own butter, baking bread—and finger bowls! Have you completely reverted, retracted?"

Not at all. I refuse to cry *mea culpa,* even with my fingers crossed. I believe now, just as I did ten years ago, that it is possible, given the right attitude, to achieve some fairly *haute cuisine* through the sophisticated use of processed foods—canned, frozen, dehydrated, brown 'n serve.

Still, perhaps it is retribution that I should be the one to wail: Please world, you've gone too far! Couldn't-care-less has become a cult. Not for what it achieves, but for its own sake, the shortcut is king. And the sorry difference between casual and careless, informality and indolence, is unrecognized. It is my hope that the FAST GOURMET may help to dispel some of the confusion.

No one denies that life is real, earnest and difficult, that help is scarce and time fleeting. Nevertheless we must insist that coping means caring not less but more. Elegance which transmutes the dross of dullness carries no price tag; and it can be achieved, in many instances, in a very few minutes. As for the homemade stock, fresh butter, new bread, the finger bowls, the service plates, the scented hot towels—these call for cheeringly meager investments of time, money and effort. The reward is grace.

Service Plates and Finger Bowls

Maidless hostesses have routed the service plates and the finger bowls: "Nobody uses *them* anymore." They should. Particularly when you are your own maitre d'hotel, chef and butler, the service plate has a definite function. It sets the stage and provides a background for the first course, which can be waiting when the guests appear. Even more important, the service plate allows you to keep your dinner plates really hot, or wonderfully chilled, as your menu dictates.

Finger bowls are—or should be—the delight of the do-it-all hostess. There is no easier or more charming effect than an array of finger bowls set on dessert plates, flanked by the requisite spoon and fork. Older etiquette required a doily; more avant-garde is a grape leaf or a calyx. In winter, the water, which should stand somewhat less than an inch high in the bowl, may be room temperature: in summer it should be frosty, with an ice cube a-clinking—why not? *Never* a slice of lemon in the bowl, for this belongs to the commercial fish house. Float a delicate leaf—as of mint, lemon-verbena, borage or burnet—a rose petal, a tiny flower. Or you can drop in interesting small shells, or bits of obsidian, agate, or amber. Droplets in the water of such fragrance as you might use on the towels—not heavy or musky, but spicy, fresh—are fit companions for food.

News On Napkins

Just as practical as the ubiquitous paper napkin, no more expensive and almost as easy, if you have an automatic laundry on the premises, are terry-cloth fingertip towels. These come in white as well as a spectrum of heady colors. They are lovely to the touch, blissfully sturdy and never need ironing.

When serving lobster or other "finger" foods, have the towels dipped in hot water scented with lime or lemon extract, cologne, with orange-flower water, rose water or an extract of roses. In hot weather the water may be icy cold. Take care the towels are not dripping and that they look smooth. Steamy or iced, they can be readied ahead of time: the hot towels kept in a warming oven; the chilled, in the refrigerator.

The Great Unwashed Wooden

In what would seem to be the most promising places— certainly the otherwise most fastidious homes and restaurants, you find The Great Unwashed Wooden. Salad bowl, I mean—wooden by the decree of some nameless, ancient and thoroughly pernicious dictator of decorum— sticky from bygone oils, redolent of garlic long deceased. It is in the nature of an outrage to submit fresh greens of spring, virgin oil and delicate vinegar to so rancid a trough. The French have been carelessly accused. But they use pottery, china or opaque glass (clear glass becomes unpleasantly smudged by oils). Those who may be bowl-proud, in thrall to their teak or Haitian mahogany, will find other uses for the wooden salad bowl: pile it high with breads for buffets; fill it with ice and raw vegetables or leaves and fruits. In any case, wash it!

Ease and Elegance

Ease is not always the sworn enemy of elegance; sometimes it is its handmaiden—as when you cook a ragout, later freeze, and subsequently reheat and serve it all in the same flame-to-oven-to-freezer-and-back vessel.

Or when you store perhaps half a dozen glasses in the refrigerator for the iciest of Martinis.

Or let the dinner plates and the coffee cups, along with two or three of the serving dishes, rest between meals in the warming oven. Any oven, even a table-top oven, becomes a warming oven when set at 180 degrees— Voilà!

THE ONE-FOR-ALL GLASS

In our headlong lunge to reduce everything to its lowest common denominator, the canard has been perpetrated that the glass doesn't matter. Obviously, any wine can be gulped from any mug, but, like a jewel, it cannot be properly appreciated except in its proper setting. Only in the right glass will it wholly delight, not just the tongue, but the eye, the nose and even the ear (the clink of crystal).

To the wine-wise, most glasses in most pantries, and in all but a handful of superior restaurants, are an anathema: wrong shape, wrong size. Conscientious householders still cling despairingly to the classic edict that different glasses should be provided for white wines and red, for Burgundy, Bordeaux, for Champagnes, cocktails, sherry and port. Feebly, they try to comply: the result is usually a mishmash or a menace. Others brazen the situation out with tumblers.

Take heart. There is a glass that is all things to all drinks, practically and esthetically. This is an eight-ounce crystal goblet slightly tapered at the top, so that the bouquet is held and the nose pleasured. With table wines—white, rosé or red—you fill it only half full; with Champagne, a little less than half; with sherry and port, only about a third. For Cognac and liqueurs, you use it as you would a brandy snifter, pouring into the bottom only about a jigger, three tablespoons. Furthermore, this obliging goblet makes a perfect cocktail glass for singles or doubles, or for any drink on the rocks. It is a new high fashion for old-fashioneds. Even for highballs—Scotch and soda, bourbon and branch water, gin or vodka and tonic—this glass is fine. It is excellent also for beer and ale; two of these glasses can be filled from a twelve-ounce bottle. As any beer connoisseur will tell you, it is best to pour portions that can be quickly quaffed since beer loses its head and changes its flavor when it stands.

At first glance, this goblet may impress you as small. In truth, it is larger than the traditional straight-sided highball glass, which holds six ounces, and as large as an ordinary water tumbler, which generally holds eight. The stem has the advantage of sparing your fingers being chilled by the drink, and the drink losing its chill from your fingers. A number of firms make such an eight-ounce all-purpose glass. Sometimes it is called a claret. At Baccarat and Tiffany, in the department stores, even in some of the larger Woolworth's and Kress's, you will find it. (In a pinch, you can even use one instead of a standard measuring cup.)

WINE AND THE FAST GOURMET

The mores of this new era of instant elegance dictate that whenever a meal is served for joy and socialability —and not just nourishment—wine is imperative. Wine makes an OCCASION. It is in many cases the easiest, quickest (and it can be a most inexpensive) way to lift a mere meal into the memorable category.

In wine too the rules have been changed. A generation ago the choice of the right wine to serve with each course and almost every dish was clearly defined even though it might not be widely known. Any one with any pretensions to vinous sophistication was aware that a dry sherry or Madeira should be served with the soup. A dry white wine accompanied fish. With red meats you must, on pain of banishment from gourmet circles, serve a red wine. With white meats, only a white wine could be permitted. What one did about a bird like chicken or turkey sporting dark and light meats—was never, in the tomes of these times, definitely explained.

The proper mating of wines and foods is the most fascinating game in the world. There are many rules . . . most of them designed to be broken.

Although red meats, roast beef and steak do seem to have a glorious affinity for the full-bodied red wines of Burgundy and Bordeaux you will find that in Germany, Alsace and in Vienna, too, beef is regularly served with a robust white wine.

Certain kinds of fish like salmon steaks and swordfish go well with certain red wines. Foods with a great deal of flavor require a wine that can stand up to them. On the other hand, foods with delicate flavors find their soul-mates in lighter, subtler wines.

Certain foods fight with wines. Curry is definitely quarrelsome unless it is quite mild. Sweet and sour dishes can ruin the taste of a wine and so can vinegary salad dressings. If you are particularly proud of the wine at your little dinner party make your salad dressing with lemon juice or serve raw vegetables without dressing.

There is one rule that is practically never broken with impunity. Never serve a sweet wine with any course except dessert.

The proper temperature of wine is another matter that causes confusion. Red wines should be served at room temperature, we are told. White wine should be chilled. But a red wine served on a warm day at a temperature of 75 degrees tastes heavy and cloying. And even the finest white wine loses most of its fragrance and much of its flavor if it is icy.

Obviously, the old rules need some modernizing. Room temperature is fine if you are referring to the temperature in the dining room of an old stone chateau or an English country house at almost any season of the year . . . about 68 degrees, at most 70.

White wines are lovely when they are cool as they might be in an ice bucket. Even Champagne is best when the temperature is between 40 and 45 degrees. The better the wine, and this goes for still white wine as well as Champagne—the more careful you should be to avoid excessive chilling. If a wine is not so special serve it very, very, very cold.

Great wines are for great moments. The grand wines of vintage years deserve the most ceremonious treatment. They are not necessary, nor are they even appropriate, for even the sit-down buffets we advocate. The stylish thing right now seems to be discovering and serving "small wines of the land" . . . like the good little California or New York State that comes in a gallon or half gallon jug. Generally these are served in decanters which are set on the buffet or on individual tables.

BEEF: BURGERS TO FILET

BEEF

⊷⧆⊶

When time is important, beef is the meat that comes first to mind. Hamburgers . . . steaks?! But these are neither the beginning nor the end.

One of the major breakthroughs in the field of Fast Gourmet cookery is the discovery—pioneered by chefs —that steak-type, quick-cooking cuts of beef like sirloin and tenderloin may be transformed in a few minutes into goulashes, ragouts, carbonnades, by the use of prepared gravies, plus herbs, spices, wines and beers.

Not wild extravagances either, since quick cooking reduces shrinkage. The cost in many cases is just about the same as it might be if you used ordinary stew meat. The flavor is richer; the texture, better . . . no strings. More of the nutritive values are retained.

If the thrifty soul rebels at the thought of putting sirloin into stews, you can still make use of the new lightning fast techniques by resorting to a meat tenderizer. Made from enzymes of tropical plants, these tenderizers date back to the days of the ancient empires in Africa when Timbuctoo was one of the intellectual and gastronomic capitals of the world and the wild doves used for ragout were wrapped then, as they are now, in papaya leaves to make them tender.

Today, meat tenderizers come in powdered form, seasoned or unseasoned. They have been improved so that their action is almost instantaneous. Using a tenderizer has another advantage—it allows you to cut cooking time in most instances about 25 per cent. Less time— less shrinkage—less vitamin loss.

Classical Speed

According to the classic tenets, the methods suitable for

speed cooking include broiling or grilling, pan-broiling, frying or sautéing and roasting. These are known technically as dry heat methods. When meat is cooked in this manner, heat seals the surfaces; those inner juices —savory and nutritious—are caught and held.

Only 22 per cent of the beef animal is by nature suited to this type of treatment . . . without tenderizers.

Different cuts of steaks have an endless number of different names, not only in different parts of the world, but in various sections of the country. Without going into local terminology, there are eight different steak cuts procurable almost anywhere in the United States. These include the boneless loin or strip steak, the pinbone sirloin, the wedge-bone sirloin, the T-bone steak, the club steak or Delmonico, the porterhouse, the rib steak and the tenderloin or filet mignon.

In addition to these tender and luxurious cuts, there are also flank, round, chuck and rump steaks. These must be cut very, very thin or pounded to break the fibers if they are to be cooked by broiling or sautéing —unless, of course, you use a tenderizer.

For broiling, steaks should be cut one-and-a-half to two-and-a-half, or three-inches thick. The one-inch steak is, in my opinion, more suitable for pan-broiling. Regular broiling, unless you are very careful, is likely to make it dry.

Most people overcook steaks. Steaks vary. So does heat; so do people and their tastes. So, it is difficult to give accurate timetables. However, as a rule of thumb, a steak one-inch thick, if you insist upon broiling it, should be cooked three inches from the heat source; a two-inch steak, four inches from the heat; a three-inch steak, six inches away. Broil until one side is brown, turn with tongs, broil other side until brown. A thick steak, like a roast, is improved—and much easier to slice—if it is allowed to rest for a few minutes in a warm place before slicing. Thin steaks should be served immediately.

A steak cut one-and-a-half inches thick should be cooked eight minutes on the first side, seven minutes on the second side for rare. Add an extra minute on each side for medium rare, and another minute on each side for medium. If you like your steak well done . . . you are on your own. We will not be a party to such desecration.

To test for doneness, make a little cut close to the bone and look.

1. BLAZING STEAK ON A PLANK

Highly dramatic is a steak on a plank! Even more stupendous when the board is borne in a blaze of bourbon into a dusk-dim dining room. In spite of its theatrical appearance and the noble taste, a plank steak is no more difficult to prepare than just plain everyday broiled.

You can buy an oak plank specifically designed for this purpose, or contrive one out of a piece of hardwood cut about 1 inch thick. Lacking a plank . . . a heat-prooof platter can be pressed into service.

This is a meal that would impress and enchant the heart of any male. A dinner in the great American tradition with all-American accompaniments—succotash and wilted greens. For dessert, apple pie à la mode, if you will, and served in the manner of Old Virginia with a little pitcher of warmed buttery syrup and chopped nuts.

Blazing Steak on a Plank
Garnished with Mashed Potatoes and Mushrooms
Succotash
Wilted Greens
Warmed Apple Pie, Old Virginia

BLAZING STEAK ON A PLANK . . . To serve four, have the butcher cut a 2-pound sirloin steak about 1-inch thick. Score the fat to keep it from curling. Massage all over with 2 teaspoons *Kitchen Bouquet* mixed with 1 teaspoon ground ginger. Allow to stand uncovered at room temperature until you are ready to cook it.

About 20 minutes before serving time, set under the broiler and broil about 4 minutes on each side for medium-rare. Season with salt and pepper.

Meanwhile, pre-heat in a very hot oven (425°) a well-seasoned oak plank or heat-proof platter. Place the steak on the plank. Arrange all around the steak a ring of mashed potatoes and set in the hot oven about 10 minutes or until the potatoes are gilded. Garnish with a 6-ounce tin of broiled mushrooms that have been heated in their own juices.

Slightly warm 4 tablespoons bourbon in a metal cup or ramekin. Set ablaze and pour over the steak. Serve at once.

SUCCOTASH . . . Use quick-frozen or canned.

WILTED GREENS . . . An epicure who has roamed the world to eat says, "The height of everything is wilted greens made with a hot bacon dressing." Combine 3 parts hot bacon drippings, 1 part cider vinegar. Season with a little dry mustard, a touch of sugar, salt and pepper. Pour hot over any tender young greens such as garden lettuce, young spinach or watercress.

WARMED APPLE PIE, OLD VIRGINIA . . . Sprinkle top of an apple pie with a little light brown or maple sugar and a few grains of cinnamon or nutmeg. Heat in the oven. Meanwhile heat together equal parts melted butter and maple syrup and add a couple of tablespoons coarsely chopped nuts. Pass syrup in a small pitcher to be poured at will over the apple pie. A small scoop of vanilla ice cream? Never hurt anyone!

II. BŒUF À LA BROCHE

Abijan, Ivory Coast, West Africa—The President and Madame Houphouët-Boigny were our official host and hostess at a dinner party for the opening of the luxurious new Hotel Ivoire. There were 400 guests in a lofty ballroom whose walls were lined with what looked like planks of gold. As hotel openings go (and we have gone to quite a few in various parts of the world) it was a fine dinner. Six courses beginning with a paté from Strasbourg and ending with a type of Baked Alaska served in a pineapple shell and billowing with meringue. In France, it would have been a swan, but in this part of the world, they preferred to say it was a white ostrich.

Chef Maurice Filleul, originally of France but lately from New York, had his problems. As yet, not enough ovens had been hooked up. So he used a blow torch to make gold tracings of wings and feathers on the meringue. However, since he used an Italian meringue, browning was not really necessary, for Italian meringue is nothing more nor less than our own fluffy boiled frosting for cakes.

Paté en Gelée
Bœuf à la Broche (Beef broiled on a spit)
Potatoes Parisiènne
Artichoke Hearts Clamart
Pineapple Ostrich Surprise
Les Mignardises (That's cookies, pet!)

PATÉ EN GELÉE . . . If money is no object, you will of course provide yourself with paté de foie gras from Strasbourg—with truffles, of course! But the rest of us will chill and slice into ¼ inch circles, a 4½ ounce tin of liver paté. Place 3 slices on each individual plate and garnish each slice with half of a black olive—shiny side up. Around the paté, arrange a half-inch circle of canned tomato aspic that has been broken into tiny bits with a fork. Garnish with watercress.

BŒUF À LA BROCHE . . . To serve 4, get yourself a 2-pound tenderloin of beef which should be at least 2 inches thick. Anoint with olive oil and rub with dry mustard. Then broil on a spit or in a very hot oven (450°) about 10 to 12 minutes per pound. If you use a meat thermometer, *do* ignore their suggestion that 140° is rare beef. According to most chefs, 120° or 125° is much better. To serve, slice beef on the slant about ½-inch thick.

POTATOES PARISIÉNNE . . . Heat a package of quick-frozen rissolé potato balls in 2 tablespoons butter or margarine and, just before removing from the stove, add 1 teaspoon beef extract.

ARTICHOKE HEARTS CLAMART . . . Cook quick-frozen artichoke hearts according to package directions. Stand them up in a small dish and place in each heart a spoonful of junior food pureed carrots which have been tastefully seasoned with salt, pepper and a dash of *Tabasco*.

PINEAPPLE OSTRICH SURPRISE . . . To serve 4, use 2 pineapples. Cut lengthwise in halves right through the fronds. Remove and dice some of the pineapple, leaving a shell about one inch thick. In the bottom of each shell, place 2 ladyfingers that have been dipped into fruit juice or sherry wine. Then add a scoop of pineapple sherbet or ice cream. Sprinkle with diced pineapple. Cover generously with fluffy boiled frosting made from your own favorite recipe or from a package.

To make the head of the bird, Chef Maurice used the cream puff dough, but pie pastry will do very well, or even a large pretzel. These desserts may be prepared beforehand and kept in the freezer.

III. CAMILLE'S MEATLOAF

In many families, including ours, a meatloaf—a real old-fashioned honest-John meatloaf—has always been a symbol of the cosiest kind of meal at home. Although meatloaf is a simple dish to prepare, it generally takes at least an hour and a quarter to bake. For months we have been obsessed by the search for a meatloaf recipe that could be cooked within the limits that we have set for the Fast Gourmet. Nothing can take more than thirty minutes to cook.

The clue came from our editor, Camille Bourgeois, who said in an offhand way, "Why not cook the meat a little beforehand?" So we did. The Fast Gourmet meatloaf was achieved . . . perfectly seasoned in no time flat (without any chopping or browning of onion) by means of a package of dehydrated soup mix; beautifully textured with a cup of packaged breadcrumbs.

Everything about the technique is different. But the look and taste are Right.

Camille's Meatloaf   Mushroom Gravy
Chantilly Potato Puff
Romaine, Cucumber and Grapefruit Salad
Bottled Italian Dressing
Devil's Food Parfait Cake

CAMILLE'S MEATLOAF . . . First light the oven so that it will be preheated to 500°. In a large bowl place a package of dehydrated onion soup mix. Cover the mix with 1 cup sour cream and 2 slightly beaten eggs. Allow to stand while you brown in the skillet 2 pounds chopped beef. Unless the meat is very lean, it should not be necessary to use any fat. In any case, use very little.

Cook the meat *only* until the red color disappears. Stir lightly with a fork from time to time to prevent it from sticking. Sprinkle over the onion soup and sour cream mixture, 1 cup breadcrumbs. Then add the meat. Place in a buttered loaf pan or a ring mold. Bake 20 minutes in a very hot oven (500°) and, during the last 5 minutes of baking, turn on the broiler so that the top will be crusted and beautifully browned. Serves 6 to 8.

MUSHROOM GRAVY . . . From a can, dear!

CHANTILLY POTATO PUFF . . . To serve 6, prepare 3 cups quick-frozen or dehydrated mashed potatoes adding milk and butter according to package directions. Place in a shallow, ovenproof baking dish. Whip 1 cup heavy cream. Fold in ½ cup grated cheese. Season with salt, pepper, a few grains of nutmeg if desired. Top the potatoes with the cream mixture and set under the broiler next to the meatloaf until golden brown—4 or 5 minutes should do it.

DEVIL'S FOOD PARFAIT CAKE . . . This is one of the new frozen parfait cakes . . . very good, tender, light cakes with a filling and a topping of whipped parfait. These cakes are available nationally in five flavors; strawberry parfait, chocolate parfait, white cake with chocolate filling, devil's food and pineapple.

IV. CHATEAUBRIAND EN PAPILLOTE

From the luxurious Quo Vadis restaurant in New York —haunt of the Greats—comes this recipe for a most luxurious production . . . a filet of beef cooked in parchment paper that blows up in the oven like a golden balloon.

This recipe follows exactly the technique except that our sauce is contrived from a can of beef gravy.

The original recipe calls for a whole filet mignon, the piece that is usually sliced to make individual filet mignons. But if you would rather not mortgage the old homestead, you could tenderize a 3-inch-thick (3-pound) boneless piece of beef cut from the top or bottom round, rump, arm chuck, or top sirloin. Use unseasoned meat tenderizer and follow package directions. Then proceed in exactly the same fashion.

Smoked Trout or Sturgeon   Sauce Raifort
Chateaubriand en Papillote   Bordelaise Sauce
Chateau Potatoes   Artichoke Hearts with
Lemon and Butter
Bibb Lettuce and Watercress Salad
Tray of Cheeses
Fresh Fruits of the Season in a Leaf-Lined Basket

SMOKED TROUT OR STURGEON, SAUCE RAIFORT . . .
Raifort is French for horseradish. To ½ cup heavy cream
whipped, add 2 tablespoons bottled horseradish, ¼ teaspoon salt, ½ teaspoon sugar. Makes 1 cup.

CHATEAUBRIAND EN PAPILLOTE . . . To serve 6, have
the butcher give you a beef filet weighing about 3 pounds.
Ask him to leave a little fat around it, but not too much.
Flatten the filet to 3-inch thickness. Season with salt
and pepper. (If you have used meat tenderizer, omit the
salt.) Broil under a medium flame or on a spit 20 to 25
minutes.

Now for the Papillote (or balloon) effect. Cut a piece
of parchment paper into the shape of a heart 25 inches
in diameter. Brush with salad oil on both sides. Set the
cooked filet on one side of the heart. Pour on 1 cup
Bordelaise Sauce. Sprinkle with parsley. Fold the parchment over and roll and press edges together as if you
were rolling a hem, so that the meat is completely sealed.
Place Papillote on an ovenproof serving dish and set in
a very hot oven (475°) about 5 minutes or until the
steam builds up and blows up the package and the paper
takes on a golden shade. At the table, cut open the
paper. Slice beef thin across the grain and slightly on the
bias at a 30-degree angle. Pass more of the sauce.

BORDELAISE SAUCE . . . To a 10 ¾-ounce tin beef
gravy add 1 cup dry red table wine which has been
cooked down to ½ cup with 1 chopped shallot (or 1
tablespoon chopped onion; ½ clove garlic, crushed).
Simmer together 5 minutes, remove from heat. Stir in
bit by bit 2 tablespoons butter, 2 teaspoons chopped
parsley.

CHATEAU POTATOES . . . This classic accompaniment
to a Chateaubriand—small whole potatoes sautéed in
butter without previous cooking—can be approximated
with great nonchalance. Use 2 packages quick-frozen

rissolé potatoes. Heat according to package directions. Place in a large heated skillet. Combine 2 tablespoons softened butter; 2 tablespoons minced chives, fresh tarragon, or a mixture of fresh green herbs. Add a big pinch of pepper. Roll and toss the potatoes in the skillet until they glisten with herbs and butter.

ARTICHOKE HEARTS WITH LEMON AND BUTTER . . . For 6 servings, cook two 10-ounce packages frozen artichoke hearts in chicken broth instead of water. Bedew with 2 tablespoons melted butter and juice of half a lemon.

V. COLLOPS OF BEEF ESCOFFIER

One of the finest of leftover dishes is Collops of Beef, prepared in a fashion described by none other than the king of modern gastronomy, the great Escoffier himself.

After the Collops, a lemon soufflé that is non-temperamental; easy to make, for the base is a lemon pudding mix. Bakes while you dine. If you want to spend an hour at the dinner table, use a moderate oven. Want it ready in half an hour? Raise the temperature! Moreover, this soufflé is so adaptable, you may, if you wish, serve it cold. Then it is more like a pudding.

Collops of Beef Escoffier
Delmonico Potatoes
Easy Ring of Kale
Harvard Beets
Obliging Lemon Soufflé

COLLOPS OF BEEF ESCOFFIER . . . For 1 pound (i.e., 2 cups) cooked or roast beef, "chop 2 fine onions somewhat finely," or use 2 cups chopped frozen onions. Toss them into 3 tablespooons melted butter until they are evenly and well browned, but not the least bit burned.

Sprinkle with ½ tablespoon flour. "Set to cook for a moment and then moisten with ½ glassful of white wine," says M. Escoffier. We use ¼ cup white wine or dry vermouth or 2 tablespoons white wine vinegar and 2 tablespoons water. Add 1 cup concentrated consommé. Bring to a boil. Leave to cook gently 7 or 8 minutes. Cut the roast or cooked beef into very thin slices and lay these on a dish. A minute before serving, add 1 teaspoon vinegar to the onions. Cover the meat with the onions and sauce. Stand the dish for 2 minutes on the side of the fire. Sprinkle slightly with chopped parsley. Notice that you do not actually cook the meat in the sauce for it might get tough.

DELMONICO POTATOES ... To serve 6, heat 2 packages frozen Delmonico Potatoes according to package directions. Sprinkle generously with packaged breadcrumbs, mixed with grated cheese, using 2 parts crumbs to 1 part cheese.

EASY RING OF KALE ... Cook 2 packages quick-frozen kale according to directions. Drain, season to taste, press into a well-buttered ring mold. Allow to stand in a warm place about 10 minutes. Cover with a plate, tenderly turn upside down and ease onto plate.

HARVARD BEETS ... To 1 jar of Harvard beets, add 1 tablespoon grated orange peel, ¼ teaspoon ginger. Heat and arrange inside and around the ring of kale.

OBLIGING LEMON SOUFFLÉ ... Combine 1 package lemon pudding and pie mix with 1¾ cup milk. Cook and stir until mixture comes to a full boil. It will look curdled but never mind. Remove from heat. Beat 3 egg yolks until thick and lemon colored. Add the pudding mixture gradually, stirring all the while. Beat the 3 egg whites with a dash of salt until foamy; add 4 tablespoons sugar (2 at a time) beating until whites stand in stiff peaks. Fold into pudding mixture. Pour into an ungreased 1½ quart baking dish. Bake in a hot oven (425°) 30 minutes, or in a moderate oven (350°) 1 hour.

VI. THE COLONY'S THIN STEAK

Easter Monday at the renowned Colony Restaurant in New York has become a tradition. This is the day of days when the sons and daughters and now the grandsons and granddaughters join their paters or their maters—rarely the two together—for lunch.

Some of the Brady family are sure to be there, Vanderlips and Vanderbilts, Whitneys, Pratts, Goeltes; Beth Leary, of course, for she is queen of the Colony regulars, Bernard Baruch, James Farley.

The most popular item is always the Colony's flattened steak which practically covers the plate. With a curious kind of reverse elegance, the Colony prides itself on serving not the thickest, but the thinnest steak on earth. Wonderfully juicy and salubrious.

Crabmeat Cocktail, Fines Herbes
The Colony Thin Steak
Mustard Sauce
Broccoli
Shoestring Potatoes
Fresh Blueberries
"Homemade" Macaroons

CRABMEAT COCKTAIL . . . Use fresh Maryland crabmeat as the Colony does, or canned or quick-frozen. Instead of the usual cocktail sauce, a light French dressing with chopped herbs—i.e., chives, parsley, chervil.

THE COLONY'S THIN STEAK . . . Start with individual steak about one inch thick—whatever cut you like and can afford. The Colony uses prime sirloin. Inexpensive round steak is excellent too, especially if you use a little meat tenderizer. The bone, if any, should be removed.

Pound the steak until it is only ¼ inch thick, using a strong, flat piece of metal or wood. At the Colony, they do not use the usual corrugated meat cleaver because they believe it tears the meat and allows the juices to run out. They broil the meat on a heavy wire mesh over charcoal. It can be done on a heavy frying pan very lightly greased. Most important—cook steak only about 30 or 40 seconds on each side. Season with salt and pepper. Serve immediately. Always at the Colony there is hot mustard sauce.

MUSTARD SAUCE . . . Add 1 or 2 teaspoons prepared mustard to 1 cup canned beef gravy; serve hot.

SHOESTRING POTATOES . . . From a can, warmed.

"HOMEMADE" MACAROONS . . . Set bought macaroons in a hot oven for 2 minutes and they will look, smell and taste deliciously fresh and different.

VII. FILET OF BEEF WITH SPRING VEGETABLES

At the Hotel Regency in New York, the Chevaliers du Tastevin (Knights of the Wine Cup) held a dinner to honor Clifford T. Weihman, recently elevated to the position of Grand Pilier, and H. Gregory Thomas who was taking his place as Grand Senechal of this organization dedicated to Burgundy wines and food.

There were seven courses, seven wines and liquors. Here are some of the highlights, slightly adapted for ease and speed. Soup à la Wooden Leg (consommé accompanied by a shinbone surrounded by vegetables). Then a filet of beef with spring vegetables, Queen of the May Salad, a procession of cheeses.

The Apotheosis or dessert was fresh pineapple with an "orbiting" sauce named for Mrs. Weihman.

Soup à la Wooden Leg
Filet of Beef with Spring Vegetables
Queen of the May Salad with Chablis Dressing
Pineapple Marjorie with Sauce Orbite

SOUP À LA WOODEN LEG . . . Serve any good rich homemade or canned consommé in soup plates. Pass on a platter a shinbone of beef (cooked, of course) surrounded by cooked carrots and celery cut into inch strips, which you help yourself to and put in your soup.

FILET OF BEEF . . . To serve 4, roast a 2 pound filet in a hot oven (375°) 12 minutes per pound (for rare). Eye of round may be used instead of filet mignon but should be sprinkled with meat tenderizer according to directions.

VEGETABLES OF SPRING . . . (As prepared by Chef Ernest Didier.) Cook medium-sized artichokes in the usual fashion and remove all the leaves and fiber, leaving only the bottom. On each artichoke bottom place the tip of a small, lightly-cooked carrot. Arrange very young, small, lightly cooked green beans in bundles. Broil, for each person, two small tomatoes which should be first brushed with melted butter and sprinkled with well-seasoned crumbs. Cut fresh asparagus into pieces about 1 inch long and cook very briefly. Anoint with lemon butter.

Most unusual were the potatoes, which had been cut to look like wooden shoes, almost as typical of Burgundy as Holland. Small potatoes are cut first into ovals. Take out a little nick for the heel and scoop out the top. Into the top of the "shoe" place a few tiny cooked peas.

Whisper: You may use canned artichoke bottoms, canned Belgian carrots, vertical pack green beans and baby peas, packaged seasoned bread crumbs and frozen asparagus cuts and tips.

QUEEN OF THE MAY SALAD . . . Use the youngest and tenderest of leaf lettuce. Toss with a dressing made of 1 part Chablis (or any dry white table wine), 2 parts olive oil, a little salt and pepper, a touch of dry mustard.

PINEAPPLE MARJORIE WITH SAUCE ORBITE . . . Use a large pineapple complete with leaves. Cut off top; take out meat; cut into thin slices; sprinkle with sugar; chill. Replace in pineapple and pass separately Sauce Orbite, made by combining equal parts Grand Marnier Liqueur and pineapple juice.

VIII. FLEMISH BEEF STEW WITH PRUNES

"For supper she gives him a can of beef stew and would you believe it . . . he thinks she's the greatest cook that ever happened!"

"Some women!" her companion mused. "What they get away with!" Both shook their heads sadly, brooding over the plight of the poor man who was given canned beef stew for supper. It occurred to us when we overheard this conversation that the lady in question might have done a thing or two or three to that can of stew. She could, for instance, transform it quickly and easily into this Flemish *spécialité de la maison,* by adding prunes and honey and cinnamon!

A little extra simmering is required to marry the flavors and, since canned stews are all too easily overcooked, it is a good idea to drain the juices from the stew, combine them with prune juice, add the stew at the last minute, heat to a sizzle and serve.

For dessert, we are suggesting a cheese cake. Could be a bought cheese cake, but it will take on a look and taste of luxury with a glimmering fruit glaze made from a package of gelatin dessert mix.

Flemish Beef Stew with Prunes
Cole Slaw in Green Pepper Cases
with Old-Fashioned Boiled Dressing
Cheese Cake with Black Cherry Glaze

FLEMISH BEEF STEW WITH PRUNES . . . To serve 4, cook ½ cup chopped onion in 2 tablespoons butter or fat until soft and golden, but not brown. Add the gravy drained from two 1 pound, 3-ounce tins of beef stew. Add also 1 cup prune juice; ½ teaspoon cinnamon; ¼ cup honey or dark brown sugar; ½ of a lemon cut into thin slices. Cook uncovered about 10 minutes. Then add 2 cups cooked or canned prunes—pitted if you are feeling particularly gracious.

Now, add the solid part of the beef stew. Bring to a boil and serve with a goodly sprinkle of chopped parsley and a garnish of fresh lemon slices.

COLE SLAW IN GREEN PEPPER CASES WITH OLD-FASHIONED BOILED DRESSING . . . Cut 2 large sweet green peppers in halves crosswise; remove seeds and fill with cole slaw. If you have a blender, this dressing is no trouble at all: Place in the blender 2 whole eggs, 2 tablespoons butter, 1½ cups milk, 4 tablespoons flour, 1 teaspoon salt, 1 tablespoon dry mustard, 2 tablespoons sugar, 3 drops *Tabasco*. Blend 40 seconds. While blender is still going, pour into the center ½ cup boiling hot cider vinegar. Blend ten seconds longer. Dressing should thicken immediately. If not, cook and stir over very low heat for a few minutes.

BLACK CHERRY GLAZE . . . Dissolve one 3-ounce package black cherry-flavored gelatin in 1 cup hot water. Add 2 tablespoons currant jelly. Swift-chill in freezer about 8 minutes or until thick as unbeaten egg whites. Spoon on top of cheese cake or cream pie. Chill either in freezer or in refrigerator.

IX. FIVE MINUTE GOULASH FROM LIMA

All over the world Hungarian goulash is a specialty of talented home cooks and also of chefs. Always it has been a dish which required many hours of "loving simmer" to make it smile.

Last summer in Lima, Peru, in a restaurant, once the palace of a Spanish conquistador, an Austrian chef prepared one of the most delicious Hungarian goulashes we have ever tasted. He did it at the table right in front of our eyes. And it took 5 minutes.

The sauce, of course, had been prepared beforehand.

In lieu of the chef's sauce, you may use a can of beef gravy. For this goulash no "stew meat" but excellent steak cut into tiny pieces.

Raw Vegetable Hors d'Œuvres
Five Minute Goulash from Lima
Broad Noodles with Poppy Seeds
Harvard Beets
Chestnuts Gabor   Cheese and Fresh Fruit

RAW VEGETABLES HORS D'ŒUVRES . . . Arrange attractively on a platter or on individual plates: Cole slaw (made from red and green cabbage if possible).

Tomatoes cut into eighths sprinkled with vinegar, salt, pepper, a little sugar.

Cold baked beans seasoned with vinegar and black pepper.

Finely shredded or grated carrots with mayonnaise.

FIVE MINUTE GOULASH FROM LIMA . . . To serve four to six, have 2 pounds of steak cut ½ inch thick and then cut into pieces ½ inch wide and 1 inch long. In 2 tablespoons lard or cooking fat, brown, until pale golden and slightly soft, ½ cup chopped onions. Push onions to one side and in the same pan brown the meat which has been seasoned with salt and pepper. Then add 1 can beef gravy; 1 tablespoon vinegar; 1 teaspoon caraway seeds; ½ teaspoon marjoram; 1 tablespoon sweet Hungarian paprika and ¼ cup dry sherry wine, if you desire. Bring to a boil and cook just about 2 minutes. The goulash is ready to serve.

BROAD NOODLES WITH POPPY SEEDS . . . To serve 4, cook ½ pound noodles according to package directions. Drain, toss with 3 tablespoons melted butter and sprinkle with 1 tablespoon poppy seeds.

HARVARD BEETS . . . They are canned and very good, too.

CHESTNUTS GABOR . . . With a sharp knife cut an X on top of each chestnut. Coat with oil, using only about 1 teaspoonful for each cup of nuts. Bake in a very hot oven (450°) about 20 minutes or place in a heavy frying pan and shake over the fire or embers about 10 minutes. Remove peel. For each pound of chestnuts heat ½ cup butter in a skillet. Add chestnuts and toss until all are completely covered with butter. Sprinkle with salt and pepper.

X. HAMBURGER "21"

At "21" Club restaurant in New York, the specialties of the house, such as Scotch grouse, Maryland terrapin, Malayan hens *and* Hamburgers "21" are—priceless. All appear on the bill of fare unaccompanied by telltale figures.

Only when the check arrives will you learn that this is one of the world's higher priced burgers—and worth every cent.

Half a pound of the finest prime beef goes into each burger—the kind of beef that has been proved over the years to produce the juiciest, tastiest hamburgers. Chef Louis prefers meat taken off the short ribs. It must be chopped to order just before cooking, "handled as lightly as though it were breakable," seasoned with practically nothing at all except—and this is a secret rarely revealed—"a very small amount of cooked celery, chopped very fine with a knife."

Caviar Salad Irongate
Hamburger "21"   "21" Sauce Maison
Fresh Asparagus   Allumette Potatoes
Fresh Berries with Devonshire Cream

CAVIAR SALAD IRONGATE . . . The freshest and youngest of lettuce (Romaine or Bibb preferably), is served with a very plain French dressing, made of 2 tablespoons fine wine vinegar, ½ cup of the best olive oil, and 2 tablespoons black caviar.

HAMBURGER "21" . . . To make 2 kingly hamburgers in the "21" fashion, you will need a pound of chopped beef "from the short ribs or chuck steak is best." Add no salt, no pepper, nothing but a single 4-inch stalk of cooked, well-drained celery, cut into pieces and then chopped very fine with a knife. Celery must not be mushy. Mix lightly with sopping-wet hands. And with wet hands shape meat into 2 oval burgers 1 inch thick.

The "21" technique combines sautéing and broiling. "Sauté on one side, then on the other, on a very heavy, very hot pan or griddle, cooking about 2 minutes on each side." Just before serving, anoint each burger with 1 tablespoon heated Sauce Espagnole (or canned beef gravy). Set under broiler 2 or 3 minutes longer. To give an exceptional savor as a finishing touch, "pour on a spoonful of slightly browned butter."

"21" SAUCE MAISON . . . This "secret condiment" is now available in gourmet shops and supermarkets throughout the U.S.A. A very good homemade facsimile can be produced by adding 1 tablespoon dry English mustard that has been stirred to a paste with warm water and allowed to stand 10 minutes, to ½ cup tomato ketchup.

ALLUMETTE POTATOES . . . Use the match-like potatoes julienne that can be bought in a can.

FRESH BERRIES WITH DEVONSHIRE CREAM . . . Have your Devonshire Cream airborne from England as they do at "21." Or you could make out with 1 cup sour cream to which you add a couple of drops of yellow coloring and ½ teaspoon sugar.

XI. KIRK'S BEAVER

Author, lecturer, world-wanderer, village squire and justice of the peace in Mecosta, Michigan, Russell Kirk writes a syndicated column called "To The Point," which indeed, it very much is! Points are widely divergent— ranging from travel to obscure places, politics, moods and moments of history. "The Bohemian Tory," he has been called. At the Vienna Opera, he was once introduced as the Duke of Mecosta, for he often wears a cape or cloak, while a Scottish antique stickpin in his necktie adds to his air of a Victorian dandy.

One of his non-writing interests is food. When we asked for his favorite recipe—"fast and practical, please," we pleaded—he wrote a small and pleasant treatise on the beaver; how to catch and cook . . .

Later he admitted that his favorite beaver dish—"like the Scotch Woodcock, the Welsh Rabbit and the Cape Cod Turkey, is not what it sounds like . . . not in fact a beaver at all, but a minute steak. When properly cooked," says he, "beaver meat is excellent, tender beef with a faint pleasant wild taste. It is less gamey than are most wild animals."

Kirk's Beaver with Proper Beaver Gravy
Fried Onion Rings
Mecosta, Michigan Spuds
Pittenween Salad
Cherry Strudel with Vanilla Ice Cream Sauce

KIRK'S BEAVER WITH PROPER BEAVER GRAVY . . . Panbroil or sauté to your liking a bevy of steaks ¾ to 1 inch thick. Give them the "taste of the wild" by rubbing lightly with crushed juniper berries or, if you have no juniper berries rattling around in a jar in your kitchen, sprinkle the meat judiciously with a little gin.

Meanwhile, prepare a Proper Beaver Gravy. Add to a can or cup of rich beef gravy, 1 cup red wine, ¼ teaspoon each: ground cloves, powdered mace or nutmeg, ground thyme, cayenne pepper. Add 1 bay leaf, 1 teaspoon dehydrated parsley. Cook down rapidly uncovered until it is reduced to half its original volume. Then stir in 2 tablespoons red currant jelly and heat just long enough for the jelly to melt.

FRIED ONION RINGS . . . Canned or frozen.

MECOSTA, MICHIGAN SPUDS . . . Thaw or heat small whole frozen potatoes. Drain. Roll in flour seasoned with salt and paprika. Drop a handful at a time into deep, hot oil and fry at 375°, 1 or 2 minutes or until golden brown. Remove and drain on paper towels. Sprinkle with freshly ground black pepper. These, by the way, make an excellent, simple, man-appealing tidbit to serve with cocktails.

PITTENWEEN SALAD . . . In addition to his ancestral home in Mecosta, Michigan, where five generations of Kirks have lived, Dr. Kirk now owns a little stone house in Scotland at Pittenween, which he uses on frequent visits to the land of his forebears. There they make this salad of well-flavored sliced tomatoes. Sprinkle with salt and pepper. Lay slices overlapping in a long, narrow dish. Generously strew with finely chopped green onions or coarse cut chives. Pour on a little French dressing.

CHERRY STRUDEL WITH VANILLA ICE CREAM . . . Heat quick-frozen cherry strudel according to directions and serve in slices. Pass, in a separate bowl, a sauce made by beating into 1 cup vanilla ice cream, 2 tablespoons concentrated orange juice. Sprinkle lightly with nutmeg.

XII. LONDON BROIL

So you are having a dinner party. Your guest of honor says, "How sweet of you, darling, but don't forget, I'm on a diet . . . high protein, low calorie, no potatoes, no bread, no rich sauces." And, she adds wistfully, "How am I going to resist dessert?"

You accept the challenge. Let us suppose oysters are in season. Eggplant is purpling on the stands. There is a special on flank steak which suggests London Broil.

As for dessert—hail and hallelujah . . . Here is a mousse with no cream, no butter. Takes less than 5 minutes to make in the blender . . . adds up to just about 100 calories per serving including the Soft Meringue Sauce.

Oysters with Red Caviar   Thin Breadsticks
London Broil with Mushrooms
Grilled Eggplant
Leaf Spinach Japanese Art
Cucumber Ovals with Chives and Mint
Mousse à l'Orange with Soft Meringue Sauce
Sauce Wafers

OYSTERS WITH RED CAVIAR . . . In a soup plate, on a flat bed of shaved ice, arrange 4 to 6 oysters on the half shell for each person. Instead of the usual cocktail sauce, provide half of a lemon with the edges cut into points. On each oyster place a tablespoonful of red caviar and, at one end, a tiny dab of freshly grated or prepared horseradish.

LONDON BROIL WITH MUSHROOMS . . . To serve 6, order 3 pounds flank steak about 1 inch thick. Panbroil on a hot frying pan about 5 minutes on each side. Remove steak; keep warm. Add to drippings in the skillet, one 3-ounce tin sliced, broiled mushrooms, 1 cup water, 2 bouillon cubes. Stir and bring to a boil. Pour over the steak. To serve, slice on the bias ¼ inch thick.

LEAF SPINACH JAPANESE ART . . . Heat 3 tablespoons sesame seeds in a hot skillet until they begin to brown and pop. Add 2 tablespoons soy sauce and sprinkle over cooked spinach.

GRILLED EGGPLANT . . . Cut unpeeled eggplant into

½ inch slices. Brush with olive oil or melted butter, salt and pepper. Broil until tender and lightly browned.

CUCUMBER OVALS ... Slice young unpeeled cucumbers slightly on the bias, about ¼ inch thick. Sprinkle with salt, pepper, chopped mint and chopped chives.

MOUSSE À L'ORANGE WITH SOFT MERINGUE SAUCE ... Into the container of your electric blender, place 2 envelopes plain, unflavored gelatin. Bring to a boil ¾ cup orange juice, ¼ cup lemon juice. Pour over gelatin. Cover; blend 40 seconds. Add 3 whole eggs and 2 egg yolks; the peel of ½ lemon or ¼ orange; 3 tablespoons sugar; ¼ teaspoon salt. Cover; blend 5 seconds longer. With motor still running, add 1 heaping cup cracked ice cubes. Continue to blend until ice disappears—about 10 seconds. Mousse may be served immediately in sherbet glasses. Or pour into a quart-sized mold. Chill. Unmold, garnish with apricot halves. Sprinkle lightly with nutmeg. Pass Soft Meringue Sauce, made by whipping the 2 egg whites and, when almost stiff, adding 2 tablespoons sugar, ½ teaspoon vanilla. Whip to stiff peaks.

XIII. MICHIGAN SECRET POT ROAST

This miracle pot roast takes only 3 minutes' time and attention. Sounds incredible because it is not pre-cooked or frozen or canned.

We discovered the idea in a little book *Secrets of Michigan Cooks* by Kay Savage, renowned Food Editor of the *Detroit Free Press*.

To Toni Milby of Traverse City, Kay Savage gives credit for a "Pot Roast In Foil" which is merely wrapped with dried onion soup mix and baked in a slow oven 4 to 5 hours. "Toni does it occasionally when she goes home for lunch."

But how often can anyone get home for lunch? Every time you think of fixing pot roast, isn't it always a solid chunk in the freezer?

So we thought and fussed and experimented. Finally we found that a solid frozen pot roast can be put in a slow oven before you leave in the morning. When you get home at night, you will find it lusciously brown and tender, deliciously seasoned and moist. The gravy that emerges from the heart of the beef ... a concentrated glory!

Crudités
Michigan Secret Pot Roast
Potato Pancakes
Red Cabbage with Apples
Honeydew Melon with Ginger and Lime

CRUDITÉS . . . That's French for crisp, raw vegetables served with coarse salt.

MICHIGAN SECRET POT ROAST . . . Fold a double
thickness of aluminum foil large enough to wrap completely around a 4-pound chuck roast. In the center of
the foil sprinkle a package of onion soup mix and sprinkle
another package over the meat. Fold foil both ways to
form a snug package and place in an open pan in a slow
oven (300°). Allow to bake 4 to 5 hours. If meat is
frozen solid, proceed in exactly the same fashion, but
cook in a very slow oven (225° to 250°) 8 to 10 hours.

Slice the leftovers. Place wax paper between the slices
and store in the freezer so you can always have some
pot roast ready to thaw and/or serve cold or reheat
in gravy.

POTATO PANCAKES . . . Use quick-frozen potato pancakes. Heat in ½-inch salad oil at 370° until thoroughly heated, crisp and brown.

RED CABBAGE WITH APPLES . . . Add 1 cup sliced
canned apples to 1 jar sweet and sour red cabbage. Season with ¼ teaspoon Allspice.

HONEYDEW MELON WITH GINGER AND LIME . . . An
English inspiration! Pass powdered ginger. Just a sprinkle
is added, then a squeeze of lime.

XIV. MINUTE RAGOUT FRONTENAC

As might be expected, the ragout served at the Chateau
Frontenac has all the richness, delicacy and finesse of
its Parisian ancestors but—miracle of miracles—it is prepared in less than 10 minutes instead of 6 hours. For
the meat is cut in small pieces and sautéed rather than
long simmered. The winey, herb-enchanted sauce, which
at the Frontenac is chef-produced, may be happily approximated by a can of beef gravy.

The day we lunched at the Chateau Frontenac, our
gala luncheon began with a chilled cream of cucumber

soup. The ragout flamed and finished at the table was accompanied by matinée potatoes (a Gallic version of O'Brien). And the dessert was nothing more than fruit on toast, but raised to divinity.

Chilled Cream of Cucumber Soup
Minute Ragout Frontenac
Matinée Potatoes
Green Beans
Pineapple Croute

CHILLED CREAM OF CUCUMBER SOUP . . . Peel, remove seeds and dice 1 small cucumber. Cook 3 or 4 minutes until tender, and whir in a blender 1 minute along with 1 can cream of chicken soup, 1 soup can milk, 3 tablespoons lemon juice. Chill thoroughly. Garnish with finely chopped cucumber peel.

MINUTE RAGOUT FRONTENAC . . . For 4 servings, have 1½ pounds tenderloin, sirloin, round or chuck steak cut about ½-inch thick. Cut into ½-inch cubes. If you use any except the tenderest (probably highest priced) meat, sprinkle with meat tenderizer according to package directions. Begin the sauce by draining a small (4-ounce) tin of broiled mushrooms. Add the mushroom liquid to ½ cup red table wine. Cook uncovered over high heat until reduced one-half. Add reduced liquid to 1 tin beef gravy. Season with 1 teaspoon chopped parsley; ½ teaspoon fresh, chopped tarragon or ¼ teaspoon dried tarragon; 1 pinch thyme. Simmer 2 minutes. Gradually stir in bit by bit 2 tablespoons butter. Cook 3 minutes longer. At serving time, heat 2 tablespoons salad oil in a heavy frying pan or electric skillet at 380°. Sauté the meat quickly on both sides about 2 minutes along with the drained mushrooms, stirring with a fork so that meat browns evenly and is nicely tanned. Slightly warm in a tiny pan or ramekin, 4 tablespoons Cognac or Bourbon whiskey. Set alight with a match and pour over the meat, tossing lightly so that flavor permeates the beef. Add the sauce, correct the seasoning, adding salt and pepper if desired. Reheat, but do not boil.

MATINÉE POTATOES . . . Prepare according to directions 1 package French fried cubed potatoes, known as "Tiny Taters." Cook 1 slice onion in 1 tablespoon butter 3 minutes. Remove onion, add 2 tablespoons chopped fresh, or frozen green peppers, 2 canned pimientos, drained and diced. Heat thoroughly and add heated potatoes.

PINEAPPLE CROUTE . . . Drain 1 small tin sliced pineapple. Cook down the liquid to one-half. For each half-cup, add 2 tablespoons Kirsch or white rum. Remove crusts from 4 slices home-style white bread. Toast and butter immediately. Pour 2 tablespoons cooked-down syrup over each piece of toast. Allow to stand a minute or two. Top each slice with 1 or 2 slices pineapple. Garnish with whipped cream or whipped topping and bright red berries.

XV. QUICK CARBONNADE OF BEEF

As much a part of the tradition of Belgium as the paintings of the Old Flemish Masters is a Carbonnade Flamande. A type of beef stew some might call it—cooked with beer, richly redolent with onions and goodly scent of thyme.

In the more elegant versions of the Carbonnade, the meat is not cut into chunks, but sliced into "collops" about 2 inches square and only about a quarter-inch thick.

In the older recipes, the less tender cuts of beef were used and the Carbonnade was usually prepared on top of the stove and then set to bake in a slow oven for several hours. This new swift version can be prepared in just about 15 minutes, *if* you use sirloin steak or any other tender beef. Or—thriftily—you may use chuck or round steak and sprinkle with a packaged meat tenderizer according to directions. Either the seasoned or unseasoned tenderizer may be used. If you use a tenderizer, you will not need salt.

Tomato Stuffed with Shrimp
Quick Carbonnade of Beef
Boiled Potatoes
Broccoli
Heated Rye Bread
Swiss Chocolate Mousse

TOMATO STUFFED WITH SHRIMP . . . Slice the top off 6 firm medium-sized tomatoes. Skin if you wish. Carefully remove seeds and inner part. Sprinkle with a little salt, turn upside down to drain. Combine 2 cups small cooked shrimp (the tiniest possible) with 1 cup mayonnaise. Add ½ teaspoon yellow mustard. Place into hollowed tomatoes; sprinkle with fresh chopped parsley or chives.

QUICK CARBONNADE OF BEEF . . . To serve 6, have 3 pounds of sirloin or any good, tender, quick-cooking beef sliced ¼-inch thick. Sprinkle meat with freshly ground black pepper. Cut 3 slices of bacon into small bits, fry out slowly. Remove bacon from the pan and brown the meat, a few slices at a time. Keep meat warm and cook in the same bacon fat, 2 cups chopped onions —adding a little more fat if necessary. The onions should be soft but not browned. Add ½ teaspoon dried, powdered thyme; a 12-ounce can or bottle of beer; 1 cup canned beef gravy and 2 tablespoons chopped parsley. Combine all the ingredients. Bring to a boil and simmer about 5 minutes longer. Just before serving, stir in ¼ cup vinegar. Carbonnade is traditionally served with a fluffy, boiled potato, but some iconoclasts recently have suggested noodles!

SWISS CHOCOLATE MOUSSE . . . Grate ½ poud of sweet chocolate and place in a saucepan with 3 tablespoons hot water. Stir over very low heat until melted. Add slowly the well-beaten yolks of 6 eggs, stirring always in the same direction. Add ½ cup crème de cocoa liqueur. Cook a minute or two longer; remove from heat. Then gently fold in the stiffly beaten whites of 6 eggs. Pile in a serving bowl and chill in the refrigerator. Or, to save time, place in the freezer. Serves 6 to 8.

XVI. ROQUEBURGERS

Hard to believe that such excitement could be engendered by yet another hamburger! The Roquefort cheeseburgers known as Roqueburgers at the London Chop House have, for years, been the topic of much conversation, comment and curiosity. They are amongst the most popular items on the menu at the London Chop House; also across the street at the Caucus Club, which thrives under the same inspired Les Gruber management.

Chef Pancho, outstanding Detroit gourmet, was on vacation when we first began our Roqueburger investigations. So we tried on our own to reproduce the effect by taste and from memory. Not much luck! When he got back we learned what we did wrong. There *must* be an egg mixed into the meat to hold it together. And the proportions of cheese, butter and Cognac are crucial.

Crabmeat Venezia
Roqueburgers
Pancho's Broiled Potatoes and Mushrooms
Tomatoes Basilica
Pineapple Duo with Honey and Crème de Menthe

CRABMEAT VENEZIA . . . Most delicate and elegant appetizer. To serve 6 you will need 1½ cups cooked, canned or frozen crabmeat, very well chilled. Sprinkle with 3 tablespoons lemon juice and a little freshly ground black pepper. Dribble on 2 tablespoons of the very best virgin olive oil. Toss lightly.

ROQUEBURGERS . . . At the London Chop House they use the trimmings of prime aged beef to make their burgers. Moral: Get good meat and have it freshly ground. To make 6 Roqueburgers, you will need 2½ pounds chopped beef. Stir in 2 eggs, 2 tablespoons finely chopped onion, 1 tablespoon finely chopped parsley, 1 teaspoon salt, ¼ teaspoon pepper. Form into 12 patties ½-inch thick. For the filling: blend together ¼ pound Roquefort cheese or any other good sharp blue cheese, 4 tablespoons butter, 1 tablespoon Cognac. Stir until smooth, form into 6 balls. Chill until needed. Place each ball between 2 patties. Press edges firmly together. Broil quickly 3 to 5 minutes on each side or to the doneness of your desire.

PANCHO'S BROILED POTATOES AND MUSHROOMS . . . Slice peeled or unpeeled potatoes ½-inch thick. Arrange on buttered heatproof dish. Brush with melted butter, broil until brown. Turn, surround with button mushrooms. Another good brush of butter! Broil until brown and tender; sprinkle with salt and pepper.

TOMATOES BASILICA . . . Dice garden tomatoes and remove seeds. Sprinkle with olive oil and very little wine vinegar; a goodly amount of fresh or dried basil. Allow to stand covered in refrigerator until serving time. Garnish with watercress.

PINEAPPLE DUO . . . Cut a ripe pineapple in half lengthwise, right through the leaves and stalk. Remove the core as if it were the core of an apple. Cut around the edges to loosen the flesh and then cut the pineapple into slices on either side of the core cavity. The slices should be about ½-inch thick. On one side of the pineapple, dribble 2 tablespoons honey, on the other side 2 tablespoons Crème de Menthe. Insert decorative picks. Place the pineapple in the center of the table and let all help themselves.

XVII. SALT-BROILED STEAK

Woodsmen taking natural salt out of the salt licks are said to have been the first to "invent" the method of broiling meats in or on beds of salt.

Recently, salt-broiled steaks have been the subject of much discussion. The technique is greatly admired by people concerned about low cholesterol and low calorie diets. Salt broiling requires no extra fat. There is no spatter or smell or smoke.

Salt-broiling has been greatly simplified. No longer do we consider it necessary to encase the meat in masses of damp salt. Only a thin layer is used on the pan and the cooking is as fast as pan-frying. The steak emerges salted enough, but not too salty.

Salt-Broiled Steaks with Herbs or Garlic in "Butter"
Toasted Paprika Rolls
Broiled Hashed-Brown Potato Patties
Sliced Beefsteak Tomatoes and Onion Rings
in Wine Vinegar Dressing
Cranberry Brown Betty   Ice Cream Sauce

SALT-BROILED STEAKS . . . Use a heavy iron skillet or an electric skillet. Pre-heat the pan, getting it very hot—close to 400° if possible. Cover the entire surface with salt—about ¼ inch thick. Allow salt to heat another minute or two, then place steaks on salt, searing quickly—first on one side, then on the other. For individual ½-inch thick steaks, continue cooking about 5 minutes longer or till cooked to your liking. Brush with melted margarine to which you have added crushed garlic or finely chopped herbs.

TOASTED PAPRIKA ROLLS . . . Brown 'n serve rolls need not be browned in the oven. They are completely cooked already. Cut crusty French or club rolls lengthwise in halves. Toast lightly in the toaster and spread the top with butter or margarine. Sprinkle with paprika, coarsely ground black pepper and chopped chives.

BROILED HASHED-BROWN POTATO PATTIES . . . Quickest and easiest way to prepare them: place unthawed in a greased, shallow oven-proof dish that can go to the table. Brush with butter or bacon fat and broil till crusty on the top. They need not be turned.

WINE VINEGAR DRESSING . . . This is a very old-fashioned dressing made without oil: Use ½ cup wine vinegar, 3 tablespoons water, ½ teaspoon salt, ¼ teaspoon pepper, ½ teaspoon sugar, a slight dab of mustard if desired.

CRANBERRY BROWN BETTY . . . Canned whole-berry cranberry sauce and packaged crumbs make a highly sophisticated, fast and easy Brown Betty; a joy for your own modern woodsman.

Combine 1 cup bread crumbs or graham cracker crumbs with ¼ cup melted butter or margarine. Line the bottom of a shallow baking dish with half the mixture. On top of the crumbs, spread the contents of 1 can whole cranberry sauce. Sprinkle with 2 tablespoons brown sugar, ½ teaspoon cinnamon, ¼ teaspoon each nutmeg and cloves. Add 4 tablespoons warm water and cover cranberries with the rest of the crumbs. Dot with butter and bake in a hot oven (425°) about 20 minutes or until hot, bubbly and lightly browned. Serve with cream or ice cream sauce. Serves 4 to 6.

ICE CREAM SAUCE . . . With a fork, stir 1 cup ice cream until it is the consistency of hard sauce. If desired, a tablespoonful of orange juice or sherry wine may be added. Butter-pecan ice cream makes a particularly good sauce for the Cranberry Brown Betty.

XVIII. SIRLOIN MARCHAND DU VIN

In the midst of a phantasmagoria of lights and luxury you dine at the Tower Suite on the forty-eighth floor of New York's Time and Life Building as if you were a pampered guest in your rich uncle's penthouse with your own Edwardian waitress and butler hovering over your table. No à la carte ordering. Course after course appears in an elegant processional.

First a little silvery tray of miniature appetizers surrounding a tiny nosegay; a choice of soups from silver tureens; a fish course followed by a thimble-sized sherbet known here as the Intermezzo. Then the roasts; vegetables; a salad; cheeses; desserts followed by nuts and figs, fresh fruits, home-sized cups of coffee; the Tower Suite's own tiny pastries. This little dinner is a mere excerpt from one enjoyed at the Tower Suite.

Tower Suite Miniature Appetizers
Beet Vichyssoise
Sirloin Marchand du Vin
Tiny Carrots   Baby Lima Beans
Potato Puffs
Raspberries Romanoff

TOWER SUITE MINIATURE APPETIZERS . . . Arrange on a silver tray: Small pitted ripe olives topped with well-seasoned raw beef; tiny baby shrimps on slices of water chestnut; cherry tomatoes filled with cream cheese; Lilliput sandwiches only an inch square, using thin slices of salami instead of bread, cream cheese for the filling; Pascal celery cut only ½-inch long, filled with Roquefort cheese spread.

BEET VICHYSSOISE . . . To a 10-ounce can frozen cream of potato soup add 1 cup canned chicken broth, 1 jar chopped junior-food beets, ½ cup cream, 1 or 2 drops *Tabasco* sauce. Beat with rotary beater or whir in blender. Heat or chill as desired. Serve with chopped chives: 4 small servings.

SIRLOIN MARCHAND DU VIN . . . At the Tower Suite they charcoal-grill individual 6-ounce sirloin steaks and serve with sauce Marchand du Vin which may be "copied" by heating 1 can beef gravy with ½ cup red table wine. Simmer gently 10 minutes.

POTATO PUFFS . . . Use quick-frozen.

RASPBERRIES ROMANOFF . . . Strawberries are the usual, but raspberries are remarkably good. To serve 4, use a quart of berries. At the table, squeeze over the berries the juice of 1 small orange or lemon; add 4 tablespoons Grand Marnier or Cointreau. Cover with a deep swoosh (2 cups) heavy cream, whipped and sweetened to taste.

XIX. STEAK AND MUSHROOM PIE

Geraldine Fitzgerald is a lady of many lives—a renowned and serious actress, a star, and a writer for television and the movies. But the role she plays with the greatest zest is that of mother to her grown-up son and 12-year-old daughter and wife to Stuart Scheftel, a prominent real estate man and television producer with more than a passing interest in high-level politics.

Their apartment on Park Avenue has the air of a country house that might be found in County Wicklow, where Geraldine Fitzgerald was born and raised. The floors are of white vinyl. In the dining room, which opens off the drawing room, there are English chintzes of green and yellow on a white background; chair covers of white Irish linen piped in green. The food has an Irish county elegance with traditional recipes adapted to the swift New York tempo.

I remember a steak and mushroom pie served in frozen patty shells, taking the place of the old-time *vol-au-vent*. "The meat is cooked in 5 minutes instead of 5 hours," says Miss Fitzgerald proudly.

County Wicklow Fish Paté
Steak and Mushroom Pie
Tossed Green Salad
Kathleen McGuire's Applesauce Fool

COUNTY WICKLOW FISH PATÉ . . . Like a great many other delicacies of Ireland, this one has a French name and what might be called a French mood. In the Old Land it would be made with a mortar and pestle.

Here Geraldine Fitzgerald uses an electric blender. Place in the blender 1 can of anchovy filets cut into smallish pieces and the oil in the can, 1 small can tuna, drained. Add the yolks of 2 hard-cooked eggs, 1 tablespoon heavy cream, 1 tablespoon lemon juice or enough lemon juice and cream to make a paté thick enough to mold with your hands. Mold on a green leaf or a leaf-shaped plate. Sprinkle with the finely chopped whites of 2 hard-cooked eggs, garnish with chopped chives and a dash of paprika. Serve with thinly sliced crusty French rolls or melba toast.

STEAK AND MUSHROOM PIE . . . To serve 6, have 2 pounds round steak cut into one-inch squares about ½-inch thick. Sprinkle liberally with seasoned meat tenderizer, according to package directions. In a large skillet, heat 3 tablespoons vegetable oil. Cook ¾ cup chopped onion until soft and pale golden. Add meat and cook about 5 minutes or until meat is browned and tender.

Meanwhile cook uncovered about 6 minutes one 10-ounce can beef gravy, 1 teaspoon Worcestershire sauce, ½ teaspoon *Kitchen Bouquet,* the liquid from a 6-ounce tin of broiled, canned mushrooms. Combine browned meat and mushrooms with sauce. Simmer 2 minutes longer. Serve in 6 frozen puff-paste patty shells which have been baked according to package directions.

KATHLEEN MCGUIRE'S APPLESAUCE FOOL . . . Kathleen was a housekeeper when the children were small and is remembered for many reasons, including this dessert which is remarkably good and distinctive yet couldn't be simpler. Place in a shallow serving dish or an attractive pie plate a half-inch layer of chilled canned applesauce. Cover with a half-inch layer of sweetened whipped cream. Sprinkle generously with shavings of bittersweet chocolate or chocolate "shot."

XX. TAHITI KABOBS, SAUCE CHORON

Excitedly, a friend writes from Papeete on the South Sea island of Tahiti, "I just learned about and ate a wonderful-tasting dish . . . really gourmet, yet so simple to prepare.

"Here, and on the other Polynesian Islands, they have

an ancient culinary art that is different from anywhere
else in the world. When you add to this a strong French
influence, the combination is hard to beat."

The dish that sent my wandering friend into such a
whirl is a beef-lobster kabob served with a tomato-
flavored Bearnaise sauce whose official gastronomic
name is Sauce Choron.

"Beef," she mentions, "is at a premium in the South
Sea islands and is not often tender. People have always
wrapped meat in papaya leaves in order to tenderize it.
Now they use meat tenderizer that comes in a jar . . .
even as you and I."

This is a delicious menu for elegant outdoor cooking,
particularly when it is served in the manner of Tahiti
with French bread and white wine.

Tahiti Kabobs   Sauce Choron
French Fried Sweet Potatoes
Grilled Eggplant
Green Chive Butter
French Bread   White Wine
Pineapple in Orange Juice

TAHITI KABOBS WITH SAUCE CHORON . . . To make 4
skewersful, get 1½ pounds cubed beef from the top or
bottom round. Cubes should be about 1½ inches thick.
Sprinkle with meat tenderizer, following directions on
jar. On each skewer place a cube of beef, than a chunk
of lobster tail meat (if frozen it should be thawed first),
then another beef cube, followed by another lobster
chunk. Brush with melted butter or salad oil. Broil or
grill over hot coals about 8 minutes or until the lobster
flakes at the touch of a fork. During the cooking, turn
several times, basting with a blend of 4 tablespoons
each white table wine or dry vermouth and peanut oil
mixed with 1 tablespoon lemon juice. Remove meat and
lobster from skewer and serve with . . .

Sauce Choron is made by adding 2 tablespoons canned
tomato sauce to ½ cup homemade or prepared Sauce
Bearnaise.

FRENCH FRIED SWEET POTATOES . . . Peel and cut
sweet potatoes into strips or slices about ½-inch thick.

Fry in deep fat at 360° until lightly tanned. Just before serving, reheat in deep fat at 375° about 1 minute or until hot, crusty and cooked through. Drain on paper towels and sprinkle with salt (or see page 76 for cold-start method).

GRILLED EGGPLANT . . . Cut eggplant, peeled or unpeeled as you choose, into half-inch slices. Season with salt and pepper. Brush on both sides with olive or peanut oil. Broil until delicately browned.

GREEN CHIVE BUTTER . . . 1 tablespoon chopped chives, 1 tablespoon heavy cream, 2 drops Tabasco and 1 small clove garlic, crushed, added to ¼ pound softened whipped butter. This butter should be delicately green in color so you may want to add 1 or 2 drops green coloring.

PINEAPPLE IN ORANGE JUICE . . . Cut fresh pineapple into cubes or use quick-frozen pineapple chunks and cover with orange juice. If fresh pineapple is used, you may want to add a little honey or sugar.

XXI. TENDERLOIN TIPS EN BROCHETTE

Jimmy's Harbourside Restaurant on the bustling Fish Pier is as much a part of the Boston scene as the Sacred Cod that hangs in the State House. Known far and wide as the Chowder King, Jimmy Doulas vaulted to national fame when some years ago he was implored by the former Governor (now Senator) Leverett Saltonstall, to bring his chowder down to the Senate dining room in Washington, D.C., so that the nation's lawmakers could know how a real fish chowder ought to taste. Since that time he has made many such official trips to Washington.

But the creamy chowder of such renown is by no means all of Jimmy's repertoire. Almost as famous are the Broiled Scallops, Jimmy Style; served to everyone as a welcomer after 5 o'clock.

His fish is of course, the top-of-the-catch, incredibly good. He is almost as proud of his tenderloin tips served *en brochette* with a touch of oregano. The salads too show the influence of Greece, his native land. So does the rice pudding (*rizogalo*) served with squares of *baklava*.

Broiled Scallops, Jimmy's Style
Tenderloin Tips en Brochette
Sautéed Corn
Greek Salad
Rizogalo (Rice Pudding)
Baklava

BROILED SCALLOPS, JIMMY'S STYLE . . . To serve 4
to 6, you will need 1 pint (1 pound) sea scallops. Cut
crosswise in halves. Butter a platter or other oven-proof
serving dish. Arrange scallops in a single layer. Brush
with melted butter. Sprinkle with ½ teaspoon salt, ¼
teaspoon pepper, ½ teaspoon garlic salt, 1 tablespoon
lemon juice, 2 tablespoons fine cracker crumbs. Broil
slowly, well below a pre-heated broiler, about 8 minutes.
Do not turn. Bless with a couple of tablespoons of dry
sherry wine. Harpoon with toothpicks.

TENDERLOIN TIPS EN BROCHETTE . . . Since he serves
so many tenderloin steaks, Jimmy uses only the tapering
tips. But the rest of us will find it more practical to cut
inch-thick tenderloin steaks into cubes or use less expensive cuts like round steak, tenderized according to
directions on the package of meat tenderizer. Brush with
olive oil, salt and pepper. Broil 4 to 5 minutes, turning
frequently, or until done to suit you. Sprinkle with Greek
oregano, which is sometimes known as wild marjoram.

SAUTÉED CORN . . . At Jimmy's, during fresh corn
season, they cook corn just one minute in a pressure
cooker. Scrape it off the cob with a long sharp knife, or
thaw frozen corn and sauté about 2 minutes in butter.
Season to taste with salt and freshly ground black pepper.

GREEK SALAD . . . Cut a head of lettuce into pieces.
Add 2 tomatoes cut in wedges; 1 onion, thinly sliced; 1
chopped green pepper; 1 sliced cucumber. Mix in a bowl.
Add 1 teaspoon salt; ¼ teaspoon pepper; ½ cup salad
or olive oil; ¼ cup lemon juice. Garnish with anchovies
and radish roses.

RIZOGALO (RICE PUDDING) . . . To 1 quart hot milk,
add ½ cup converted rice. Simmer about 15 minutes,
stirring occasionally. Add ¾ cup sugar, the rind of ½
lemon. Cook about 8 minutes longer. Stir in 1 egg mixed
with 2 tablespoons cold milk, ½ teaspoon cornstarch.

Serve warm or cold sprinkled with cinnamon, along with . . .

BAKLAVA . . . A sweet, rich pastry which can now be bought frozen. Simply cut into squares.

XXII. TOURNEDOS ON GOLDEN PEDESTALS

Lord Rumbottom is a name to remember when you get to St. Thomas. Milord's was, a few years ago, slightly rowdy and noisy . . . a dancing and drinking not-much-for-eating spot about four miles out of town.

All this has changed: Lord Rumbottom now brings to the minds of knowing Virgin Islanders a vision of some of the best food on the island. Not at all "native," either! The new Lord Rumbottom is a red-headed young giant of a man by the name of Bill Bligh, as in captain of the Bounty. His father was a disciple of the great chef Louis Diat. Bill assumes that he might have inherited a passion for food and cooking.

Bill Bligh is chief cook as well as captain, host and maitre d'. His place is already famous for rib roast served with Potatoes Anna. But he "hates to be typed as a roast beef joint" . . . has a standing wager with the world that he can produce any dish in the Larousse *Encyclopedia of Classical French Cooking,* providing he gets twenty-four hours notice and the ingredients are available.

Nobody ever forgets his carrots in a miraculous orange sauce, a classic Parisian dish with some tropically personal touches. Up to this moment—from all we have been told—he has refused to divulge the Secret. But here we have it step by step just as he does it.

Lord Rumbottom Salad
Tournedos on Golden Pedestals
Artichoke Hearts with Lime Butter
Carrots à l'Orange
Coupe Royale

LORD RUMBOTTOM SALAD . . . Appears automatically on the table as soon as a guest is seated . . . mixed greens served in a frosty-chilled bowl. Arranged over the greens are very thin slices of onion and green pepper, tomatoes cut in wedges. The salad is tossed at the table with what Bill calls his Number One French dressing, made of "2 parts Italian olive oil, 1 part tarragon wine vinegar, salt, pepper. That's all." Serve with a generous dusting of grated Parmesan cheese.

TOURNEDOS ON GOLDEN PEDESTALS . . . Tiny 4 ounce steaks served two to a person on rounds of white bread that have been gilded in butter on both sides.

ARTICHOKE HEARTS WITH LIME BUTTER . . . Cook quick-frozen artichoke hearts, drain and serve with melted butter to which has been added 1 or 2 tablespoons lime (or lemon) juice, a few grains of cayenne pepper. Serve with lime sections.

CARROTS À L'ORANGE . . . For six servings use 6 medium-sized peeled and sliced carrots. Cook quickly in very little water—about ¾ cup boiling water with 1 teaspoon salt. When the water is half cooked away, add 4 tablespoons butter, ¾ cup orange juice, the rind of 1 lemon cut into strips, ½ cup sugar, 4 whole cloves. Cook uncovered until carrots are tender. Just about 5 minutes before serving (this is the real wizardry) add 1 tablespoon good white Cruzan rum.

COUPE ROYALE . . . Over a package of frozen mixed fruit pour 4 tablespoons Cointreau and allow to stand until almost, but not completely, thawed. Serve in champagne glasses.

XXIII. TOURNEDOS MARK TWAIN

A quarter of a mile from the inn that still bears his name, Mark Twain built his last home on a hilltop in Redding, Connecticut. Some of the neighbors still remember that . . . always hatless, with his dramatic white hair and his famous white-flannel suit, he loved to walk down the hill in the late afternoon to have a beer and a snack at what was then a country pub. Now it is a cozy but elegant eating place. Lorraine's Mark Twain . . . owned by Lorraine Hunt, a dynamic, sparkling brown-eyed blonde.

Celebrities continue to find their way to Redding and the inn. One may discover, as we did the other evening, conductor-composer Leonard Bernstein dining on the specialties of Chef Louis Hus from Brittany. Dinner began with *soupe du jour;* on that occasion—cream of cauliflower. The main course, tournedos with Sauce Chasseur, green beans, a salad and afterwards one of Chef Louis' quite remarkable *cakes du jour* with a bottom crust of puff paste like a Napoleon, a deep lemon-tangy filling, another layer of cake, then lemon-flavored whipped cream.

Admittedly our menu is a copy, but very good.

Cream of Cauliflower Soup
Tournedos Mark Twain
Braised Celery   Green Beans
Chef Louis' Lemon Cake

CREAM OF CAULIFLOWER SOUP . . . Add to 1 can condensed chicken soup 1½ soup cans milk, one 10-ounce package frozen cauliflower cooked and mashed or pureed. Simmer about 4 minutes; add a few grains of cayenne pepper. Garnish with chopped chives. Serves 4.

TOURNEDOS MARK TWAIN . . . The proper cut for this elegant entrée is the heart of a filet mignon. There is no reason why you should not use any small individual steak or even a good thick hamburger. Grill the meat so that it is crusty on the outside, rosy in the middle. Serve with this a quick version of the famous *Sauce chasseur* (Hunters' sauce).

Drain the juice from a 4-ounce can of sliced broiled mushrooms. To the juice add ¼ cup white wine and cook rapidly uncovered until reduced by half. Add to one 10-ounce can beef gravy and ½ cup canned tomato sauce. Cook for a few moments; add the mushrooms and 1 tablespoon fresh or 1 teaspoon dried chopped parsley and tarragon. Simmer 5 minutes longer. Pour sauce over steak or pass separately.

BRAISED CELERY . . . Heat a 12-ounce can of celery hearts in the liquid from the can. Drain and brown lightly in butter.

CHEF LOUIS' LEMON CAKE . . . This is a long, narrow cake about 4″ x 12″. To make the first layer, thaw and roll out 2 quick-frozen patty shells, the kind intended for making chicken patties. Bake according to package directions. When cool, cover with an inch layer of lemon pie filling made from 1 package of mix. On top of the lemon pie filling place an inch-thick layer of sponge cake or ladyfingers and cover the top with a deep layer of sweetened whipped cream, seasoned with lemon juice.

XXIV. VIENNESE BOILED BEEF UNDER PRESSURE

Once we had the temerity to serve a boiled beef dinner to a gourmet who has spent considerable time in Austria. We knew it was temerity even before he told us that boiled beef has always been in Vienna "not merely a dish, but a way of life. Not just something to eat, but a philosophy, a state of mind, the subject of endless discussion and controversy."

As the gentleman in question accepted another serving—his third—he said loftily, "Obviously this is not one of your fast half-hour dishes." When we assured him it was, he seemed not only stunned but furious. He wouldn't even let us explain that our secret weapons were a pressure cooker, some canned consommé and a package of gelatin that gives to the broth something of the same texture as the slow, slow cooking of beef bones.

Cup of Beef Broth
Viennese Boiled Beef Under Pressure
Horseradish with Applesauce
Baby Carrots with Chopped Dill
Boiled Potatoes
Lettuce and Cucumber Salad
Chocolate Pudding Viennese

VIENNESE BOILED BEEF UNDER PRESSURE . . . To serve 4, place a 2-pound pot roast or brisket of beef into a pressure cooker along with an onion stuck with 2 cloves, 4 peppercorns, 2 stalks of celery. Cover with 2 cans condensed consommé. Add 2 soup cans water, 1 package unflavored gelatin. Cook under pressure according to manufacturer's directions 20 minutes. Bring down pressure immediately by letting cold water run down the side. Remove cover. The meat at this point should be just about tender. Nevertheless, allow it to cook slowly, uncovered, on top of the stove for another 10 minutes or until done. This last uncovered cooking takes away any steamy taste and gives to the meat and broth a mellow richness.

In Austria, the presentation of boiled beef is a ritual. A cup of the broth is generally served first with some simple garnish—perhaps a little parsley or a slice of toast. The beef is cut into slices about an inch thick and served on a heavy heated silver dish under a silver cover. Several accompaniments are provided, including pickled gherkins, coarse salt and always horseradish in some form or another—often mixed with applesauce.

HORSERADISH WITH APPLESAUCE . . . To 1 cup applesauce, add 2 teaspoons lemon juice, 2 teaspoons vinegar, 1½ tablespoons grated horseradish. Season to taste with a little additional sugar if desired; a dash of salt and a few grains of white pepper. Makes 1 cup.

LETTUCE AND CUCUMBER SALAD . . . Serve thinly sliced cucumbers on leafy lettuce or romaine with a very light dressing of equal parts salad oil and cider vinegar. Season with a little salt, pepper, a touch of sugar. Garnish with sliced hard-cooked eggs.

CHOCOLATE PUDDING VIENNESE . . . Make up a package of bittersweet chocolate pudding according to directions. Add 1 teaspoon almond extract, ¼ teaspoon cinnamon. Serve in small coffee cups or wine glasses. Top each serving with a macaroon.

BIRDS OF PARADISE
TO EAT

❧❦❧

POULTRY

❦

Chicken poses a problem when you put a half-hour limit on cooking time. On first thought, a turkey or a duck seems impossible. But, as you will see from the following pages, The Fast Gourmet is not easily fazed. When all else fails, she turns with aplomb to the rotisserie and the corner delicatessen or the highway grill, where the barbecues keep turning.

With such wiles as these, she produces a Thanksgiving turkey (page 235) or a chicken flambée with black cherries (page 66).

A duckling, cut into serving pieces, roasts in twenty to twenty-five minutes, and becomes *à l'orange* or *Bigarade,* when marmalade and wine and herbs are added to canned beef gravy (page 74). A pressure cooker produces old-fashioned fricassee in twelve to fifteen minutes (page 80). There is no tell-tale taste of steam if you bring down the pressure immediately, uncover the cooker and let the chicken simmer for a few minutes longer on top of the stove.

Present-day broilers and fryers (1½ to 2½ pounds) are so young and tender that they can be cooked by broiling or frying in 20 to 25 minutes. If you want to broil larger chickens, say up to 3½ pounds, you may want to use a tenderizer. As in any other case, when you use a tenderizer, the cooking time is reduced by one-quarter.

Broiled chicken should never show the slightest tint of pink. Generally they are started flesh side up, broiled five to six inches away from the heat and finished skin side up. This method makes the skin crisp and crackly.

I. ARROZ VOLCANO WITH BANANAS
AND PEAS

Grenville Walker is a tall, dark, handsome man who, as he puts it, travels to eat. For, if he didn't travel and induce other people to travel, he couldn't eat. Travel is his profession; cooking his hobby. Several times he has circled the globe, visited every continent except Antarctica. Wherever he goes he picks up ideas. Buffet parties are his forte.

His cucumber canapés are particularly tasty, easy, inexpensive . . . quite low in calories. The recipe for his *arroz con pollo* (chicken with rice) comes, he says, "from central South America and on shipboard to Spain." He has recreated his own "no knife" version. Knives he considers a nuisance and a menace at buffets. He calls his *arroz* "*Volcano*" because it is shaped like a mountain and has a large pimiento crowning the top like a glowing crater.

Grenville Walker's Cucumber Canapés
Arroz Volcano with Bananas and Peas
Lettuce, Tomato and Avocado Salad
Bel Paese Cheese
Frozen Pineapple Chunks with Kirsch or Rum

GRENVILLE WALKER'S CUCUMBER CANAPÉS . . . To make a dozen canapés, "peel a long cucumber carelessly, leaving a bit of the skin here and there." Slice ¼ inch thick. Cover with 2 cups water to which you add ½ cup vinegar, 1 tablespoon salt. Allow to stand at least an hour. Dry well. Place on rounds of salty rye bread, spread with mayonnaise. Top with another dab of mayonnaise and sprinkle with cayenne pepper or paprika, depending upon whether you want your canapés hot or not.

ARROZ VOLCANO . . . Although the original recipe calls for chicken, Grenville Walker uses turkey. Since his recipe is designed to serve 20, he starts by roasting a 10-pound turkey which is later cut into ½-inch cubes. To serve 5 or 6, you will need 2½ to 3 cups cooked turkey or chicken. (A fine use for leftovers!)

Chop, rather finely, 1 large sweet green pepper, 1 good-sized onion. Sauté till tender in 2 tablespoons oil or butter. Prepare 1½ cups pre-cooked packaged rice according to directions, but use good strong chicken or turkey broth instead of water and add ¼ teaspoon saffron. If you don't happen to have saffron use 1 teaspoon curry powder. (The color is somewhat the same but the flavor is different.) Add about ½ cup beer to the diced chicken and heat. Combine with cooked rice, sautéed onions and pepper. Add 1 package lightly cooked frozen peas; season to taste with hot pepper or *Tabasco*. If mixture is on the dry side add a little more beer.

Meanwhile, slice 6 bananas in half lengthwise. Place in buttered pan, sprinkle with brown sugar, dot with butter, bake at 375° about 10 minutes or until sugar and butter have melted. Pile the rice mixture on a heated platter in a mound. Cover the top with a large canned drained pimiento—"that's the crater." Arrange bananas over the mountain "like streams of lava flowing down." Garnish base with greenery.

FROZEN PINEAPPLE CHUNKS . . . To serve 6, you will need two 10-ounce packages of frozen pineapple chunks. At the beginning of dinner, place in a bowl, sprinkle with 2 or 3 tablespoons kirsh (white spirit made from black cherries) or white rum. Garnish with mint.

II. BALINESE CHICKEN

What the chafing dish was to the belles of the Naughty Naughts . . . the electric skillet is to the modern hostess . . . and a great deal more. It is, in fact, almost indispensable. Versatile and obliging when you are in a mad rush and graciously elegant when you are entertaining.

You don't need an electric skillet to prepare this interesting, quick and knowingly off-beat Balinese chicken dish. It can be done in any deep skillet or Dutch oven. So can the *Pommes Washington*—named not for the Father of This Country—but for the tart Washington State winesap apples which are ideal for this dish.

> *Oriental Egg Flower Soup*
> *Balinese Chicken*
> *Two-Finger Hominy Poi*
> *Baby Peas and Onions*
> *Pommes Washington*

ORIENTAL EGG FLOWER SOUP . . . To a quart of boiling chicken broth, add ½ cup drained, canned water chestnuts sliced or chopped. Simmer about 5 minutes. Beat 2 eggs and pour into the chicken broth, stirring slowly "until small flowers form." Add a touch of *Tabasco* to taste.

BALINESE CHICKEN . . . Brown in a hot skillet (electric or otherwise) 2 pounds chicken parts in 2 tablespoons shortening at 400° until well gilded and slightly crisp. Sprinkle with salt and pepper. Add one 10¾ ounce can chicken gravy, ½ cup drained, canned or frozen pineapple chunks and ½ teaspoon ground cinnamon. Turn down the heat to 200°. Cover and simmer about 20 minutes or until chicken is tender. Makes 4 to 6 servings.

TWO-FINGER HOMINY POI . . . In the South Sea Islands *poi* is made from the root of the taro plant. Here quick-cooking packaged hominy grits may be substituted. Prepare according to directions as for breakfast cereal. A Two-Finger Poi is medium thick so that it can be scooped up with two fingers. A thicker *poi* is called One-Finger; thinner . . . it becomes Three-Finger.

BABY PEAS AND ONIONS . . . Comes quick-frozen. Heat according to package directions.

POMMES WASHINGTON . . . Peel, quarter and remove cores from 6 medium-size tart Washington winesap apples. Place in a 2 quart saucepan, adding ½ cup hot water. The idea is to use as little water as possible. Cook with cover on until apples fall apart. Mash coarsely to form a thick puree. Add ⅓ cup sugar, ⅛ teaspoon salt, 1 teaspoon vanilla. While apples are cooking, pour 1 tablespoon caramel maple syrup or dark cane syrup or honey in each of six 6-ounce custard cups, swirling the syrup to coat the entire inside surface. Spoon the apple mixture into the cups. Place in a pan of hot water. Cover and cook over moderate heat 15 minutes. Serve warm or cold with soft custard or whipped cream.

III. BREAST OF CHICKEN CACCIATORE

St. Thomas, Virgin Islands—What does one wear to a cook-out at the Henry Kimmelmans? (He is Minister of Commerce on the islands.) "Just a little cotton . . . but it could be by Dior."

Henry and Charlotte have a way of combining warm

informality with suave elegance. At their house, indoors and outdoors flow into each other. The buffet is set under a tropical velvety sky beside a lily pool lit by Hawaiian flares.

Specialty of the house is Charlotte's chilled lemon soufflé which has many obliging features. Can be prepared hours or even a full day ahead of time. Despite its delectable taste and luscious airs this soufflé is amazingly low in calories. If you use a non-caloric sweetener and low-calorie whipped topping . . . only about 100 calories per serving.

Assorted Hors d'Œuvres
Breast of Chicken Cacciatore and/or
Spaghetti with White Clam Sauce
Green Beans
Tossed Salad
Charlotte's Slimming Lemon Soufflé
After Dinner Coffee with Rum

ASSORTED HORS D'ŒUVRES . . . Serve before guests sit down to table. The Kimmelmans always include a number of different vegetables such as chick peas and celery root marinated in French dressing, pimientos, various types of salami, ham, sardines, anchovies.

BREAST OF CHICKEN CACCIATORE . . . Comes quick-frozen in pliofilm packages all ready to drop into boiling water and heat. Sprinkle with a little rosemary and garnish with button mushrooms.

SPAGHETTI WITH WHITE CLAM SAUCE . . . There are a number of very good clam sauces on the market, some with tomatoes, some without. Garnish with whole clams, fresh or canned.

CHARLOTTE'S SLIMMING SOUFFLÉ . . . Sprinkle 1 envelope unflavored gelatin over ¼ cup cold water. Separate 4 eggs. Mix the yolks with ½ cup lemon juice, ½ teaspoon salt. Add ½ cup sugar or, if you are really serious about calorie counting, use the equivalent amount of liquid non-caloric sweetener—about three teaspoons. Cook in the top of a double boiler over boiling water, stirring constantly, 4 to 5 minutes or until thick and custardy. Stir in the gelatin and 1 teaspoon grated lemon rind. Cool. Meanwhile beat 4 egg whites until stiff. Beat 1 cup heavy cream or use 1 package low calorie dessert topping mix. Pile on top of the egg whites. Gently stir in the lemon mixture. Pour into 2-quart bowl or soufflé dish. Even more dramatically use a 1½ quart soufflé dish and make a collar of brown paper or foil to stand at least 2 inches above. Brush the inside of the strip with salad oil. Chill until firm. At serving time sprinkle with crumbled graham crackers or macaroons. Serves 8.

AFTER DINNER COFFEE WITH RUM . . . Serve instant espresso coffee with a twist of orange peel that has been studded with whole cloves. Add a touch of Virgin Island rum if desired.

IV. CHICKEN WITH BLACK CHERRIES

At four o'clock on a Monday afternoon, a certain young woman picked up the phone in her boss's office. It was her husband.

"What," he asked in a tone of voice she had learned to distrust, "are we doing about supper tonight?"

"I hadn't thought, but you might pick up a chicken at the delicatessen on your way home," said she, vaguely.

"You don't suppose . . ." he began.

The upshot of the matter was that he had invited two people to dinner. He simply couldn't get out of it.

Her vagueness vanished. She went into high gear. The chicken, hot off the spit, saved the day—aided, of course, by a can of black cherries, beef gravy, a jar of Hollandaise and some frozen cream puffs.

Asparagus with Mousseline Sauce
Chicken with Black Cherries
Potato Puffs
Sliced Tomato-Cucumber Salad
Profiterolles or Frozen Ice Cream Roll au Chocolat

ASPARAGUS WITH MOUSSELINE SAUCE . . . To make Sauce Mousseline stir ½ cup heavy cream, whipped into 1 cup warm Hollandaise sauce, homemade or you can buy it in a jar.

CHICKEN WITH BLACK CHERRIES . . . You can buy your bird from the rotisserie or roast or broil your own. Broiled or roasted, the bird takes on the look and the taste of a Paris production when presented with this ravishing sauce and garniture.

Sorcery begins with a can of gravy . . . beef, not chicken gravy as you might expect. To the gravy add the juice drained from a large (No. 2) can of pitted black cherries. Add also 1 clove garlic crushed, ½ cup sherry wine, ¼ teaspoon dried marjoram; allow to simmer gently about 5 minutes, stirring from time to time. Add the drained cherries. Heat but do not boil. At serving time, pour the sauce and cherries over and around the chicken. Garnish with bouquets, rather than sprigs, of watercress.

POTATO PUFFS . . . Buy them quick-frozen and heat according to directions. Sprinkle with a little paprika and chives or parsley.

PROFITEROLLES AU CHOCOLAT . . . Little cream puffs filled with ice cream. Buy your cream puffs or make them from a mix. Fill with ice cream, place in the freezer. At serving time thaw only a little and serve with heated chocolate sauce to which you have added a little cinnamon and a dash of rum. In some markets these tiny frozen cream puffs can be procured ready-to-serve.

V. CHICKEN IN A COCOON

Deep in the heart of Broadway, surrounded by the glittering theatre marquees on West 48th Street, is the Restaurant Vesuvio. Some New Yorkers still remember it as it used to be on Mulberry Street in Little Italy years ago. It is dressier now, but the atmosphere hasn't changed a great deal. There is the same Neapolitan air about it and the scent of oregano. A realistic mural of the Bay of Naples still dominates the back room with the sunken liner *Andrea Doria* added as a wistful afterthought to the painting.

The two most famous dishes are the Baked Seafood Vesuvio generally served as a first course and the chicken, which is lovingly seasoned, wrapped first in bacon then baked and served in a silver cocoon.

Baked Seafood Vesuvio
Chicken in a Cocoon
Shoestring Zucchini

Fresh Spinach Salad
Basket of Fresh Fruit
Amoretti (Italian macaroons)

BAKED SEAFOOD VESUVIO . . . For each serving, arrange on a heatproof plate a small Danish lobster tail split as for broiling, 2 or 3 scampi or shrimp, 3 scallops and 3 clams in the shell. The clams may be omitted if desired. Pour on 2 tablespoons clam juice combined with 1 tablespoon each fine breadcrumbs, parsley and Parmesan cheese. Add ¼ teaspoon dried oregano and a sprinkle of salt and pepper. Sprinkle this mixture over the seafood. Dribble with olive oil and set in a moderately hot oven (375°) about 15 minutes or until the seafood is done. Serve on the baking dish with crusty French bread.

CHICKEN IN A COCOON . . . At Vesuvio the chicken is deboned, but this is not absolutely necessary. Provide half of a small broiler for each person. Divide into 2 parts, leg and breast. Roll a strip of bacon around each part. Beat up 1 egg; season the egg with salt, pepper and a speck of oregano. Dip the chicken into the seasoned egg and then roll in fine breadcrumbs, wrap in foil and bake in a hot oven (400°) 20 minutes.

SHOESTRING ZUCCHINI . . . For each person you will need 1 medium-size *zucchini* (Italian green squash). Wash but do not peel. Cut into long thin strips about ¼-inch wide. Coat strips with flour, shake to remove any excess flour and drop a handful at a time into deep hot oil at 370°. Cook just about 1 minute or until pale golden and crisp. Remove with a slotted spoon. Drain on paper towels. Serve hot.

FRESH SPINACH SALAD . . . You can now buy ready-washed crisp young green spinach in plastic bags. Tear the leaves into eatable pieces and serve with a light mayonnaise which has been made even thinner by adding sour cream or yogurt.

VI. CHICKEN MOUTARDE WITH GRAPES

A writer friend headlines the story that my daughter "Claudia's *haute cuisine* comes out of a lowly tin." Quite true that, after a year of study at Maxim's Academie in

Paris, she did feature, at her first "personal" dinner party, a dish borrowed from one of Mama's quick recipes. But added several of her own improvements.

When we asked her, "What's for dessert?", she looked at us haughtily, "Baked Alaska, Mother, what else!" At that instant we felt that whoever once said we begin learning all over again from our children *must* have been a mother . . . A mother who stepped back as we did—and learned. For to save herself the trouble of cutting into the Alaska (sometimes hazardous) she made hers into individual servings . . . A Baked Alaska per person.

Chicken Moutarde with White Grapes
Sea Shell Pasta
Argenteuil Carrots
Belgian Endive Salad with French Dressing
Claudia's Individual Baked Alaskas

CHICKEN MOUTARDE WITH GRAPES . . . To serve 6, use 3 cans chicken in golden gravy. Rinse each tin with 6 tablespoons dry white table wine or 2 tablespoons lemon juice and 4 tablespoons water. Stir in 3 to 4 teaspoons yellow prepared mustard. Mix thoroughly; bring to a boil. Cook gently about 2 minutes, then add 1 small tin or 1 cup white seedless grapes which have been drained and heated for a couple of minutes in 2 tablespoons butter.

SEA SHELL PASTA . . . You can buy small or large sea shell-shaped pasta, bowknots, even curlicues. Cook according to package directions.

CARROTS AUX ASPERGES . . . After thawing 1 package frozen asparagus tips, cut them into ½-inch bits. Combine with 8 small white onions, 1 sprig parsley, 4 tablespoons hot water, ¾ teaspoon salt, ½ teaspoon white pepper. Cover and simmer gently about 10 minutes. Just before serving, sprinkle with 1 teaspoon sugar. Serves 6.

CLAUDIA'S INDIVIDUAL BAKED ALASKAS . . . There is a trick, and only one trick, about making Baked Alaska. You must start with ice cream that is very solidly frozen, keeping it in the freezer until the very last moment. In every way you must protect the ice cream from the heat of the oven. To do this, use a board 1 inch thick. Cover the board with a piece of brown paper cut to fit. On top of the paper place six slices of sponge cake ½ inch thick or 6 Mary Ann individual short cakes. On top of the cake place a slice or a scoop of ice cream. Cake must extend 1 inch beyond ice cream on all sides.

Cover the ice cream completely with this meringue: Beat 3 egg whites until stiff but not dry. Add ¼ teaspoon cream of tartar (optional) then gradually add 3 tablespoons superfine granulated sugar. Continue to beat until meringue is thick and smooth. Lightly fold in another 2 tablespoons sugar. Then cover ice cream and cake with meringue, being careful that there are no holes in the meringue. Bake in a preheated oven at 450° for 3 minutes or just long enough for the meringue to take on a golden tinge around the peaks.

VII. CHICKEN NAPOLEON

The problem of "what's for dinner" is not confined to any page in history. Even Napoleon had his troubles. His chef's solution on what to serve for the conquering hero after the battle of Waterloo has become a legend. As might be expected, it was chicken, generally known as Chicken Marengo. This version is called Chicken Napoleon. One kitchen maestro was so enamored of the recipe that he is said to have flavored it with Napoleon's own brandy. White wine is usual, but vinegar and water may be substituted. Brandy or cognac is entirely optional.

For your own favorite warrior, fresh from combat in the marts of trade, Chicken Napoleon is a fine dinner idea. Our modern tender birds cook so quickly that the dish is ready for the table in less than half an hour.

Chicken Napoleon
Green Rice
Garlic Bread Mont Royale
Broccoli with Anchovies and Lemon
Sour Cream Pie
Iced Tea with Lime and Mint Leaves

CHICKEN NAPOLEON . . . To serve 2 or 3, have a tender young chicken cut up as for frying. Season with salt and pepper. Heat 4 tablespoons olive oil and brown the pieces along with ½ cup chopped onion, 1 clove garlic, crushed.

This takes about 5 minutes. Remove chicken. Add 2 tomatoes, quartered, 1 small 4-ounce tin sliced, broiled mushrooms with liquid, 2 tablespoons vinegar and ½ cup water or ½ cup white table wine, 1 tablespoon Cognac or brandy if desired. Stir or cook uncovered about 5 minutes. Put the chicken back, cover and cook gently 10 minutes longer or until chicken is tender.

GREEN RICE . . . To 2 cups hot cooked rice, add ½ cup finely chopped parsley which has been heated in 2 tablespoons melted butter or margarine. Toss lightly with a fork. Serves 2 to 3.

GARLIC BREAD MONT ROYALE . . . From Montreal comes this inspiration: Brush a small loaf of crusty bread with melted butter. Sprinkle with 1 teaspoon sweet Hungarian paprika mixed with 1 teaspoon garlic salt. Wrap in foil and heat in the oven. Serve in thick slices.

BROCCOLI WITH ANCHOVIES AND LEMON . . . Lightly cook fresh or quick-fozen broccoli. Garnish with filets of anchovies and squeezable sections of lemon.

SOUR CREAM PIE . . . A dazzlingly simple and easy version of a famous American specialty. Buy a ready-baked peach pie and remove the top crust, or get a one-crust pie. Warm in the oven. Cover with 1 cup sour cream to which you have added 1 egg well-beaten, 2 tablespoons sugar, ¼ teaspoon salt, ½ teaspoon vanilla. Sprinkle lavishly with crumbled macaroons, graham crackers or other tasty cooky crumbs. Lightly powder with cinnamon.

VIII. CHICKEN TANDURI RITA'S TRANSLATION

Daughter of Madame Vijaya Lakshmi Pandit and niece of the late Prime Minister Nehru, Rita Pandit Dar is the wife of India's Minister in Washington, D.C. A graduate of Wellesley, she has, although still in her twenties, lived and cooked in practically every corner of the globe. Like her mother, she has an intense interest in food and cooking. Her little dinner parties at the house on California Street have a light, imaginative, one-worldly elegance.

Although there is a talented chef from Kashmiri to help her, Rita insists that she must have a number of menus that she can prepare herself when one of those crucial social situations arises.

A recent triumph is her own less-than-twenty-minute version of Chicken Tanduri . . . one of India's most famous dishes. Most famous in India, that is! A barbecued chicken cooked traditionally on a revolving spit inside a *tandur,* which is a clay oven with a narrow neck that holds a banked fire. The chicken is cooked by heat and smoke and the soft ashes that collect below receive the drippings without burning or smoking, giving to the food an extraordinary savor. Rita prepared an amazingly good translation in the serving pantry of her mother's apartment in the Hotel Carlyle using, if you please, a chicken still warm from a rotisserie on Madison Avenue.

Rose Petal Consommé
Chicken Tanduri Rita's Translation
Pineapple Pilaf   Plain Yogurt with Mint Leaves
Mandarin Oranges with Sake   Coconut Cookies

ROSE PETAL CONSOMMÉ . . . To 3 cups clear chicken broth (homemade or canned) add ½ cup *rosé* wine and, if you have it, ½ teaspoon rose flavoring. Simmer a few minutes to blend the flavors. Rita Dar serves this soup in small silver bowls garnished with rose petals or a thin slice of lime studded with 1 or 2 cloves. Serves 4.

CHICKEN TANDURI RITA'S TRANSLATION . . . To 1 cup yogurt, add the juice of 1 lemon (about 3 tablespoonsful), 1 teaspoon powdered coriander, 1 teaspoon powdered cumin, ¼ teaspoon chili powder, ½ teaspoon ginger. Let stand a few minutes. Meanwhile, rub the barbecued chicken inside and out first with cut onion and garlic and then with the spiced lemon-yogurt mixture. Sprinkle generously with 2 tablespoons sweet paprika so that the bird takes on "a glow like red embers." Wrap in foil. Set in a hot oven (400°) 5 minutes to the pound. During the last 5 minutes remove the foil.

PINEAPPLE PILAF . . . Prepare 2 cups packaged precooked rice according to directions using 1 cup pineapple juice, 1 cup water, ½ teaspoon powdered saffron, curry powder or tumeric. Scatter with slivered almonds.

YOGURT WITH MINT . . . Place plain yogurt in bowl. Sprinkle with fresh or dried mint.

Mandarin Oranges with Sake . . . Chill canned mandarin sections. Drain. Cook down syrup to ½ of original volume. Add an equal quantity of Japanese *sake* and pass the warm *sake* sauce to be poured, as desired, over the chilled fruit. Dry sherry may be used instead of *sake*.

IX. CORNISH ON THE COALS

Ann Sargent is the latest model of a proper Bostonian. Just a few years out of Briarcliff College, she has already made a name for herself in public relations. That shining platinum page-boy coif bobs up wherever things are doing. During the work week, she lives with her mother in the family home in Chestnut Hill. But on weekends—winter and summer—she hies to Whip-O-Will farm in southern New Hampshire, which, as she says, is her Independence. One of her admirers describes her as Miss Boston '64. But, he admitted, "She has a streak of *seventeen* along with *nineteen* sixty-four." For she loves the traditional and antique. Her hobby is making dandelion blossom wine. She would like to try elderberry too, if she had a proper recipe.

The cooking that she enjoys the most is done over, in and around the fire on a winter's evening at Whip-O-Will. On New Year's Day, she often serves baked little nubbin potatoes—"the kind most farmers throw away," Cornish game hens on the coals, broccoli with black butter. (She once set the place ablaze blackening the butter, but never mind.) Dessert at this time of year is a ritual that dates from Merrie Olde England: a blazing Snapdragon of raisins in a ring of fire.

Baked Nubbin Potatoes
Cornish on the Coals
Broccoli   Black Butter
Green Salad
Toasted Garlic Bread
Winter Pears with Gorgonzola Cheese
Snapdragon

Baked Nubbin Potatoes . . . Nubbins are tiny potatoes no bigger than a golf ball. Ann Sargent bakes them in a hot oven. Because they are so tiny, they take only 8 to 10 minutes. Served with meat, there should be 4 to 6 for each person. "They are best of all," she says, "as an appetizer, with a dab of sour cream and a bit of caviar in the center."

CORNISH ON THE COALS . . . Split Cornish game hens and flatten them out. Sprinkle with salt and pepper. Massage lavishly all over with butter. Place in a well-greased foldover wire grill and broil slowly over the coals, basting from time to tmie with equal parts melted butter and white vermouth.

BROCCOLI WITH BLACK BUTTER . . . Cook ¼ pound butter in a pan to a dark brown shade—not really black. When just right, it should give off a nutty fragrance. Add 2 tablespoons finely chopped parsley, 1 tablespoon capers, 1 tablespoon vinegar. Serve with broccoli, asparagus, cauliflower or green beans.

SNAPDRAGON . . . Arrange heaps or clusters of large raisins on a heatproof platter or tray. Slightly warm in a porringer or a metal cup: ¾ cup rum, whiskey or brandy. Turn off all the lights. Gather around the platter. Set a match to the spirit and pour flaming over the raisins. The idea is to snatch as many raisins as possible out of the flames. The more you get, the greater your luck during the next year.

X. DUCK À L'ORANGE

Speaking of a new arrival in her town, a woman said with awe in her voice, "Of course I know she's a gourmet cook. She can make duck *à l'orange.*"

Paris, to many dedicated eaters, means that most Parisian of specialties, duck. Some epicures have been known to walk the streets of Paris, map in hand, searching for restaurants famous for duck.

Cooked in this incredibly swift way, duck *à l'orange* has a completely authentic look and flavor—even the whiff of the famous four spices that you can buy in the Burgundy country already blended or concoct yourself.

For even greater speed in cooking and because ducks are so devilish to carve, we suggest that you have the butcher cut the bird into quarters or even smaller serving pieces like a frying chicken.

Red Wine Consommé, Hot or Jellied
Duck à l'Orange
Green Rice   Broccoli with Lemon Butter
Glazed Strawberry Tartlets

RED WINE CONSOMMÉ . . . To 1 can condensed consommé, add ½ soup can water, ½ soup can dry red table wine. Simmer 5 minutes; do not boil. Serve immediately. Or, for jellied consommé, stir in a teaspoonful of gelatin. To speed the jelling process, place in freezer no more than 10 minutes by your timer. Garnish with lemon slices.

DUCK À L'ORANGE . . . To serve 4 to 6, you will need a 4 or 5-pound duckling. Rub each piece skin and flesh-side with butter, sprinkle with salt and pepper and a blend of the Four Spices, i.e., equal parts of powdered cinnamon, clove, nutmeg and ginger. Place the pieces well separated skin-side up on a rack above a deepish pan that will catch the drippings. Roast in a moderately hot oven (375°) 20 to 30 minutes or until done, basting from time to time with orange juice. Five minutes before the duck is done, brush lightly with *Kitchen Bouquet*. Turn the oven up high to 450°. This will crisp the skin.

Meanwhile, prepare the orange sauce by heating together ¼ cup orange juice, 2 tablespoons lemon juice, ½ teaspoon *Kitchen Bouquet*, a few grains of cayenne pepper, 1 tablespoon orange marmalade, 1 can beef gravy. Simmer gently about 5 minutes. At serving time, garnish with drained canned mandarin oranges or slices of un-peeled navel oranges. Sauce may be poured around the duck or served separately.

GREEN RICE . . . Add 4 tablespoons melted butter or margarine and one 8-ounce jar chopped junior food spinach to 3 cups cooked rice. Serves 6.

BROCCOLI WITH LEMON BUTTER . . . Melt 4 tablespoons butter; stir in 1 tablespoon lemon juice, 1 tablespoon chopped chives, a goodly sprinkle of freshly ground black pepper. Heat but do not boil. Serve over lightly cooked broccoli.

GLAZED STRAWBERRY TARTLETS . . . Buy tart shells or bake from pastry mix. Place a tablespoon of ready-whipped cream or instant vanilla pudding in baked tart shells. Cover with strawberries, fresh or quick-frozen and well-drained. Slowly melt ½ cup currant jelly; pour carefully over berries. Chill.

XI. FRIED CHICKEN AU MARJORAM

Not too often in a gourmet's lifetime does a brand new technique appear on the scene. Recently it happened. The art of frying has been revolutionized by what is known as the cold-start method, where the oil stands only a half inch deep in the skillet. You don't preheat. You don't do anything but turn on the heat medium high (about 375°). No special equipment is needed—no fry baskets, no strainer. Accurate measurement of the temperature is not too important. There is no smoke, practically no odor, no danger of hot oil bubbling over; practically nothing in the way of spatter. Flavor and texture are unbelievable. Food is crisp and dry on the outside. Strange as it may sound, there is no more absorption of fat than by the old, deep-fry method.

This Fried Chicken *au Marjoram* is a minor miracle. To go along with it—because we were heady with delight over this new discovery—we prepared skillet-baked sweet potatoes which we even didn't parboil or peel. The skins had a marvelous nutlike crunch and the cut surfaces were as crispy as the best French fries.

Fried Chicken au Marjoram   Quick Sauce Allemande
Skillet-Baked Sweet Potatoes
Buttered Green Beans
Salad of Endive and Grapefruit Sections
Frozen Strawberry Icebox Cake

FRIED CHICKEN AU MARJORAM . . . For 4 or 5 servings, use a 2½ or 3-pound frying chicken cut up. Dip the pieces into a mixture of ⅓ cup flour, 1 teaspoon salt, ⅛ teaspoon pepper, ½ teaspoon dried marjoram. Pour vegetable oil ½ inch deep in a large skillet. Place the seasoned chicken in a single layer in the skillet. Turn on heat to medium high (375°). Cover and fry 15 minutes. Remove cover. Turn chicken and continue cooking uncovered another 8 minutes or until done. Drain on paper towels.

Quick Sauce Allemande . . . To 1 can heated chicken gravy add 1 slightly beaten egg yolk diluted with a little of the hot gravy. Season with 1 teaspoon lemon juice, a few grains of nutmeg (optional); stir in 3 tablespoons grated Parmesan cheese. Keep warm but do not boil.

Skillet-Baked Sweet Potatoes . . . Cut 4 sweet potatoes into quarters or eighths lengthwise. Do not pare. Place in a single layer in a large skillet. Pour in vegetable oil until it just covers the potatoes. Stir so that the pieces are well coated. Fry at medium high heat (375°) until golden brown, stirring occasionally. Takes about 15 minutes. Turn off heat. Remove with slotted spoon. Drain on paper towels. For a second batch, put more potatoes in the skillet. Proceed as before.

Frozen Strawberry Icebox Cake . . . One of the newer prepared frozen products . . . ready-to-serve without defrosting. If you can't find it yet at your grocer's, settle for a strawberry ice cream sandwich made with strawberry ice cream between thin slices of sponge cake or ladyfingers, with a garnish of sliced, sugared strawberries fresh or frozen.

XII. INDIVIDUAL TURKEY PIES

The Coach House (which really *was* the old coach house of the Wanamaker estate) in New York City has a devoted clientele among gourmets who have been everywhere, know food in all languages and long to dine on the prize victuals of the land.

Consistent with the American dream is the fact that the man behind one of the few truly American gourmet restaurants is by birth a Greek. Yet he has the most knowing ways with crabmeat chunks. The fried chicken is a Down-South dream; his black bean soup flavored with Madeira is a velvety wonder. The Coach House reaches the heights when maestro Leon Lianides adds to American fare certain personal and ancestral touches, such as a spoonful each of olive oil and wine vinegar added to that black bean soup. The appetizer of fresh mushrooms must not be missed nor the special dessert of meringue circles, light as flying saucers, which he puts together with a rich egg-gilded filling and calls *Dacquoise*.

Fresh Mushrooms à la Grecque
Black Bean Soup au Madeira
Individual Turkey Pies
Tossed Green Salad
Dacquoise

FRESH MUSHROOMS À LA GRECQUE . . . Combine 1 cup dry white wine, 1 cup water, ½ cup olive oil, 4 tablespoons lemon juice, 1½ tablespoons wine vinegar, 1 small stalk celery diced, 1 clove garlic crushed, 1 bay leaf, 2 sprigs parsley, 12 peppercorns, ½ teaspoon oregano. Cook 10 minutes. Add 1½ pounds fresh mushroom caps. Cook 5 minutes longer. Chill. Sprinkle with 1 tablespoon fresh chopped dill. Serve with crusty bread.

BLACK BEAN SOUP AU MADEIRA . . . A gastronomic miracle is the black bean soup at the Old Coach House! Not the same, of course, but very good indeed, is a quick version made by adding to 1 can condensed black bean soup 1 can condensed consommé, ¼ cup Madeira wine. Heat but do not boil.

At serving time, garnish with a finely chopped hard-cooked egg and add a spoonful of olive oil, a spoonful of wine vinegar.

INDIVIDUAL TURKEY PIES . . . Heat quick-frozen turkey pies according to directions. When half done, brush with sour cream or slightly beaten egg yolk to give a beautiful glaze and interesting taste to the crust.

DACQUOISE . . . A wondrous party dessert, to serve at least 8. Subtle, unusual, to all appearances incredibly complicated; yet it can be prepared in half an hour, if you work the filling while the meringues are baking.

Beat 10 egg whites with ¼ teaspoon cream of tartar until stiff but not dry, adding gradually while beating 1 cup of sugar. Fold in ½ pound blanched almonds finely ground. Spread this meringue in 2 circles on buttered cookie sheets or in cake pans and bake in a moderately slow oven (300°) 20 to 25 minutes or until they are dry.

Meanwhile, cook together ⅔ cup sugar and ¼ cup water until the syrup spins a thread and registers 234° on a candy thermometer. Cream 1 cup butter with 2 tablespoons instant coffee. Beat 5 egg yolks until they are thick and alternately add to the egg yolks, the syrup and the butter mixture. Flavor with 2 tablespoons of

Grand Marnier or undiluted frozen orange juice concentrate. Chill (in the freezer to save time).

At serving time, spread between the 2 meringue layers. Sprinkle with confectioners' sugar and chocolate shavings.

XIII. LOYALIST HOUSE POT PYE

Oldest and most beautiful of the Georgian houses in St. John, New Brunswick, oldest incorporated town in Canada, is Loyalist House, built in 1810 by David Merritt, a gentleman of Virginia, who, in the new United States of those days, would have been called a Tory; in Canada —a Loyalist.

Never out of the hands of the Merritt family, Loyalist House is filled with many of the original furnishings and accessories. The old blue Canton china, the heavy silver, candle-snuffers, sugar crushers, warmers, trivets and kettles . . . all in place. You can almost smell the chicken stewing with potherbs for a pot pye; the berries waiting to be crushed for the syllabub . . .

Loyalist House Pot Pye
Pickled Peaches
Broccoli New Brunswick
Radishes and Carrot Sticks
Raspberry Syllabub   Ladyfingers

LOYALIST HOUSE POT PYE . . . A wonderfully old-fashioned heartiness, a marvelously authentic look and taste. Yet this pot pye goes together like a flash because instead of an ancient hen or wiry old rooster, you reach for canned chicken fricassee (sometimes known as chicken in golden gravy) and other cans of chicken gravy and canned white onions. For the topping, instead of making a batter, you roll or pat thin some oven-ready biscuits.

For 6 to 8 servings, heat together two 15½-ounce tins chicken fricassee, one 10½-ounce tin chicken gravy, 1 can small white onions drained, 1 teaspoon parsley flakes, 1 tablespoon lemon juice. Top with ready-to-bake buttermilk biscuits rolled out thin. Lay them on top of the chicken, rather than anchoring them around the edge of the dish like ordinary pie crust. Brush biscuits with 2 egg yolks slightly beaten with 1 tablespoon cream. Bake in a hot oven (425°) about 15 minutes, or until the pot pye is bubbly and the crust golden brown.

PICKLED PEACHES . . . Not only peaches but also apricots, pineapple, pears or purple plums can be pickled in this swift and easy fashion. And the result is not too different from the fruit pickle of Loyalist days. Begin by draining the juice from a No. 2 can. To each cup juice add 1 cup sugar, ½ cup white distilled pickling vinegar, 10 whole cloves, a small stick of cinnamon (optional). Cook uncovered 10 minutes. Add fruit; bring to a boil. Simmer 5 minutes. Chill and serve.

BROCCOLI NEW BRUNSWICK . . . Cook broccoli lightly. Serve with melted butter and a sprinkle of white vinegar.

RASPBERRY SYLLABUB . . . Beat together with an electric beater until stiff enough to hold shape: 1¼ cups crushed fresh or frozen raspberries, 1 cup confectioners' sugar, 2 egg whites. Pile lightly on a chilled dish. Chill and surround with ladyfingers. Serve plain or with soft custard. Serves 6.

XIV. OLD-FASHIONED CHICKEN FRICASSEE

Funny how it stays in the mind and somehow clings nostalgically in the memory that chicken is Sunday Best . . . a treat, a joy and a luxury.

So it comes as a surprise to find that chicken is often the least expensive of leading meats. All of which makes a really old-fashioned chicken fricassee appealing from many points of view. Right now we are chortling over a recipe that makes it fast as fast. Instead of dumplings— inclined to be heavy sometimes—we suggest baked biscuit balls.

Old-Fashioned Chicken Fricassee
Baked Biscuit Balls
Tomato Aspic Salad on Chicory Leaves
Apricots Melba   Butter Pecan Ice Cream
Ginger Wafers

OLD-FASHIONED CHICKEN FRICASSEE . . . Place in a pressure cooker two 3-pound broiler fryers cut into pieces.

Add 3 cups water, ¼ of an onion stuck with 2 cloves, 1 tablespoon dried celery flakes, 1 bay leaf, 2½ teaspoonsful salt, ¼ teaspoon pepper, 4 whole allspice berries. Cook at 15 pounds pressure 6 minutes. Bring down pressure immediately; add 6 carrots scraped and cut lengthwise into quarters and then into eighths. Add also 12 small whole onions. Cook 10 to 15 minutes or until chicken and vegetables are tender. Bring down pressure. Stir 4 tablespoons flour into ½ cup cold water. Add some of the hot broth to the flour mixture. Stir until smooth; add to the fricassee. Cook while stirring until thickened. Serve in a deep hot dish. Sprinkle generously with chopped chives and garnish with thin slices of lemon. Surround with Baked Biscuit Balls. Makes 6 servings.

If you would rather not use a pressure cooker, you can cook the chickens in a kettle on top of the stove about 30 minutes. Then proceed as above.

BAKED BISCUIT BALLS . . . Add ⅔ cup milk all at once to 2 cups prepared biscuit mix. Stir with fork into a soft dough. Beat 15 strokes. Turn onto lightly floured board. Knead gently 10 times. Cut into 24 pieces. Roll into balls. Bake on an ungreased baking sheet in a hot oven (450°) 8 to 10 minutes.

APRICOTS MELBA . . . Drain the syrup from a can of apricot halves and also from canned or quick-frozen raspberries. Place the apricots on a shallow serving dish. Arrange the raspberries around the apricots. Combine the syrup from the apricots and the raspberries. Cook uncovered over fairly high heat until reduced by half. Flavor syrup with 2 tablespoons sherry or undiluted frozen orange juice concentrate. Serve warm or chilled.

XV. PUFFED-BROWN CHICKEN

For years I had heard about Ann Robinson's low lowcalorie recipes, especially the chicken she used to serve at Sunshine Terrace, in Croton-on-Hudson; a Beauty Farm she called it. The chicken was prepared partly under the broiler, partly in the oven, with not a smidge of butter, fat or oil, yet it tastes savory all the way through. The skin, wonderfully crisp and brown, puffs up like a soufflé potato!

Puffed-Brown Chicken
Sunshine Terrace Salad
with
Rose Cream Dressing
Popovers

PUFFED-BROWN CHICKEN . . . To serve 2, have a small broiling chicken cut into quarters, or even smaller pieces if you want it to cook more quickly. Sprinkle with salt and pepper, brush with lemon juice (lemon keeps the flesh white and firm). Place rib side up in a shallow pie pan or broiler pan. Broil quickly about 5 minutes or until brown. Turn skin side up. Cover the bottom of the pan with about ¾ inch boiling water and place in a very hot oven (480°) 20 to 25 minutes or until the chicken is tender and the skin beautifully brown and crisply puffed. An amazing recipe!

SUNSHINE TERRACE FRUIT SALAD . . . "Don't make a hash of your fruit salad," Ann Robinson warns. Fruits should be cut into large king-size bites. Into a nest of crisp lettuce and watercress place half of a large pear or apple unpeeled, whole orange, half banana, melon—all cut into inch chunks. Cover with Rose Cream dressing. Decorate with fresh berries.

ROSE CREAM DRESSING . . . Like so many of the specialties at Sunshine Terrace this one is most handily done with a blender. But you could, if you are energetic, mash the cream cheese and the berries beforehand and whip with a rotary beater.

Best way: Put four tablespoons unsweetened pineapple juice or orange juice into a blender. Add ½ of a 12-ounce package frozen strawberries or about 20 fresh berries. Blend well. While blender is running add a little at a time a large (6-ounce) package cream cheese. Dressing should be thick as mayonnaise. Makes about ¾ cup . . . enough for 4 salads.

XVI. QUEEN JINGA'S DISH

A young woman with the lovely name of Arminda d'Almeinda, who is now studying at Asheville, North Carolina, gave me a recipe for which I had been searching a long time. It is "the national plate" of her homeland —Angola, on the West Coast of Africa.

Queen Jinga's Dish it is called, named for a woman who is probably the most famous historical personality from Africa of the sixteenth century. A noted Portuguese historian of the time wrote that her beauty was greater than that of Semiramis or Cleopatra and compared her in nature with Catherine the Great of Russia. For 25 years she defended her queendom against the Dutch and the Portuguese and, when her armies were encircled and her country conquered . . . like Cleopatra, she killed herself.

Whether or not Queen Jinga actually invented the dish that bears her name, nobody really knows. But in all parts of the land it is prepared, enjoyed and ascribed to her.

We have taken only one liberty with the original recipe —instead of grinding the peanuts, we use peanut butter.

Queen Jinga's Dish
Fungi
Cooked Leaves
White Wine
Bananas and Oranges
Dolce de Coco

QUEEN JINGA'S DISH . . . To serve 3 or 4, you will need a young frying chicken or broiler weighing about 3 pounds. It should, for true authenticity, be cut through the bones Chinese fashion into pieces about an inch long, or as small as feasible. Crush 2 or 3 cloves of garlic into 2 tablespoons salt and add 2 tablespoons vinegar. Rub this seasoning mixture into the meat. Place in a pan along with 2 small bay leaves, 1 onion thinly sliced or chopped and 2 tomatoes cut into pieces, 2 tablespoons peanut oil and 2 cups chicken stock. Cook about 10 minutes or until the chicken is almost tender. Then stir a little of the hot broth into 2 tablespoons "chunky" peanut butter and gradually add the peanut butter to the chicken. Cook gently, stirring occasionally, about 8 minutes longer or until the chicken is completely tender and the gravy slightly thickened. Season to taste with pepper and *Tabasco*. In the Queen's country this dish is always served with *Fungi* which is similar to our cornmeal mush or hominy grits.

FUNGI . . . Cook 1 cup white or yellow cornmeal or packaged hominy grits according to package directions for mush. Spread out about 1 inch thick on a lightly buttered deep platter or in a very shallow bowl. Serve in slices or squares with the chicken and gravy alongside.

COOKED LEAVES . . . This is the Angolan term for a wide variety of leafy vegetables, many of which are unavailable in this country. Quick-frozen leaf spinach makes an admirable substitute.

DOLCE DE COCO . . . An excellent version of this Angolan sweet can be made from a package of the new toasted coconut frosting mix. Follow the package directions for toasted coconut fudge but, instead of pouring the mixture into a buttered pan, drop by spoonfuls onto a buttered cooky sheet. One 13-8/10-ounce package should make about 3 dozen candies.

FOOD FROM THE SEA

FISH, SHELL AND OTHERWISE

❧❦❧

Of all the foods provided by nature, those from the sea would appear to be the fastest to cook. Bake, broil, boil, poach, simmer, fry, or sauté . . . whatever the method, whatever the fish, from swordfish to sole, shrimp, lobster, or crab . . . the time is little. The big problem in cooking seafood or fish is to guard against overcooking—serve straightaway.

Fish is the most difficult of all foods to keep warm. It may be cooked and served cool, not icy, but just cool. However, if you try to keep a fish dish hot for any length of time, it seems to lose all its juices, grows hard, tastes dry. Covering the fish with a sauce helps to some extent, but not much.

Fish steaks, as of salmon or swordfish, should be cut at least 1 inch, or possibly 1½ inches, thick. Brush well with melted butter, margarine or oil, even though the fish is fatty, and broil four to five inches away from the heat. Unless the steak is quite thick, it is not necessary to broil both sides. If you broil only one side, the broiling may be done in a baking dish that can go to the table. You need not use a rack.

Another way to guard against dryness when you are broiling fish . . . pour about one half inch of hot water into the bottom of the broiling pan. Usually it is not necessary to turn the fish. If you do not use a rack, use less water, just enough to cover the bottom of the dish.

I. BAKED FISH WITH FENNEL AND FLAME

Chef Albert Schnell, originally of Zurich, now Montreal, has collected an imposing array of awards and honors. He is also one of the youngest, handsomest and most affable of culinary maestros.

Generous with recipes, he will, with slight urging, reveal what are supposed to be top level secrets, like his baked fish served with fennel and flame.

Montreal epicures will tell you that only their local Dore deserves this drama. Chef Albert assures soothingly that striped bass is excellent and so is whitefish. His recipe using a 2-pound fish is designed for two. To serve more . . . use more fishes. Or, if the fish is larger, increase the baking time.

Baked Fish with Fennel and Flame
Garnitures of Onion and Potatoes
Eggplant Nicoise
Bibb Lettuce Salad
Bagatelle (a Trifle)

BAKED FISH WITH FENNEL AND FLAME . . . "The fish in this instance must keep its head." Begin by heating 6 tablespoons olive oil in a baking pan. Add 1 onion and 2 medium potatoes sliced ⅛-inch thick. Mix lightly with a fork. Rub fish with a large handful of fresh or dried leaves of fennel and a small amount of thyme. (In the States, fennel is often called finocchio, and is available in Italian markets.) Place the fish on top of the potato-onion combine. Bake at 375° for 5 minutes. Pour on 2 tablespoons *Pernod*, ¼ cup white wine. Continue baking 20 minutes longer, basting frequently with juices from the pan.

"This," says Chef Albert Schnell, "is a very spectacular dish and should be finished at the table as follows: Remove the fish carefully to a service platter. Surround with potato garniture. Divide the fish lengthwise into 2 filets. Remove all bones and the head. When the eyes of your audience are full upon you, heat in a small skillet, 4 tablespoons *Pernod*. Light it and pour, flaming, over the fish. If you use fresh fennel, serve it with the fish as a garniture. Dried fennel should be removed. In France, Cognac is used instead of *Pernod*. The flavor is less pronounced."

EGGPLANT NICOISE . . . Peel and cut eggplant into 1-inch cubes. To serve 4 there should be 2 cupsful. Remove the skin from 4 fresh tomatoes. Cut in halves, scoop out seeds and dice. Heat 2 tablespoons olive oil.

Add 2 crushed shallots, or 1 small white onion—chopped and 1 clove garlic, crushed. Sauté 1 minute. Add the diced tomatoes and eggplant. Sprinkle with ¼ cup water. Season to taste with salt and pepper. Cover, bring to a boil, then reduce heat and simmer about 15 minutes or until tender, stirring from time to time.

BAGATELLE . . . Cut a day-old sponge cake into 2-inch cubes. Soak in ½ cup sweet sherry, ¼ cup white wine. Add ¾ cup strawberry jam, 2 tablespoons lemon juice. Toss lightly with a fork. Place in glass or silver bowl. Make up half a package of instant vanilla pudding according to directions, adding 1 teaspoon pure vanilla extract. Cover with ½ cup heavy cream whipped and sweetened with 2 tablespoons sugar. Sprinkle with nutmeg.

II. BROILED FILETS OF SOLE BASILICA

In ancient Persia, Greece and Rome and in Tudor days in Merrie England, sweet basil was a treasured herb. It was said to "cause sympathy between human beings." In certain areas of Italy the tradition still exists that a lad is certain to love a lass from whose hand he accepts a sprig of the plant.

Even in our own Jet Age the old superstition has some merit, particularly when the sweet basil is used to flavor and garnish broiled filets of sole—or flounder—or sand dabs of San Francisco, fresh-caught or fresh-snared from the depth of the frozen food bins!

Sole, by the way, is available fresh and frozen at all times of the year in just about all parts of the country.

Broiled Filets of Sole Basilica
French-Fried Onion Rings
Lyonnaise Potatoes
Pickled Beet Salad
Pears in Port   Ladyfingers

BROILED FILETS OF SOLE BASILICA . . . To serve 6, you will need 2½ to 3 pounds of filets of sole fresh or frozen. Sprinkle lightly with salt and pepper. Place the fish on a well-oiled broiler rack, lined with aluminum foil for easy cleaning. Brush with a mixture of 4 tablespoons butter, melted, and 3 tablespoons lime juice.

Sprinkle with 1 teaspoon fresh basil chopped or ½ teaspoon dried basil which has been soaked for 5 minutes in lime juice.

Place in preheated broiler 4 inches away from the heat. Broil 6 to 9 minutes or until the fish loses its translucent appearance, looks snowy white and flakes easily when touched with a fork. Do not turn. Do not overcook. Garnish with sprays of fresh basil, if available, or parsley, preferably Italian parsley. Give to each filet a ruddy dash of paprika. Serve immediately. Fish hardens quickly as it cools.

FRENCH-FRIED ONION RINGS . . . Use quick-frozen French-fried onion rings, but ignore package directions for heating. Instead, heat vegetable oil 1½ inches deep to 370°. Toss onion rings a few at a time into the hot oil and cook just about 30 seconds. Drain on paper towels. Sprinkle with coarse kosher salt and freshly ground pepper.

LYONNAISE POTATOES . . . Place in a large frying pan 3 tablespoons butter, 1 small onion chopped fine. Cook until onion is pale yellow; add 2 cups sliced cooked potatoes. Sprinkle with ½ teaspoon salt, ¼ teaspoon pepper. Add 2 tablespoons condensed consommé. Cover and cook slowly until potatoes are brown underneath. Fold like an omelet. Sprinkle with chopped chives.

PICKLED BEET SALAD . . . Drain canned pickled beets. Serve on romaine lettuce. Sprinkle with caraway seeds and serve with French or Italian dressing on the side.

PEARS IN PORT . . . Drain a large can of pears. To the syrup add a cinnamon stick broken in half. Cook quickly uncovered until reduced one-half. Add an equal quantity of ruby port wine. Pour over the pears and serve warm or chilled.

III. BROIL-POACHED FISH

Fish is most important in any figure-conscious diet and should be served at least once a week. This special way combines the advantages of poaching and broiling. Almost any delicately flavored fish may be cooked in this fashion, even salmon, a "fatty" fish, since by this method the oils cook out of it. The fish retains, to an extraordinary extent, a rich trove of iodine and other minerals.

Ice Pyramid of Celery, Olives, Spring Onions
Broil-Poached Fish
Fresh Asparagus
Small Baked Potato with Yogurt (no butter)
Steamed or Canned Whole Tomatoes aux Fines Herbes
Grapefruit

ICE PYRAMID OF CELERY . . . Fill a bowl with crushed ice and allow to stand in the freezer until serving time. Turn out on chilled platter and cover with celery curls, olives, spring onion or whatever.

BROIL-POACHED FISH . . . For each portion, use a thick filet of fish or a small steak about 1 inch thick. Place in a shallow baking dish. Almost cover the fish with cold water, measuring the water as you pour it in. For each cupful add 1 tablespoon lemon juice, ½ teaspoon salt, ¼ teaspoon pepper. Place the fish in its pan under the broiler. After the water comes to a boil, cook just about 8 minutes. At this time the top should be brown, the fish should be opaque and flake off easily when touched with a fork. The water will be flecked or coated with oil. Pour off the liquid or lift the fish carefully with a wide slotted spatula. Serve with sections of lemon and bouquets of parsley.

WHOLE TOMATOES AUX FINES HERBES . . . Cut top off large firm tomatoes and set in a serving dish on a trivet in a steamer or electric skillet with ½ inch boiling water in the bottom of the pan. Cover closely and steam about 3 minutes or heat whole canned tomatoes. In either case at serving time sprinkle with finely chopped parsley, chives and any other garden herb that is handy.

IV. BROILED SWORDFISH OR HALIBUT STEAKS

In all the realm of fishdom there is nothing more delightful than a fresh-broiled swordfish steak. But be advised and be careful: swordfish can be dry, so the steak should be cut at least 1½ inches thick.

Although swordfish is an American delicacy, the best of all sauces for it came originally from Sicily. But, as often happens in this gastronomic melting pot of ours, we encountered it at the height of perfection when it was served in New Bedford, Massachusetts by a lady of Portuguese descent.

Everyone around the table tried to guess how the sauce was made. No one succeeded. Perhaps because it is too simple.

Chilled Vichyssoise à la Ritz
Broiled Swordfish or Halibut Steaks
Very Particular Sicilian Sauce
Wax Beans with Pimientos
Heated Parker House Rolls
Cucumber Fruit Salad

CHILLED VICHYSSOISE À LA RITZ . . . To a tin of condensed or frozen cream of potato soup prepared according to directions and chilled, add ¼ cup chilled tomato juice, ½ teaspoon Worcestershire sauce. Serve in chilled cups garnished with a thin slice of tomato or a spoonful of chili sauce and a sprig of parsley.

BROILED SWORDFISH OR HALIBUT STEAKS . . . If swordfish is unavailable, settle for halibut and proceed in the same fashion. To serve 6, order 2 pounds of swordfish steaks. Arrange on a buttered shallow baking dish, preferably one that can go directly from the broiler to the table. Sprinkle fish with salt and pepper. Dot generously with butter or margarine. Cook about 3 inches below the heat about 12 minutes on one side. Turn; season the other side with more salt and pepper, more dots of butter. Cook 8 to 10 minutes longer or until the fish flakes easily at the touch of a fork and is snowy-white and opaque. Immediately pour on the following:

VERY PARTICULAR SICILIAN SAUCE . . . This sauce makes such a stir in epicurean circles that you might not wish to admit it is nothing more than a French dressing. Beat together ½ cup olive oil, ¼ cup lemon juice. Add ¼ teaspoon salt, a few grains of hot cayenne pepper and 4 tablespoons each of fresh chopped mint and parsley. If the fresh herbs are unavailable, use 2 tablespoons each of the dried herbs and allow them to stand covered with lemon juice for a few minutes before adding them to the dressing. If you add them dry to the oil, they do not freshen and soften so readily.

WAX BEANS WITH PIMIENTOS . . . Cut garden-fresh yellow wax beans into inch pieces or prepare quick-frozen or canned wax beans in the usual manner. Drain and serve garnished with pimientos cut into tiny pieces.

CUCUMBER FRUIT SALAD . . . This salad, often served in cucumber boats, makes an excellent first course or combination salad-dessert. To serve 6, cut three large cucumbers in halves, lengthwise. Hollow them out, discard the seeds, cut into strips or dice. Combine with your favorite fresh or frozen fruit salad mixture and add 2 cups romaine lettuce cut into pieces. Pile back into the shells and serve with French dressing that has been sweetened with a touch of honey.

V. BROILED OR SAUTÉED SHAD ROE

The Farmer's Almanac marks the day when the first shad arrives in New England and the first white shad blow blossoms can be found shyly flowering in the woods. In Connecticut the shad (fish) and the shad (blossoms) can almost always be counted upon to appear at the same time.

Whether you catch or find a fresh shad with its roe, or discover shad roe in a can, which is very good too, shad is an excellent choice for a simple but epicurean supper.

Cream of Tomato Soup with Crisp Cucumber Garnish
Shad Roe, with or without Canadian Bacon
Lemon Wedges
Parsley Potatoes
Green Peas with Pearl Onions
Apple Strudel

CREAM OF TOMATO SOUP . . . Use canned condensed tomato soup and garnish at the table with thin slices of unpeeled cucumber.

SHAD ROE WITH CANADIAN BACON . . . Older cook-books and even some of the standard works of today have proved the ruination of many a fine roe, for they instruct the hapless neophyte to poach the fresh roe for *20* minutes! This is just about 10 times too long.

Poaching 2 or 3 minutes in simmering hot water should be enough.

Whether you use fresh, slightly poached shad roe or canned, brush roe with melted butter or salad oil and heat in the broiler or in the frying pan, turning only once. Don't go away. The roe should be cooked in 6 to 8 minutes. Roe is often served with bacon; Canadian bacon being particularly good, when cut in ¼-inch slices and broiled or fried as usual.

Sprinkle with lemon juice and chopped chives or parsley, and serve immediately. One roe or 1 can of shad roe makes 2 servings.

PARSLEY POTATOES . . . Buy quick-frozen whole peeled potatoes. They come in a plastic bag, ready to be dropped into hot water. Directions may recommend 7 minutes of cooking but we find this too long; 5 is enough. Drain, toss over heat and dry and sprinkle with chopped parsley.

GREEN PEAS WITH PEARL ONIONS . . . A vegetable combination which is already cooked and quick-frozen.

APPLE STRUDEL . . . Notable apple strudel is available quick-frozen. Heat in the oven and serve warm in inch-thick slices with whipped cream or sour cream.

VI. FINNAN HADDIE COOKED IN MILK

Sweetcake Cove on Briar's Island near Westport, Nova Scotia, is where writer Phil Shea—and his Betty and babies—spend their summers.

Why the name? Because one of his lady ancestors . . . a great-great-great-aunt (he thinks it was) seems to have been famous for her sweetcakes. We would call them sugar cookies. As a small boy, Phil remembers finding in one of the bedroom closets a small white box containing a single cookie that had long before turned to stone. According to family legend, the lady of Sweetcake fame, when she knew that the time was growing near for her to depart this world, sent to each of the children in the huge family a sweetcake for remembrance of her.

Whether or not her original Sweetcake Cove recipe actually was willed to a favorite grandniece is still a moot question. But the Shea women treasure this recipe. It is remarkably good. Being a drop cookie, it is also very quick and easy to make.

Finnan Haddie Cooked in Milk
Potatoes Baked with a Nail
Nova Scotia Navets (Turnips)
Red Cinnamon Sauce
Sweetcake Cove Cookies

FINNAN HADDIE COOKED IN MILK . . . To serve 4, you will need 1½ pounds finnan haddie. Place in a shallow flame-proof dish that can go to the table. Add a thinly sliced onion separated into rings. Cover the fish with milk. Put on lid and cook over moderate heat 20 to 25 minutes. Drain or not, as you wish. Dot with butter and sprinkle with freshly ground black pepper. No salt needed.

POTATOES BAKED WITH A NAIL . . . Through the center of a medium-sized potato (1 or more for each person, of course) run a long galvanized nail. Potatoes will bake in much less time than usual—20 to 25 minutes in a 400° oven.

NOVA SCOTIA NAVETS . . . An Acadian recipe. Peel and slice thinly 1½ pounds young and tender yellow turnips. Melt 2 tablespoons butter in a frying pan and sauté turnips until they begin to take on a little color. Sprinkle with 1 tablespoon sugar. Cook until lightly browned. Add ½ cup boiling water with 1 bouillon cube dissolved in it. Continue cooking until turnips are tender and all moisture cooked away.

RED CINNAMON SAUCE . . . Add 2 teaspoons red cinnamon candies (red hots) to 2 cups chunky applesauce. Stir in 1 tablespoon butter. Serve warm.

SWEETCAKE COVE COOKIES . . . Cream 1 cup butter or margarine until very light and fluffy. Beat in ¾ cup sugar. Add 1 egg and 1 egg yolk, ½ teaspoon lemon extract, 2 teaspoons grated lemon peel, 1 tablespoon cream (sweet or sour). Beat thoroughly. Sift together 1¼ cups flour, ¼ teaspoon each: salt, cinnamon or nutmeg and baking powder. (The baking powder is optional—obviously a modern touch.) Add the dry ingredients to the egg-cream mixture. Mix well. Drop by teaspoonfuls onto buttered cookie sheets or sheets of heavy-duty aluminum foil, 1 inch apart. Bake about 7 minutes in a moderately hot oven (375°). Remove from oven. Brush with melted butter. "Then," the old receipt says, "sprinkle with crushed loaf sugar." Granulated sugar will do. Put back in the oven a minute or two longer or until sugar starts to melt and shine. Remove cookies with a spatula. Makes about 5 dozen.

These keep quite well in a covered tin box *if hidden in the corner of a high shelf.*

VII. GRILLED SHRIMPS MAHOPAC

In Washington, D.C., or any other capital of the world, Commissioner Emma Rothblatt would be Chief of Protocol. Hers is the task . . . and, she says, the joy . . . of arranging entertainment for New York's official guests. A tall, striking brunette with flashing, crinkly dark eyes, Commissioner Emma has been called the Elsa Maxwell of Gracie Mansion. But when she gets home to her East Side apartment or the rambling house on Lake Mahopac, she is weary of being a hostess. So her husband Henry, a distinguished lawyer with the look and air of a Spanish grandee, does most of the cooking.

Particularly when it comes to food, Henry Rothblatt has leanings toward Spain and Puerto Rico. Amongst his favorite recipes is a quick version of the Puerto Rican *Habichuelas,* (red beans and rice) . . . a dish served daily in most homes in Puerto Rico and in the many little Puerto Ricos of Manhattan. Along with red beans, the Rothblatts might serve a soy-graced steak or Grilled Shrimps Mahopac. These have a Japanese tang.

Grilled Shrimps Mahopac
Puerto Rican Habichuelas (Red Beans and Rice)
Fresh Fruit Salad Bowl with Mint Dressing
Puerto Rican Crusty Bread
Guava Jelly and Cream Cheese

GRILLED SHRIMPS MAHOPAC . . . To serve 6, heat ¼ cup salad oil in a large skillet. Toss in 2 pounds shelled, cleaned, fresh or frozen shrimp. If the shrimps are large, they should be split lengthwise, but not completely divided so they lie flat. They may be shelled or not, as you prefer. Sprinkle with 1 teaspoon salt and 1 teaspoon black sesame seeds. Cook about 3 minutes, then turn and season the other side with another teaspoon of salt, another teaspoon of sesame seeds. Cook 3 minutes longer or until shrimps on the inside are pink and tender. Add 4 tablespoons soy sauce; heat and stir until blended. Serve with a sauce made of equal parts lemon juice and soy sauce.

RED BEANS AND RICE . . . Dice 2 slices of bacon and fry until crisp. In the bacon fat, brown ½ cup chopped onion. Add ½ cup canned tomato sauce or marinara sauce. Cook slowly about 5 minutes. Then add 2 cans kidney beans with the liquid. Bring to a boil and simmer uncovered a few minutes longer. Just before serving, add ½ cup chopped sweet green peppers. Serve over fluffy cooked rice. (Councillor Rothblatt is devoted to frozen chopped onions and frozen chopped green peppers which he only recently discovered.)

FRESH FRUIT BOWL WITH MINT DRESSING . . . A huge bowl of green salad to which is added a package of not-completely-thawed frozen fruit salad. Toss at the table with a dressing made from 3 tablespoons salad oil, 1 tablespoon lime juice, ½ teaspoon salt, ⅛ teaspoon pepper and 2 tablespoons of fresh chopped mint leaves or 1 tablespoon dried mint that has been soaked for 5 minutes in warm water to cover.

VIII. INCREDIBLE SALMON MOUSSE

Height of elegance for a summertime supper is a salmon mousse. At the White House, Jacqueline Kennedy liked to serve it as a first course at a formal dinner party. More often it was a main course for luncheon or a Friday dinner. A beautiful addition to a buffet at any time of the year.

Conventional recipes require time and considerable fussing. Not this one, made in an electric blender with a heaping cup of crushed ice added. The actual preparation takes less than 1 minute.

You can, if you like, spoon it immediately onto individual plates or mound it into the center of a spread-out head of Boston lettuce.

Cream of Mushroom Soup
Incredible Salmon Mousse
Macedoine of Vegetables   Mayonnaise à la Russe
Pommes Chip
Lemon Sherbet with Fresh or Canned Nectarines
Thin Crisp Ginger Wafers

INCREDIBLE SALMON MOUSSE . . . A blender is absolutely necessary. A mixer will not do. Into the container put 2 envelopes unflavored gelatin, ½ cup *boiling hot* clam broth, white wine, or chicken broth, 2 tablespoons lemon juice, 2 slices onion. Cover and blend 40 seconds. Add 1 large (16-ounce) can salmon including the liquid. Blend 5 seconds longer. With motor on, add 1 cup light cream, ¼ teaspoon pepper, a few grains cayenne pepper. After 5 seconds, with motor still going, add 1 heaping cup crushed ice. As soon as all the ice disappears, the mousse is ready. Serve immediately on crisp lettuce or pour into a quart-size fish mold rinsed in cold water. Refrigerate 10 minutes. Unmold and garnish with crisp greens, sliced cucumbers and ripe olives.

MACEDOINE OF VEGETABLES . . . To serve 6, cook according to directions 2 packages quick-frozen mixed vegetables. Drain; cover with French dressing. Chill in freezer to save time. Drain again; serve in lettuce cups.

MAYONNAISE À LA RUSSE . . . Made by combining equal parts mayonnaise and chili sauce.

POMMES CHIP . . . Even at Maxim's in Paris you will sometimes see them listed on the menu. As you might expect . . . they are potato chips. Buy and warm. Sprinkle with coarse salt.

IX. MERLAN EN COLÈRE

When a whole, small, golden, crispy fish was brought—a perfect circle upon the plate—everyone within sight in the dining room at the Hotel Ivoire wanted to know, "What is that fish? How is it cooked?" The head chef, Maurice Filleul, looking tall as tall in his high chef's hat, arrived to answer our questions.

"It is called *Merlan en Colère*—the angry fish," he explained, "and must be very fresh fish with head and tail intact. The fish you see resents being thrown into a bath of hot oil, as who wouldn't! He gets so furious, he bites his own tail."

The preparation, as it turns out, is classical. Whiting is the fish generally used, although almost any small fish may be substituted . . . perch, pickerel, even trout. "The circular form," the chef finally admitted, "is more than slightly induced." For the tail is speared to the head with a toothpick . . . a toothpick which is, of course, removed before serving.

The Angry Whiting (Merlan en Colère)
Maître d'Hotel Butter
Boiled Potatoes (Pommes au Vapeur)
Baby Peas in Tiny Boats (Petits Pois en Barquettes)
Cucumber Salad
Coupe Ivoire

THE ANGRY WHITING . . . For each person, provide one small fish weighing at least a pound. Scale and clean, but leave the head and tail intact. Season with salt and pepper inside and outside and rub with a little lime or lemon juice. This keeps the flesh firm, removes any fishy taste and gives a fine flavor.

Make a half-inch slice along the backbone. Roll the fish in flour; dip in slightly beaten egg and then in fine breadcrumbs. Fry in deep hot salad oil at 370° about 4 or 5 minutes, or until golden brown and cooked so the flesh underneath the crust is snowy-white and flakes easily at the touch of a fork. Drain on a paper towel and just before serving, place into the slit of the fish a tablespoon of:

MAITRE D'HOTEL BUTTER . . . Mix until smooth ½ cup softened, sweet butter with 1 tablespoon chopped parsley, ½ teaspoon salt, ⅛ teaspoon freshly ground pepper and 1 teaspoon lemon juice.

BABY PEAS IN BOATS . . . Make up half a 10-ounce package of pie crust mix according to directions. Roll out thin; cut into strips about 3 inches long and 2 inches wide. Prick with a fork to keep from puffing. Lift the edges and press together at both ends to make little boats. Bake in a hot oven (425°) about 5 minutes or until lightly browned. Just before serving, fill the tiny boats with canned or quick-frozen peas cooked according to directions and well drained. Makes a dozen *Barquettes*. Serve 2 or 3 to each person.

COUPE IVOIRE . . . In a sherbet glass or champagne saucer, place 2 small scoops of vanilla or strawberry ice cream. Cover with a puree of fresh or frozen strawberries (made most easily in your blender) and garnish with coarsely chopped cashew nuts, pistachio nuts or almonds.

X. "FLUTTERBY" SHRIMP

Tall, blonde, brightly sophisticated designer Marti—more formally Mrs. Bruce Huber—is the mother of three. On any number of topics she bubbles with ideas. Her great specialty is at-home clothes for mothers and daughters.

Her recipes, like her clothes, are amazingly simple, serviceable, workable; yet all have more than a touch of glamour.

To serve when she wears her famous "Flutterby" gown or any of the new long cotton sheaths, she suggests this "Flutterby" menu—particularly good for "a small Friday evening at home." It features her favorite shrimps cooked in beer.

"First," she says dreamily, "you might try my piping cheesies. There is onion hiding under a puff of mayonnaise mixed with grated Parmesan."

Marti's Piping Cheesies
Avocados Madrilene   "Flutterby" Shrimp
Chive Rice
Peas with Orange Peel
Summery Salad with Sour Cream
Fruits au Brandy

MARTI'S PIPING CHEESIES . . . The name may sound quaintsy but the taste is hearty. Especially appealing to men; goes well with cocktails of all persuasions or salad or soup. To make a dozen . . . trim the crusts from three slices of white bread and cut the bread in quarters. Place a thin slice of onion on each quarter and cover with mixture of ½ cup mayonnaise and 4 tablespoons grated Parmesan cheese. Place under broiler until brown. Crackers may be substituted for bread.

Avocados Madrilene . . . for 2 people provide 1 medium-sized avocado. Cut in half lengthwise; remove pit. Fill with red jellied madrilene consommé. Chill until serving time. One 12½-ounce tin should be sufficient for 4.

"Flutterby" Shrimps . . . Marti insists she started making this dish in order to use up leftover beer. In the beginning she served the shrimp as a snack before dinner but people insisted on making a meal of them. So she goes along. To serve 6, place 2 pounds of fresh or frozen shrimp in enough water to cover. Add 1 cup beer or a little more and cook for 3 minutes. Chill and serve with hot sauce (like *Tabasco*) or hot ketchup and lemon.

Chive Rice . . . Add 4 tablespoons chopped fresh or frozen chives to 2 cups cooked rice.

Peas with Orange Peel . . . Add grated peel of 2 oranges or 3 heaping teaspoons prepared orange peel to 2 packages frozen peas, prepared as directed on package. Serve with extra garnish of orange peel.

Summery Salad . . . Mix fresh chicory, endive and Boston lettuce. Serve with a dressing made of 1 pint sour cream, ¼ of the juice from a jar of dill pickles, 2 tablespoons vinegar, 2 tablespoons sugar, dash of salt. Sprinkle with dill, celery and caraway seeds. Keep extra dressing in the refrigerator for use on any fresh fruit or greens.

Fruits au Brandy . . . To frozen mixed fruits, canned peaches or black Bing cherries add a tablespoon of brandy for each serving.

XI. MINCED CLAM SOUFFLÉ

Caught short on a Friday night with a couple of guests coming to supper. No time for any elaborate shopping. But you want it to be a dinner of distinction.

Catch your breath. Take courage in hand. The main dish will be a clam soufflé. To keep the party happy when they first sit down to the table, provide an asparagus salad à la mimosa. Along with the soufflé, green peas and potatoes in Sauce Supreme. For dessert, Little *Pains d'Epices Normande,* which are nothing more nor less than spice-cake cupcakes made with canned apple-sauce.

Chilled Asparagus Mimosa
Hot Rolls
Minced Clam Soufflé
Green Peas and Potatoes with Sauce Supreme
Little Pains d'Espices Normande

CHILLED ASPARAGUS MIMOSA . . . Cook lightly fresh or frozen asparagus or drain canned asparagus. Arrange on romaine lettuce 5 or 6 stalks of asparagus per portion. Frost with mayonnaise to which has been added prepared mustard (½ teaspoon mustard to ½ cup mayonnaise). Leave the tips of the asparagus untouched. Sprinkle with chopped, hard-cooked egg yolks.

MINCED CLAM SOUFFLÉ . . . The most revered souf-flés in Paris are made with the least amount of flour. This one qualifies, for the recipe uses no flour whatso-ever. Although the procedure is simplified by the lack of flour, the soufflé is, of course, exceptionally delicate and perishable. With no flour or base to hold it up, it flops at a breath, so timing is most important. Other-wise, there is no trick to it.

Drain two 7-ounce cans of minced clams. Add the drained clams to 5 egg yolks, well-beaten with ½ tea-spoon salt, ¼ teaspoon white pepper, 1 teaspoon lemon juice. Beat the whites of 6 eggs (one more egg white than yolk is traditional). They should be stiff but not dry. Carefully fold the whites into the yolks. Pile the mixture into a buttered straight-sided baking dish . . . about 1½-quart size should be just about right. The soufflé should almost reach the top of the dish. Make a swirl with a spatula or a spoon so that the soufflé will break extravagantly. Bake in a moderately hot oven (370°) 15 to 18 minutes or until well-puffed and brown. Run to the table! Serves 4.

GREEN PEAS AND POTATOES WITH SAUCE SUPREME . . . A new addition to the fast-growing list of frozen pre-pared vegetables. To serve 4 generously, you will need two 8-ounce packages Green Peas and Potatoes with Cream Sauce. Prepare according to package directions. Remove from heat. Add the one egg yolk left over from the soufflé. In order to keep the egg from curdling, add a bit of the sauce to the egg before turning into the pan.

LITTLE PAINS D'EPICES NORMANDE . . . This is a kind of upside-down cake which is baked and served in custard cups. Combine 2½ cups canned applesauce with ½ cup brown sugar. Heat to boiling. Remove from heat and spoon into six or eight custard cups. Prepare a package of spice cake or gingerbread mix according to directions. Pour over the applesauce. Bake in a moderate oven (350°) about 20 minutes or until the cake is done. Garnish with whipped cream and sprinkle with grated orange or lemon rind. Serve warm or cold.

XII. SAFARI FISH STEW

On the Ivory Coast in West Africa safaris are mostly for looking or photographing, not for hunting. The animals are likely to be found some distance inland. Here, as at home, Saturday is the day for exploring, and you are likely (if you are lucky) to be served a Safari Stew made of fresh water fish, not unlike *La Pouchouse* of the Burgundy country in France.

Safari Fish Stew
Frejon or Black Bean Puree
Rice
Juju Pudding

SAFARI FISH STEW . . . To serve 6, have ready about 4½ pounds fresh water fish, cut into ½-inch pieces. In a deep saucepan, heat 6 tablespoons peanut oil and brown ½ cup diced onions until soft and golden. Add 2 cups tomato juice, 2 cups clam juice, ½ cup lemon juice, 3½ cups water, 1 bay leaf, 2 sprigs parsley, ½ teaspoon oregano, 2 cloves garlic, crushed. Bring to a boil and cook uncovered briskly 10 minutes. Add the pieces of fish and cook again 10 or 12 minutes until the fish is done. Stir in 1 tablespoon meat glaze. Add salt, pepper, *Tabasco* to taste.

FREJON OR BLACK BEAN PUREE . . . A puree of cooked black beans, often served with fish stew. Here, they add a little coconut milk. To make a quick approximation, use a tin of condensed black bean soup, undiluted. Heat carefully over hot water. Do not scorch. Stir in 1 tablespoon butter; sprinkle with coconut.

JUJU PUDDING . . . Called Juju because it is "magic," made, without cooking, from a can of sweetened condensed milk. Blend one 15-ounce can sweetened condensed milk with ½ cup lime juice. Add the grated rind of 1 lime and yolks of 3 eggs well-beaten. Cover with meringue made by beating 3 egg whites until foamy; add 2 tablespoons sugar. Beat until stiff. Set in moderate oven (350°) 10 minutes or until faintly gilded. Chill.

XII. SEAFOOD PLATTER, NICOISE SAUCE

Status symbols change from time to time. Right now in some circles it seems to be homemade mayonnaise. The earmark of an epicure. Nothing adds such cachet to cold salmon or lobster.

With a *Sauce Nicoise* which is actually a dressed-up mayonnaise, a can of tuna fish becomes a production. Particularly when it is presented with the classic Nicoise Garniture of anchovies, tomatoes, potato salad, cooked green beans and black olives. Since this belongs to the class of composite salads, the ingredients are not tossed together, but each is arranged separately in its own nest of crisp lettuce.

If you haven't discovered the ease, joy and infinite versatility of blender-made mayonnaise, this is the moment.

White Wine Chowder
Seafood Platter   Nicoise Sauce
Heated Hearth Bread   Sweet Butter
Pots de Crème Mocha

WHITE WINE CHOWDER . . . To a can of condensed New England style chowder, add 1 soup can white wine, ½ soup can light cream. Heat and simmer gently about 5 minutes.

SEAFOOD PLATTER . . . To serve 6 or 8, place 1 or 2 cups canned tuna in the center of a chilled platter. Surround with mounds of cooked or canned green beans which have been marinated in French dressing and drained. Cut 3 tomatoes into quarters. Place mounds of potato salad in lettuce and garnish with quartered hard-cooked eggs and anchovy filets. Sprinkle with fresh herbs.

BLENDER-MADE MAYONNAISE . . . Into the blender container break 2 eggs. Add 1 teaspoon dry mustard, 1 teaspoon salt, 4 tablespoons vinegar or lemon juice. Then add ½ cup oil—olive, peanut, safflower or what you will. Cover; turn motor on low. Immediately uncover container and pour in 1½ cups more oil in a slow, steady stream. As soon as the last of the oil has been added, the mayonnaise is ready to serve. Makes 2½ cups. This mayonnaise may be covered and kept in the refrigerator for at least a week. Can be varied every which way by using different flavored vinegars and different oils in different proportions.

SAUCE NICOISE . . . To 1¼ cups Blender-Made Mayonnaise, add 1 cup chopped green peppers, ½ cup canned tomato sauce, 2 teaspoons fresh tarragon or 1 teaspoon dried, 2 tablespoons chopped chives, 1 clove garlic, optional.

POTS DE CRÈME MOCHA . . . Little pots of cream flavored with chocolate and coffee! To a package of instant chocolate pudding, add 1 teaspoon instant coffee and make up according to package directions, but use half milk, half cream instead of all milk and add 1 beaten egg. Pour into demi-tasse cups, and decorate with semi-sweet chocolate morsels.

XIV. VENETIAN SHRIMP ALLA GRIGLIA

What are scampi? Ask the question and the arguments are sure to start . . . and rage on and on. On restaurant menus in the U.S.A., the word usually refers to giant-sized shrimp. In England almost any shrimp is a scampi unless, of course, it's a prawn. In France scampi are usually translated into *langoustines*. But in Venice, I was assured that we are *all* wrong. There is, I was told, only one scampi. It comes only from the Adriatic Sea and can be compared with no other seafood in the whole, wide world.

They did consent, however, to impart to me the secrets of preparing scampi in the true and authentic Venetian manner, *alla griglia*—on the grill. Now we have the temerity to pass it along with the suggestion that our jumbo shrimp may be delectably substituted.

Dessert is a variation of the French *Poires Hélène*, which combines poached pears with chocolate sauce and vanilla ice cream. Our new American version uses canned pears and a syrup flavored with instant coffee, scented with vanilla.

Venetian Shrimp alla Griglia
Crusty Italian Whole Wheat Bread
Noodles and Green Peas
Cauliflower Salad
Poires Hélène New Style

VENETIAN SHRIMP ALLA GRIGLIA . . . To serve 4, use 2 pounds jumbo shrimp. Cut them lengthwise without removing the shells. Leave one section on the outside joined. Flatten them out like a butterfly. Skewer each crosswise with a wooden toothpick to hold them flat. Baste with olive oil; season with salt and pepper; grill under a hot broiler or on charcoal—first the cut side, then the shell side. This will take 6 to 8 minutes depending on the size. Serve on a very hot dish sprinkled with chopped parsley.

NOODLES AND GREEN PEAS . . . Combine 2 tablespoons butter or olive oil with 4 slices bacon, diced, 1 package frozen green peas, ½ cup frozen chopped onion, 1 cup water. Season with ½ teaspoon salt, ½ teaspoon sugar, ½ teaspoon meat extract. Bring to a boil and cook about 15 minutes or until peas are soft and water almost absorbed. Toss in a bowl with one 8-ounce package noodles cooked and drained according to directions. Serves 4.

CAULIFLOWER SALAD . . . Cook 2 packages frozen cauliflower 1 minute less than the package directs. Place in a salad bowl with ½ cup sliced black olives, 2 tablespoons capers, 1 can anchovy filets, drained. Toss with a dressing made by mixing 4 tablespoons olive oil with 2 tablespoons red wine vinegar, ¼ teaspoon freshly ground black pepper. This salad is usually chilled but can also be served warm.

POIRES HÉLÈNE NEW STYLE . . . Drain a can of pears and cook down the syrup to ½ cup. In the syrup dissolve 4 tablespoons instant coffee, ¼ teaspoon salt.

Stir into 1½ cups corn syrup (light or dark). Bring to a boil and cook 5 minutes. Remove from heat. Stir in 2 teaspoons vanilla. Pour over pears. Serve hot or chilled, with or over vanilla ice cream.

LAMBS' GAMBOLS

LAMB

In our country, lamb suffers a sad fate on most tables. It is almost always overdone. For the best taste and the best texture, lamb in all its forms—even chops—should verge on the pink side.

On the other hand, lamb is not too attractive when it is red rare, or even medium rare. All of which entails some judgment on your part. Don't look for help from your meat thermometer, for, if you cook your lamb to the degree indicated on the standard meat thermometer, it will be grossly overcooked, grey and lifeless.

Lamb chops are not just lamb chops, as most novice cooks believe. There are at least five types: Most popular everywhere is the single loin chop. Much better are double lamb chops. Most luxurious . . . triple! These chops are deliciously flavored and have a tender, elegant nature. Then there are the rib chops, the ones with the long, narrow bone.

When the rib chop takes on airs . . . the meat is cut from the bone and the end covered with a paper frill, they become French lamb chops and are generally the most expensive. These can be single or double. Double loin chops not split through the backbone are known in some places as English chops, although they may also be known simply as double lamb chops.

Shoulder lamb chops are larger, have only a tiny bone, and are somewhat less delicate, but comfortably less expensive.

Also suitable for broiling and pan frying are lamb steaks, cut from the heavy leg and ground lamb patties, sometimes called lamburgers.

Chops cut one to two inches thick are best for broiling. Thinner chops are better pan-broiled. For an appetizing brown crust, which contrasts blissfully with slightly pink meat inside, brush the meat before broiling with *Kitchen Bouquet.*

Chops should be broiled at least three or four inches from the heat, depending upon their thickness. Lamb chops one inch thick are broiled from five to six minutes on each side. If they are two inches thick, double the time.

I. ATHENIAN LAMB CHOPS

Vivid as a flamingo in her Balmain tweeds, pixie Paris columnist Naomi Barry flitted recently through the most-fun parties in New York. Naomi writes as she talks and as she cooks—with verve and authority, a merry knowingness. What, we wanted to know, was she serving at her chic little dinner parties on the *Rue de l'Université?*

She mentioned consommé to start. Then maybe baby lamb chops, all green with enormous amounts of parsley. "We're having a run on a puree of stringbeans . . ." the invention of Auguste Guyet, owner of the restaurant Flamberge.

In her wildly popular guidebook, *Paris Personal,* she describes this dish. "Guyet gave a fresh twist to the stringbean. Bored and jaded with years of sautéing in butter or using it cold in a salad, he approached the subject with a dash of imagination and a pinch of audacity. Why not puree the stringbean and give it a whole new career?"

Her favorite dinner party dessert is "madly French-American . . . Apple Pie, *Dames Tatin.*" Naomi calls it "an upside-down pie," gorgeously *caramelized* on its bottom—or is it top?

Consommé Barry
Athenian Lamb Chops   Fluffy Rice
Puree of Stringbeans, Flamberge
Salad of Belgium Endive with Beets Julienne
Apple Pie, Dames Tatin

CONSOMMÉ BARRY . . . (In Paris, Naomi is known as The Barry without the *du.*) To make her special consommé, she adds 2 cups water and ¼ cup port wine to 2 cans condensed consommé. "What gives real character," she says, "are sliced, raw mushrooms which are put in at the very last minute so that they have a crunchy texture."

ATHENIAN LAMB CHOPS . . . To serve 4 to 6, provide 12 tiny French lamb chops. Place in a bowl with ¼ cup olive oil, 2 teaspoons salt, ½ teaspoon pepper, ¼ cup chopped chives, ¾ cup chopped parsley. Allow to stand as long as feasible and broil 6 to 8 minutes turning once.

PUREE OF STRINGBEANS, FLAMBERGE . . . To serve 4, cook 2 pounds large green beans (not small ones) or use 2 packages frozen green beans. Immediately after cooking plunge into cold water. This keeps them green. Put through a vegetable mill or whir in the blender with 2 tablespoons butter, 2 tablespoons cream. Season with salt and pepper. If necessary to reheat, do it over hot water.

APPLE PIE, DAMES TATIN . . . Into the bottom of a shallow casserole put a layer of soft butter (at least ½-inch thick). Cover with a ½-inch layer of sugar mixed with 1 teaspoon cinnamon. Add 2 tins or jars (about 4 cups) canned apple pie filling. Sprinkle with 1 tablespoon lemon juice, another half-teaspoon cinnamon. Dot with 2 tablespoons butter. Cover with pie pastry. "Tuck it in all around and down the sides as if you were making a bed," says Naomi. Bake in a hot oven (400°) about 15 minutes or until the crust is done. Place the dish on an asbestos pad over low heat on top of the stove and let it rest there while you are eating your dinner. This causes the butter and sugar on the bottom to caramelize. Turn upside down to serve. In Paris, Naomi serves it Crème Fraiche. Here she approximates Crème Fraiche by adding 1 egg yolk and 1 tablespoon sugar to 1 cup sour cream.

II. FOUTOUT WITH LAMB

The First Lady of the Ivory Coast is young, beautiful, slender and elegant. Educated in France where, before independence, her husband was a cabinet minister under three administrations, she is understandably partial to French cooking. Nevertheless, there is not a home in the Ivory Coast from the smallest grass-thatched cottage to the Presidential Palace where at least once a week they do not serve Foutout, the national dish.

The word Foutout, means literally "all mixed up together" and refers not only to the stew, but to the starchy accompaniment. The stew itself (made of any sort of meat or fish) is generally called a sauce. Many different sorts of roots and grains are used to prepare the round or doughnut-shaped balls that take the place of bread as well as rice or potatoes. You will see the market women taking the snowy doughnuts of *Foutout* out of green leaf wrappings. Pretty and most appetizing! You could use lettuce, green cabbage or grape leaves.

Foutout with Lamb
Fried Bananas
Sliced Tomatoes and Green Peppers
Melon Fingers with Lime

FOUTOUT WITH LAMB . . . Make up, according to package directions, a stiff mush of white cornmeal, hominy grits or cream of rice. Butter hands, shape into balls and make a depression with your thumbs on both sides. Wrap green leaves. Keep warm over hot water. Meanwhile, prepare the lamb.

To serve 4, have 2 pounds of lamb steak cut into half-inch cubes. Brown quickly in 3 tablespoons hot peanut oil. This should take about 3 minutes. Remove lamb and in the same skillet, lightly sauté 1 package sliced, quick-frozen okra about 3 minutes or until lightly cooked.

Stir the contents of 1 small (1¾-ounce) tin dehydrated onion soup mix into 1½ cups boiling water. Partially cover and simmer 10 minutes stirring occasionally. Stir in 4 tablespoons canned tomato sauce; 4 tablespoons chunky peanut butter. Stir till smooth. Season to taste with ½ teaspoon chili powder—or more if you like the authentic African "heat." Add the sautéed lamb and okra to the sauce. Cook together 2 minutes longer. Serve with *Foutout* or rice.

FRIED BANANAS . . . Cut the bananas into quarters lengthwise and then into halves crosswise, making 8 fingers. Allow to stand 10 minutes covered with lemon juice. Roll in fine crumbs or crushed corn flakes and cook quickly in peanut oil ½ inch deep at 370° until crispy brown on both sides. These may be sprinkled with black pepper and served as an accompaniment to meat or fish . . . with sugar and cinnamon as a dessert.

MELON FINGERS WITH LIME . . . Cut a large chilled honey-dew, Persian or cassava melon into eighths, but not quite all the way through. Sections should be about an inch wide. Spread out on a large plate like the petals of a tropical flower. Remove all the seeds, etc., and garnish with leaves. Place a cluster of lime sections in the center of the tropical flower.

III. GREEK LAMB ON SKEWERS

Warriors of old, so they tell us, impaled collops of meat on their swords and cooked them over their bivouac fires. More ancient than *shish kebab* or *shashlik* is this Greek way of roasting lamb on skewers. It is also one of the simplest and most delicate ways. Usually the lamb is allowed to stand laved in olive oil with parsley and onion for several hours before it is cooked. However, if you are in a mad rush, things can be hurried along if you will warm the olive oil slightly and then rub it into the meat.

Avocado Salad
Greek Lamb on Skewers
Pilaf Madrilene à la Muriel
Yogurt with Fresh Dill or Mint
Zucchini au Poivre
Fresh Raspberries with Cream   *Angel Cake*

AVOCADO SALAD . . . Serve, on lettuce or romaine, slices of avocado with a dressing made with equal parts vinegar and oil. Season simply with salt, pepper, a dash of paprika.

GREEK LAMB ON SKEWERS . . . To serve 4 or 6, have 2 pounds of lamb from the leg or shoulder cut into inch-size chunks. Place in a bowl 4 tablespoons finely chopped onion, 2 tablespoons olive oil, 2 tablespoons chopped parsley, 2 teaspoons salt; ½ teaspoon pepper. Mix thoroughly. Roll meat around in the mixture until well covered.

Place 5 or 6 pieces of meat on each skewer and between every 2 pieces place a whole small or half of a large bay leaf. At the end of the skewer impale a section of lemon.

(The lemon should have been cut crosswise into halves and the halves into quarters.) Broil about 10 minutes turning 2 or 3 times. As the meat broils, the bay leaves begin to glow and emit the most glorious fragrance, transmit the most exciting savor. Sprinkle with chopped fresh or dried oregano. Serve with rice pilaf . . . perhaps this one which was "invented" by my Redding neighbor, Muriel Grasmere.

PILAF MADRILENE À LA MURIEL . . . Into a heavy 3-quart saucepan, place 1 cup extra-long-grain rice. Add one 12-ounce can ready-to-serve consommé madriline, ¼ cup cold water, 2 or 3 drops *Tabasco*, 2 tablespoons butter or oil, 1 tablespoon vinegar. Bring quickly to a boil. Reduce heat to medium, stir once with fork. Cover tightly. Cook over low heat 12 to 14 minutes or until all liquid is absorbed. Serves 4 to 6.

YOGURT WITH FRESH DILL OR MINT . . . Place a container of unflavored yogurt in a chilled bowl of dillweed or mint.

ZUCCHINI AU POIVRE . . . Peel (only if necessary), slice thin and cook in a wide skillet or electric frying pan large enough to accommodate all the *zucchini* in a single layer. Cook quickly uncovered only 2 or 3 minutes. Serve *au poivre*, i.e., sprinkled with coarsely ground black peppercorns.

IV. LADY LATOUR'S LAMB SAUTÉ

On Portland Point, a rocky finger of land that juts into the gray Atlantic, archeologists are digging to learn more about one of Canada's heroines, Lady Latour. She was a tiny, blonde and beautiful French actress married to one of the First European Acadians—the dashing Lord Charles Latour who could dance a noble minuet and as nimbly negotiate a treaty with the Indians or the courtiers of France and England!

During his long absences, his wife was left in charge of the fortress. With a small garrison of fifty men she repeatedly repulsed the attacks of her husband's bitter rival across the Bay. On Easter Sunday, 1645, the fort was vanquished, not by force, but by the treachery of one of her own men. With a halter around her throat, she had to watch the execution of her garrison and a few weeks later died of a broken heart.

But her beauty, charm and courage are still remembered. So are certain of her recipes said to have been brought by her from *La Belle France*.

Baby Green Beans Vinaigrette with Pimiento
Crusty French Bread
Lady Latour's Lamb Sauté
Rice Pilaf
Buttered Corn Kernels
Crème Brulée Instante

BABY GREEN BEANS VINAIGRETTE . . . Serve cooked or canned green beans well chilled with dressing made from 3 parts olive oil, 1 part vinegar, salt, pepper, mustard to taste. Garnish with sliced canned pimiento.

LADY LATOUR'S LAMB SAUTÉ . . . Cut 2 pounds lamb from the neck, shoulder, or leg into small uniform pieces about ½-inch thick. Season with salt and pepper. Sauté in 2 tablespoons butter and 2 tablespoons salad oil at 375° about 5 minutes or until lamb is cooked and lightly browned. Then push aside and, in the same skillet, sauté ½ pound mushrooms, or 1 small (4-ounce) tin drained, broiled mushrooms. Sprinkle with 2 tablespoons chopped parsley, 1 tablespoon lemon juice, ½ cup dry white table wine. Add one 10¾-ounce tin beef gravy, 4 tablespoons tomato sauce or ketchup, and "as much chopped garlic as can be held on the point of a knife." Simmer 5 minutes longer. Serves 4 to 6.

RICE PILAF . . . Cook rice in chicken broth instead of water, adding ½ teaspoon curry powder to 2 cups liquid.

CRÈME BRULÉE INSTANTE . . . With so much on her mind Lady Latour might well have resorted to the incredibly swift version of the famous *Crème Brulée*. Place 1 pint commercial sour cream in a shallow oven-proof serving dish. Sprinkle to the depth of ½ inch with brown sugar being careful that there are no lumps. Place under broiler (watching like a hawk) until sugar is smoothly melted. Chill until top hardens. Crack top with a whack of fork or spoon. Serves 4 to 6.

V. LAMB CHOPS ROMAN

As a quick main course for a special little dinner . . . almost too readily lamb chops come to mind. Too often we dismiss them as not quite interesting or different enough.

But recently I discovered—or, more accurately, rediscovered—the Roman way with a chop. It is a method particularly suitable to the large, meaty and much less expensive chops cut from the shoulder. The seasonings are the same as those used in the preparation of the famous *abacchio* or leg of lamb . . . the touch of olive oil, the suspicion of garlic, the remembered fragrance of rosemary, the tang of an anchovy and a benison of red wine vinegar.

A meal to evoke Rome in your heart might begin with shrimps, broiled scampi fashion. Then the lamb chops, pasta in the shape of wagon wheels or shells or bowknots, a salad of leaf spinach or cooked dandelion greens and afterwards a divine and delicate walnut *torta* with two distinct personalities. If you serve it warm, it is like a soufflé; when cool, it becomes a cake.

Broiled Scampi with Crusty French Bread for Dunking
Lamb Chops Roman
Wagon Wheel Pasta
Cooked Dandelion or Leaf Spinach Salad with Beets
Italian Walnut Torta

BROILED SCAMPI . . . To serve 4 as an appetizer, remove the shells from 1 pound fresh shrimp, leaving the portion which covers the tail. Cut down center and de-vein. Simmer 3 minutes ⅛ pound butter, 1 clove minced garlic. Place shrimp on a large broiling pan, pour garlic butter over them, sprinkle with salt and pepper to taste. Broil 5 to 7 minutes or until brown and tender.

LAMB CHOPS ROMAN . . . Heat a tablespoon of olive oil in a heavy skillet. Brown well on all sides over high heat 4 good-sized shoulder lamb chops. Sprinkle with ½ teaspoon salt, ½ teaspoon freshly ground black pepper, 1 small clove garlic crushed, ½ teaspoon powdered rosemary. Continue browning 5 minutes. Add ¼ cup each wine vinegar and hot water, 1 anchovy filet chopped. Cover. Cook slowly about 5 minutes longer or until meat is tender. Garnish with parsley.

ITALIAN WALNUT TORTA . . . Combine 1¼ cups finely ground walnuts with ¾ cup sugar, ⅓ cup unsweetened cocoa. Gradually add 4 egg yolks very well beaten, 1 teaspoon vanilla extract, 1 teaspoon grated lemon rind. Beat 4 egg whites until stiff but not dry and fold into the mixture carefully. Butter a 9-inch glass baking dish, dust with 2 tablespoons packaged bread crumbs. Bake in 350° oven 30 minutes or until cake tester comes out clean. Usually served in Italy with a sweet dessert wine such as Marsala.

VI. LAMB CHOPS VILLEROI

To many Americans—like us—there is in Paris a feeling of "coming home," mostly because of Dora Miller and her husband, Allen Updegraff.

For years, Dora Miller has been the acknowledged dean of American fashion correspondents. Her husband is a poet, an essayist, a wise, amusing philosopher. Their apartment has been for years the meeting place for writers, artists, editors from everywhere . . . from Kansas City, Missouri (Dora's home town) to Athens, New York and Athens, Greece.

A Paris resident for forty years, Dora Miller knows French food almost as intimately as she knows French fashion. A recent dinner was a special delight. Lamb chops—a dream among lamb chops—enrobed in a rich covering first of sauce, then of crumbs. The *cuisinière*, Geneviève Stop, who comes from Catalan, gave me her recipe. She makes her own Bechamel sauce to cover the chops (which she calls cutlets). But we use mushroom soup.

Bouillon Floraline
Lamb Chops Villeroi
Salad Catalan
Strawberry Timbales

BOUILLON FLORALINE . . . Dora's vivacious Mlle. Geneviève does miraculous things with chicken broth

—miracles which can be approximated, if not duplicated, with broth from a tin. If you use canned broth, add to each 2 cups 1 teaspoon lemon juice, a few grains of cayenne pepper, just a suspicion of garlic salt, a teaspoon of butter or chicken fat. Cook uncovered 5 minutes. Add 2 tablespoons of the very fine pastina known in France as Floraline and cook about 4 minutes longer.

LAMB CHOPS VILLEROI . . . To serve 4, you will need 8 rib lamb chops or 4 large shoulder chops. Brown lightly in a frying pan about 4 minutes on each side. Cool. Meanwhile, combine 2 well-beaten egg yolks and one 10-ounce tin condensed cream of mushroom soup. Cover chops completely and smoothly with this sauce. Dip them into flour, then brush with beaten egg and sprinkle with fine breadcrumbs. Fry in deep fat at 370° 3 minutes or until chops are golden brown and crisp.

SALAD CATALAN . . . Mlle. Geneviève washes her spinach in seven waters. But you may use ready-washed spinach. Cook very lightly and drain. Blend 2 tablespoons olive oil with 3 tablespoons lemon juice. Add salt, pepper and a little garlic. Pour over spinach. Serve chilled—garnish with sweet red peppers or pimientos.

STRAWBERRY TIMBALES . . . In most Parsian households not much fancy baking is done. But these *timbales,* a kind of tart shell made from cookie dough, are easily put together at home. To make the *timbales,* add to a 10-ounce package pie crust mix 2 egg yolks, 2 tablespoons sugar, 1 tablespoon cream. Divide in 6 parts. Mold to the outside of tart pans or custard cups, forming a shell. Bake pastry upside down according to package directions. Cook, then carefully lift from pans. Fill with ice cream and top with sugared fresh or frozen strawberries.

VII. LAMB WITH DILL AU FAST GOURMET

Years ago we went to stay with some relatives in Sweden . . . Fru Elsvig Ankarcrona whose husband Theodor was huntmaster for the King. The King, much interested in hunting and fishing, came often to visit them at Boserup, the farm-estate in Skona, the castle at Runsa near Stockholm and the trout fishing lodge in the North.

The food must certainly have been as interesting to the King as was the chase. All these long years we have remembered . . . and tried often to recreate those luscious tastes and delicate fragrances.

There was, we recall, an appetizer made of inexpensive canned cod roe known as Swedish caviar. There was a lamb stew blessed with dill. And at the flick of a wish would appear great platters covered with the small dew-thin pancakes known as *plattär*, and served with currant jam or the lilliput cranberries of Scandinavia—lingonberries. Now easy to find in this country, too.

Relish of Her Grace
Lamb with Dill au Fast Gourmet
Duchesse Potatoes
Cucumber Salad
Swedish Plattär with Lingonberry Preserves

RELISH OF HER GRACE . . . Fru Elsvig, known as Her Grace, counted this one of her prize specialties. Whip ⅔ cup heavy cream until stiff. Stir in a small tin (about 3 tablespoons) of Swedish cod roe caviar and 2 tablespoons very finely chopped onion or chives. Place in a mound in the middle of a plate. Sprinkle with freshly ground black pepper. Arrange around the mound 3 hard-cooked eggs sliced. Surround with heated rye crisps or fingers of fresh toast. Each person spreads his own.

LAMB WITH DILL AU FAST GOURMET . . . Never in Skona would anyone have dreamed of starting this dish with such directions, but the flavoring and the final effect are quite authentic: Drop into hot water and heat for 4 minutes 6 individual packets of frozen lamb stew. Remove from plastic bags and place in a kettle with 1 can chicken gravy. Add 2 tablespoons vinegar, 2 teaspoons sugar, 2 tablespoons fresh or frozen chopped dill or 1 tablespoon dried dillweed. Bring to a boil; simmer 5 minutes. Beat 1 egg slightly, add a couple of tablespoons of hot gravy to the egg and turn the egg into the stew. Garnish with sprigs of dill or watercress. Serves 6.

DUCHESSE POTATOES . . . To 3 cups hot mashed potatoes add 4 tablespoons butter, 2 slightly beaten egg yolks, ½ teaspoon yellow mustard, 2 drops *Tabasco* or a few grains of cayenne pepper, salt and pepper to taste. Allow mixture to cool briefly. Shape into a dozen pretty heaps on a floured board. Place on buttered baking sheet.

Brush with a slightly beaten egg. Bake in a hot oven (400°) about 5 minutes or until golden. Serve at once.

SWEDISH PLATTÄR WITH LINGONBERRY PRESERVES . . . Here as in Sweden you can buy special *plattär* pans with 7 shallow depressions, 2 inches in diameter— just the right size for these tenderest of tender pancakes. However, they can be dropped by spoonfuls onto a very hot, lightly greased griddle. To serve 6, sift into a mixing bowl 1½ cups flour with 3 teaspoons sugar, ¼ teaspoon salt. In another bowl beat together 4 eggs and 3 cups milk. Gradually stir the egg-milk mixture into flour. Beat until smooth. Seven *plattär* make a proper portion.

VIII. PERSIAN LAMB

In the flare-lit garden of a friend who comes from Iran (the old name was Persia) we recently had a supper that might have been served from gleaming salvers to ladies like Semiramis and noblemen with flashing scimitars.

The jewel of the meal, as the host expressed it, was skewered lamb in the Persian manner served around Rice with a Golden Eye. A dessert of melon balls and peaches was sprinkled with rose petals and topped with crushed ice cubes that had been flavored and colored with Crème de Menthe.

Teheran Platter of Relishes
Skewered Lamb—Persian Manner
Rice with a Golden Eye
Fruit Semiramis
Coffee with Mint

TEHERAN PLATTER OF RELISHES . . . Fill a shallow bowl or deepish platter with crushed ice and cover the ice with radish roses, green onions and various types of pickles and gherkins, sprinkled with fresh tarragon.

PERSIAN LAMB . . . To serve six, have 3 pounds of leg or shoulder of lamb cut preferably into strips rather than chunks, although chunks will do. The strips should be about 6 inches long, an inch wide, half an inch thick. Marinate several hours or overnight with ½ cup finely chopped onion, 2 teaspoons saffron. Thread the meat on skewers. Brush with melted butter or olive oil and broil about 10 minutes, turning often. Season with salt and freshly ground black pepper.

RICE WITH A GOLDEN EYE . . . Cook long-grained rice according to directions. Drain. In a heavy skillet melt 2 tablespoons butter. Then add the rice a spoonful at a time. Sprinkle with 4 tablespoons melted butter, 1 tablespoon lemon juice. Cover tightly and allow to cook without stirring about 15 minutes or until a crust forms on the bottom.

To serve, place a mound of rice in the center of each plate. Into a small depression in the center of the rice place the yolk of an egg and a ball of butter. Arrange the lamb around the rice and sprinkle with chopped mint or dill. Provide a wedge of lemon. Each person mixes the butter and egg into the rice.

FRUIT SEMIRAMIS . . . To serve six, combine 2 cups honeydew or Persian melon balls with 1 cup diced or sliced fresh or frozen peaches. Add 1 tablespoon lemon juice. Serve very well chilled in champagne saucers garnished with rose petals and crushed ice cubes which have been colored and flavored by adding 4 tablespoons green Crème de Menthe to 2 cups water. Freeze cubes as usual.

COFFEE WITH MINT . . . Add fresh mint leaves to hot or iced coffee.

IX. NEW CROWN OF LAMB

"Love and kisses from the Misches," is often the sign-off on a dinner invitation, prized and blissfully remembered. Robert Misch, gourmet, advertising executive, wine lecturer, and his lovely wife, Janet (one of the wheels at Lincoln Center), give dinner parties in the grand tradition.

Usually it is Robert who composes the menu as carefully and thoughtfully as if he were writing a sonnet. At a recent party, for the first course we had fiddle-back ferns. Out of season you can find them canned or frozen. Lacking ferns, green asparagus will do. The entree was a crown roast of lamb. Since a crown roast is not too easy to get outside of large cities, we have, with Bob's help, devised a way to achieve somewhat the same elegant effect by using double lamb chops set around a mound of buckwheat *kasha* or whole wheat cereal cooked in consommé.

Fiddle-back Ferns or Green Asparagus à la Polonnaise
New Crown of Lamb
Buckwheat Groats or Quick Kasha
Creamed Spinach
French Cheese Board
Robert M.'s Compote of Plums
and Apricots au Vermouth
Vanilla Ice Cream

FIDDLE-BACK FERNS OR GREEN ASPARAGUS . . . Serve lightly cooked fiddle-back ferns or asparagus spears à la Polonnaise. Brown 1 cup fine bread crumbs in 4 tablespoons melted butter. Sprinkle lightly with about a teaspoon of lemon juice and a few grains of cayenne pepper. Garnish with 1 or 2 very thin slices of ham heated in butter.

NEW CROWN OF LAMB . . . To serve six, provide 6 double lamb chops . . . French type. Cut the meat away from the two bones, leaving them quite bare like two little handles.

Rub chops with garlic, sprinkle with salt and pepper, brush with olive oil mixed with *Kitchen Bouquet* and broil 10 to 12 minutes or until crusty brown on the outside, still pink in the middle. Meanwhile, cook, according to package directions, 2 cups fine buckwheat groats or quick-cooking whole-grain cereal. Mound the *kasha* in the center of a platter; rest the chops on the *kasha* with the bones standing up to form a crown. Traditionally each little bone should be surmounted with a paper frill but you may use, impaled on each bone, a large pimiento-stuffed olive or a tiny canned beet.

BUCKWHEAT GROATS OR KASHA . . . In many markets you can get buckwheat groats. Cook according to package directions. If groats are not available, much the same effect can be achieved by using quick-cooking, whole-grain cereal. Instead of water, use beef broth or consommé.

CREAMED SPINACH . . . Comes already cooked and creamed, quick-frozen—ready to heat. For an extra touch of continental glamour add a light sprinkle of nutmeg.

ROBERT M.'s COMPOTE . . . A delicious and most unusual compote with juices dark and gloriously caramelized. To serve 6 or 8, drain the syrup from 1 large (No. 2) can purple plums and 1 large can unpeeled apricots. Mix and set aside half the syrup. Add 1 cup sweet Italian vermouth, cook down until reduced by half. Add fruit and cook slowly on top of the stove for 25 minutes or in the oven at 400° for 2 hours. Serve warm. Pass vanilla ice cream.

X. RACK OF LAMB MADERIA

Thirty years ago Gertrude Stein wrote a book which she misnamed *The Autobiography of Alice B. Toklas* because her heroine could not be persuaded to do it herself. Now in her eighties, Alice Toklas has written *What Is Remembered*, recapturing not only the essence of Gertrude Stein's remarkable personality but the essence of those rich years in Paris when Miss Stein wrote and talked, Miss Toklas cooked and talked. The cooking was as important in its way as all the other artistic activities that flourished in that creative atmosphere.

Many gastronomical memories appeared in the first *Alice B. Toklas Cookbook* and also in *Aromas and Flavors*, a book with which we were privileged to help. Among our treasures is a chocolate mousse recipe which she sent to us not long after we had arranged her introduction to what she called the blessed blender. The addition of instant coffee and cinnamon to Miss Toklas' old and classic French recipe would probably horrify her but they do seem in some odd way to approximate the special flavor inherent in European chocolate.

Baby Asparagus Around Cream
Rack of Lamb Madeira
Green Mashed Potatoes
Alice B. Toklas Chocolate Mousse

BABY ASPARAGUS AROUND CREAM . . . Get the youngest, freshest, thinnest green asparagus. Cook only about 8 minutes. Arrange like spokes of a wheel on a round plate.

In the center place ½ cup heavy cream, whipped with ½ teaspoon salt. Serve before cream has time to melt.

RACK OF LAMB MADEIRA . . . This is nothing more than 4 or 6 French lamb chops that have been allowed to stay together. Roast in a hot oven (400°) about 30 minutes, basting 3 or 4 times with ½ cup rich chicken broth mixed with ½ cup Madeira wine or American sherry.

GREEN MASHED POTATOES . . . To serve six, mash 6 large baked potatoes or heat 2 packages frozen mashed potatoes and beat in 4 tablespoons softened butter, 1 teaspoon salt, 1 cup light cream, ¼ cup parsley and ½ cup watercress leaves (both finely chopped) and 2 tablespoons fresh basil or 1 tablespoon dried basil.

ALICE B. TOKLAS CHOCOLATE MOUSSE . . . Here are two versions; the first made with the electric blender, the second, without . . .

Into the container of an electric blender place 5 tablespoons boiling water, a 6-ounce package of chocolate pieces. Blend at high speed 6 seconds. Scrape from sides with rubber spatula. Blend 10 seconds later. Add 4 egg yolks, 2 tablespoons Cognac or rum, ½ teaspoon instant coffee, ¼ teaspoon cinnamon if desired. Blend 5 seconds or until smooth. Then add 4 egg whites; blend at low speed about 1 minute. Spoon into 6 or 8 small demi-tasse cups or wine glasses. Chill at least 1 hour. Serve plain or with whipped cream slightly sweetened and flavored with Cointreau or Triple Sec.

Without a blender . . . put into a bowl 3 tablespoons hot water, instant coffee, cinnamon and chocolate pieces as above. Place bowl over hot water and stir until melted. Beat 4 egg yolks until thick and lemon colored. Add rum or Cognac as above or substitute 2 tablespoons heavy cream, 1 tablespoon vanilla. Fold in whites of 4 eggs beaten until very stiff. Proceed as above but chill longer . . . at least 4 hours.

XI. HALF-HOUR RAGOUT OF LAMB

Almost as fast as a quick-frozen lamb stew is this delicious thyme, garlic and clove-scented ragout of lamb. With the aid of meat tenderizer, inexpensive cuts of lamb may be used. If, in addition to using a tenderizer, the meat is cut, not into the usual cubes, but into strips about ½ inch thick and 1 inch long, the lamb should be marvelously tender in about a third of the usual cooking time.

From the nutritional point of view, the ragout will be even better, for shortening the cooking time makes it possible to retain a host of vital nutrients often lost by the long moist simmering that our grandmothers found necessary.

To go along with this modernized ragout . . . an ultra-fast version of a very old Southern delicacy—Peach Leather Strips. Long, long ago peach leather was made from fresh-picked peaches, dried in the hot Georgia sun. Took at least a week of doing! Now we start with commercially dried peaches and go floatingly along to achieve this delightfully chewy confection in a few minutes.

Half-Hour Ragout of Lamb
Alabama Biscuits
Ring of Tomato Aspic Salad With Cole Slaw,
Celery and Carrot Curls
New-Fashioned Peach Leather Strips with
Peach Ice Cream

HALF-HOUR RAGOUT OF LAMB . . . To serve 6, thoroughly moisten with water the surfaces of 3 pounds lamb shoulder or breast of veal. Sprinkle with seasoned instant meat tenderizer as if you were sprinkling with salt. Use no salt. Pierce the meat deeply every half inch with a kitchen fork so the tenderizer will penetrate. Prepare one side, then the other. Cut the meat into strips 1 inch long and about ½ inch thick. Dust lightly with flour.

Heat 2 tablespoons vegetable oil in a heavy kettle. Brown the meat quickly. Sprinkle with ¼ teaspoon ground cloves, ¼ teaspoon powdered thyme, 2 cloves garlic crushed, 1 bay leaf, ½ cup white wine or water. Cover closely. Bring to a boil; simmer about 15 minutes. Add 1 pound can each whole onions, potatoes and green beans, including the juices. Continue cooking until vegetables are heated and meat is tender. This should take about 10 minutes.

Serve in heated bowls sprinkled with chopped parsley and garnished with garlic-flavored croutons.

ALABAMA BISCUITS . . . Use the new, flaky, ready-to-bake packaged biscuits, but cut each biscuit crosswise in half and prick deeply with a fork. Bake according to directions.

RING OF TOMATO ASPIC SALAD WITH COLE SLAW . . . To serve 4 to 6, use 2 tins ready-jelled, canned tomato aspic. Melt according to directions and season with 1 tablespoon beefsteak sauce. Pour into a ring mold. It will re-jell as soon as it reaches room temperature. Fill center with cole slaw. Sprinkle liberally with chopped chives; garnish with celery and carrot curls.

NEW-FASHIONED PEACH LEATHER STRIPS . . . Wash 2 cups dried peaches. Place in a sieve or colander over hot water. Cover closely and allow to steam about 15 minutes or until puffed and softened. Drain off any visible moisture and press firmly between paper towels to flatten, using a rolling pin—or your hands. When very flat, cut into half-inch strips and roll or toss in a bag with sugar. May be served immediately or allowed to dry and kept in a tin box.

THE MANY-SPLENDORED PIG

PORK

Except for various types of ham and bacon—pork stymies the cook in a great hurry, since pork, we all know, must be cooked thoroughly. This is no gastronomic whim. Thorough cooking is necessary to guard against trichinosis, caused by parasites sometimes present in fresh pork. Trichina are not so often present now as they were formerly, for it has been discovered that keeping the fresh meat at zero temperature or under for two weeks can effectively destroy the parasites. So pork that has been stored in the freezer at a temperature of zero to minus five degrees F. is quite safe. Nevertheless, most of us will continue to cook our pork very well.

In order to cook in thirty minutes or less, pork chops should be cut a scant half-inch thick. In many cases, the bone (when present) is removed and the meat pounded even thinner. Since pork contains quite a bit of fat, it is possible to broil thin pork chops without drying. They should be done in about twenty-five minutes. To make certain that the meat is thoroughly cooked, make a cut near the bone, or in the center. Be sure that the meat looks snowy white.

Although fresh pork poses a problem, ready-cooked or canned hams, ham steaks or slices, sausages and bacon are a joy and a refuge.

SO MANY HAMS

Ham is a many-splendored subject. There is a multitude of hams—so many different types, shapes and flavors. Most valued by the epicures are smoked, uncooked hams of the country type. These are becoming as scarce as dinosaurs and almost as expensive as truffles. If you don't believe it, try pricing a true Smithfield country ham.

These country-style hams are scarcely appropriate for fast cookery. They take days of soaking, scrubbing, simmering, baking, if you start from raw. Thin slices of country smoked ham are quickly cooked however and so are the much more readily available and wonderfully economical smoked and cured picnic shoulder, boneless butts, cottage rolls or Calas hams. All of these may be sliced from a quarter to a half-inch thick and cooked like ham steaks.

Aside from the country-style, old-fashioned hams, heavily salted or peppered, smoked and aged (which require parboiling as well as soaking and scrubbing), there are other types.

Most popular all over the country is a *mild-flavored* (some say *too* mild-flavored) tender ham, *processed* rather than smoked. Such hams come uncooked or fully cooked and ready to eat. None of these requires parboiling.

Scotch ham is available in many parts of the country. It is a mildly cured ham, not smoked, often budget-priced. Generally it must be cooked before eating. *Tenderized ham* is theoretically ready to eat, but most people think it requires thorough heating.

Picnic shoulder, boneless butts, cottage rolls and *Calas* are processed and marked the same as regular hams. Follow the packer's cooking directions.

Boiled or baked, *delicatessen hams* are ready to eat. This sort of ham is most often used for making sandwiches, invaluable also as the start of many excellent, quick specialties. For certain dishes, it is better to have the ham cut a little thicker than usual.

Canned hams are fully cooked and boned. They do not require any more cooking. The best (and most expensive) brands are one-piece chunks and can easily be glazed in the oven. When, as is more usual, several pieces are pushed or pressed together, the ham is likely to fall apart. In any case, be careful about over-cooking canned hams. They lose their juices and become dry and papery.

Prosciutto and *Prosciuttino* are Italian, boned, lean, dry-cured and spicy hams, delicate in flavor and delightfully sweet. These are practically never cooked and are served tissue paper thin along with antipasto, or as an appetizer with fresh fruits, such as melon, pears, apples and papaya.

Westphalian and *Parma* hams belong to the same exalted category.

HAM SLICES

Uncooked ham slices are best pan-broiled. Slash the fat edges to prevent curling. Rub a pre-heated skillet with fat, so that the ham does not stick. Pan-broil, using moderate heat, about two minutes on each side for a slice of ham about a quarter of an inch thick. A half-inch-thick slice of ham is cooked four minutes on each side. If the ham steak is an inch thick . . . 8 to 9 minutes.

Ham slices anywhere from ½ inch to 1½ inches may be broiled (from 2 to 4 inches away from the heat) 5 to 12 minutes on each side, according to thickness.

Cooked ham slices, or ready-to-eat ham, are prepared in exactly the same fashion, but in just about half the time.

BACON

Bacon is, according to one gourmet, like light, air and sunshine to cuisine. In most people's minds, bacon is married to the egg. But, if so, it has been carrying on the maddest love affairs with everything, from hors d'oeuvres and sandwiches to soups, salads, muffins, biscuits, waffles, baked potatoes and almost any casserole you can name.

It must be admitted with some sadness, however, that bacon is not what it used to be. It has, in the average supermarket, become paper-thin, dull and tasteless, especially when it is sold with all the tasty rind removed in pound or half pound vacuum-sealed glassine packages . . . about a dozen slices to the half-pound. If flavor is what you want, try the so-called country-style sliced bacon. Have your bacon cut to order from a slab and sliced at least twice as thick as usual.

Canadian bacon is generally more expensive than regular bacon, but it has more taste. So versatile, it can take the place of bacon or ham. To our way of thinking, it too is best when sliced thicker than usual.

"Breakfast bacon," in case you should come upon it,

is a misnomer. It is not pork at all, but beef, and is especially popular in kosher markets.

I. AUGE MOUNTAIN PORK CHOPS

Of all the scents in all the world there is none more inviting on a crisp September evening than the fragrance of onions and pork chops a-frying.

In the Auge mountain region of France, they have a very special way of cooking pork chops with cider and shallots—those rosy little cousins of the onion which impart a subtle flavor that is part onion, part garlic, all Heaven.

But since shallots are so hard to find in this country, we use sweet red onion instead and a little garlic. So we come quite close, we think, to the original taste. Even the aromas are hauntingly similar.

Auge Mountain Pork Chops
Straw Potatoes
Cucumber and Green Pepper Salad
Compote of Plums   Spice Cake

AUGE MOUNTAIN PORK CHOPS . . . Chop 6 shallots or 1 small red onion and ½ clove garlic. Combine with an equal quantity of finely chopped parsley. Score 4 thin pork chops lightly on each side. Sprinkle with salt and pepper and spread with the herb mixture. Brush with olive oil and broil slowly about 4 inches under the broiler.

Have ready 1 cup cider heated in a small pan. When the chops are cooked, put them in their broiling pan on top of the stove. Pour in the cider. Let it bubble over high heat about 2 or 3 minutes until all the juices of the meat have formed a sauce.

In France, at this point, they would stir in a couple of tablespoons of *calvados*, which is apple brandy—quite similar to our applejack. It is supposed to cut the richness of the pork.

STRAW POTATOES . . . These are very finely cut French fried potatoes. Canned, shoestring or quick-frozen potatoes may be substituted. In France these potatoes are reheated by being tossed in a small quantity of butter.

CUCUMBER AND GREEN PEPPER SALAD . . . Peel and

slice thinly 2 cucumbers. (If there is time, sprinkle with a little salt and let them stand for ½ hour.) Drain and place in salad bowl. Sprinkle with 1 teaspoon vinegar, 3 teaspoons salad oil. Cut a sweet green pepper in julienne strips and dress with a small quantity of vinegar and oil and salt and pepper, stirring to coat the strips on all sides. Spread the green peppers on the cucumbers. Garnish with 3 thinly sliced, firm fresh mushrooms. Frost with a little mayonnaise. Serve on lettuce.

COMPOTE OF PLUMS . . . Drain a can of purple plums and into the syrup stir ½ cup black cherry jam. Cook uncovered 5 minutes. Replace the plums in the syrup. Chill in the freezer. At the last minute you may add a few pine nuts that have been crisped in the oven.

II. BRAZILIAN PORK CHOPS

The startling statement has been made that the three best cuisines in the world are the Chinese, the French and the Brazilian! Gourmets may gasp and argue. The fact remains that the Brazilian is an exciting style of cooking based on the artistry of the Indians and the Africans as well as the Portuguese.

Brazilian poets and musicians have composed sonnets and fugues; scholars have written learned books extolling the delights of Africa-inspired Brazilian dishes . . . many of which feature that "nutty glory of Guinea" which is the peanut.

As in many parts of Latin America the tortilla is a favorite breadstuff. Although there is nothing that can compare with a freshly patted, handmade tortilla . . . you can do right well with the frozen variety or even those that come in tins if you know how to treat them properly.

South American Pumpkin Soup
Brazilian Pork Chops
Santos Salad
Toasted Tortillas
Chocolate Ice Cream with Coffee Beans

SOUTH AMERICAN PUMPKIN SOUP . . . To serve 4, add to 1 can condensed cream of chicken soup 1 can milk, 1 soup can water, 1 cup canned or frozen pureed pumpkin or squash. Season to taste with additional salt and pepper, a dash of cayenne pepper, ⅛ teaspoon nutmeg. Simmer 5 minutes. Sprinkle with chopped parsley.

BRAZILIAN PORK CHOPS . . . To serve 4, you will need 8 small thin pork chops. Season with salt and pepper. Brown slowly in a heavy skillet 15 minutes or until well browned. Add 2 tablespoons finely chopped onion. Cook 2 minutes longer. Pour off any fat in the pan; add 3 cups consommé, ½ cup sherry if desired, 1 small stick cinnamon, a dash of garlic powder. Simmer 10 minutes or until the meat is well cooked. Remove chops and keep warm. Add ½ cup peanut butter and 2 tablespoons cornstarch stirred to a paste with 2 tablespoons water. Blend smoothly and thoroughly. Cook until the gravy thickens and boils about 2 minutes. Sprinkle generously with salted peanuts.

SANTOS SALAD . . . Garnish a bowl of crisp chicory, romaine or leaf lettuce with sliced tomatoes, thinly sliced onions and pimiento-stuffed olives. Serve with a dressing made by combining 3 parts salad oil, 1 part lime or lemon juice. Season highly with garlic and onion juice. A dash of anchovy paste is often added.

TOASTED TORTILLAS . . . With your hands, dampen the flat underside of a tortilla . . . not the "face" which is slightly raised. Toast right on top of a very low gas flame or an electric unit or on a griddle. Keep turning so that tortillas heat through without burning and become delicately freckled; give off an appetizing fresh-corn fragrance. Brush immediately with melted butter fore and aft.

CHOCOLATE ICE CREAM WITH COFFEE BEANS . . . Jinx Falkenberg's brother opened one of the first ice cream parlors in Brazil some years ago; ice cream has become increasingly popular ever since. Any good chocolate ice cream can be given a Brazilian accent by adding a dash of cinnamon and a sprinkle of coffee beans or instant coffee.

III. HAM AND CHEESE SAVOURY

At Quebec's Chateau Frontenac Hotel whose lordly towers seem to guard the wide waters of the St. Lawrence . . . the old and the new, the past and the present, simplicity and elegance, French and English all seem to blend into gracious harmony.

The Frontenac's executive chef, M. Christian Hitz, prepared for us *the best* Habitant Pea Soup, followed by a Ham and Cheese Savoury that in England might have been a palate-clearer after a long dinner. For us it made a perfect main course served along with sliced tomatoes, a salad of young greens.

For dessert there was a pie, considered one of the national treasures of French Canada. Often one hears the phrase, "French as *Ferlouche*" . . . the French raisin pie that is generally made in Quebec with a mild, light table molasses. In some areas, however, dark molasses is preferred. Either will do.

Habitant Pea Soup
Ham and Cheese Savoury
Sliced Tomatoes
Salad of Young Greens
Ferlouche (French Raisin Pie)

HABITANT PEA SOUP . . . You can buy Habitant Pea Soup ready to serve in cans. Or use condensed or dehydrated split pea soup, adding one small handful of celery leaves and 2 or 3 tablespoons finely chopped onion. Garnish with finely shredded carrots.

HAM AND CHEESE SAVOURY . . . For each serving, lightly toast 1 or 2 slices of white bread depending upon the appetite and occasion. Homemade bread is preferable or at least the homemade type. Remove crusts, brush with butter, cover with thinly-sliced baked or boiled ham that has been warmed for a few seconds in a little butter. Cover with thin slices of Switzerland cheese. Sprinkle lightly with a couple of tablespoons dry white wine or white vermouth. Bake in a moderately hot oven (375°) until cheese is melted—about five minutes.

FERLOUCHE (FRENCH RAISIN PIE) . . . Combine ½ cup molasses with ½ cup brown sugar, 1½ cups hot water, 1 cup seedless raisins. Bring to a boil. Mix 4 tablespoons cornstarch with 4 tablespoons cold water to make a smooth paste. Add this to the raisins. Stir and cook until mixture thickens and becomes clear. Cool and pour into a 9-inch baked pie shell. Serve with whipped cream.

IV. HAM COTELETTES TYCOON

At the end of a business day, tycoons meet to eat in the sky on the first-class jet flight from Detroit to New York on American Airlines. Dinner accompanied by a blaze of twilight is deliciously pampering. One of the favorite specialties on the menu are *Cotelettes Cordon Bleu*. American Airlines has them prepared on the West Coast where they are generally made with chicken breasts that are boned and flattened, then rolled together with ham and cheese. A rather long and fussy process!

Ever on the lookout for ease and speed combined with elegance, we set ourselves to evolve a version of the *Cotelettes* that can be put together in minutes using slices of boiled or baked ham from the delicatessen and Swiss, Muenster or Monterey Jack cheese.

Ham Cotelettes Tycoon
Sweet Potatoes with Orange Glaze
Buttered Green Beans
Tossed Salad with Quartered Tomatoes
Currant Jelly Roll with Rosettes of Whipped Cream

HAM COTELETTES TYCOON . . . To serve 4, you will need 16 slices of ham, about ⅛ inch thick, and 4 slices of cheese.

For each *cotelette* start with 2 slices ham topped with a slice of cheese. Cover with 2 more slices of ham. Roll loosely and tuck in the edges, flattening a little to make a pillow-shaped cutlet about 4 inches long and 2 inches wide. Roll in flour; dip into slightly beaten egg to which you have added a tablespoon of milk. Coat with packaged flavored bread crumbs.

Deep-fry in salad oil at 370° about 4 minutes or until cotelettes are golden and crusty. Drain on paper towels. Serve immediately or set uncovered in a 180° oven until serving time.

SWEET POTATOES WITH ORANGE GLAZE . . . Heat 4 to 6 cooked or canned drained sweet potatoes (thickly sliced if large or halved if small) in a glaze made by heating together 3 tablespoons each: melted butter, orange juice, brown sugar. Shake the potatoes over high heat until they glisten and glow.

BUTTERED GREEN BEANS . . . For special elegance use Blue Lake canned green beans from the Northwest.

CURRANT JELLY ROLL WITH ROSETTES OF WHIPPED CREAM . . . If you use ready-whipped cream, you can easily push it out in swirls or whirls or you can keep rosettes or rosebuds of whipped cream in the freezer. Press out onto waxed paper and freeze uncovered. Then place in a candy box and use as needed.

V. HAM STEAK BIGARADE

Our friend Mabel Stegner has long been known as a creative dynamo in the world of food. New ideas and new techniques pop and crackle as she talks. Hers is a particular genius for taking plain, ordinary, get-them-any-where ingredients and turning them into distinguished dishes.

Mushroom Bouillon
Ham Steak Bigarade
French Fried Onions
Cream-Style Corn
Cherry Rolls, Allspiced Topping

MUSHROOM BOUILLON . . . Simmer together 10 to 15 minutes one 6-ounce can sliced broiled mushrooms with their liquid, 1 can condensed consommé, 1 soup can water, 4 tablespoons Madeira wine (optional). Garnish with lemon slices.

HAM STEAK BIGARADE . . . Trim any excess fat from a pre-cooked ham steak, cut about ¾ inch thick and weighing in the neighborhood of 1½ pounds. Score fat along the edges. Brush evenly on all sides with at least a teaspoon of *Kitchen Bouquet*.

Heat 1 tablespoon cooking oil and brown ham on both sides over moderate heat. Remove to a heated platter and keep warm. To the fat in the skillet add 1 cup orange juice, 1 tablespoon butter, ⅓ cup orange marmalade, ¼ teaspoon ginger, 1 tablespoon cornstarch. Cook until sauce thickens—about 5 minutes. Put the ham back in the pan; cover and continue cooking over moderate heat 10 minutes longer. To serve, cut into ½ inch slices across the grain. Makes 4 to 6 servings.

FRENCH FRIED ONIONS . . . Use quick-frozen French fried onions, but ignore package directions. Heat a handful at a time in ¾ inch salad oil at 375°. Taste and texture are much better.

CHERRY ROLLS . . . Quick-frozen. Heat according to package directions.

ALLSPICED TOPPING . . . Instant whipped cream lightly sprinkled with powdered allspice.

VI. HAM STEAK WITH RED-EYE GRAVY

Melon Slices with Lime Juice
Ham Steak with Red-Eye Gravy
Skillet Spoon Bread
Instant Café au Lait

MELON SLICES WITH LIME JUICE . . . Peel a well-chilled cantaloupe or honeydew melon and cut crosswise into circles. Remove seeds and sprinkle with lime juice. Garnish with mint leaves.

HAM STEAK WITH RED-EYE GRAVY . . . Rub a heavy skillet with a piece of ham fat and, when the pan is fairly hot, add slices of raw smoked ham cut about ¼-inch thick. Keep turning the ham frequently so that the slices stay flat and do not curl. Remove ham from skillet and keep warm. Add to the drippings in the pan about 1 cup water, 1 teaspoon instant coffee; just enough liquid to loosen the brown particles in the pan. Stir and cook until half the liquid evaporates. Season to taste with a little *Tabasco* sauce, ½ teaspoon sugar, ½ teaspoon prepared mustard and ½ teaspoon paprika. Serve promptly. If allowed to stand too long, the ham will harden.

SKILLET SPOON BREAD . . . Sift ⅓ cup cornmeal with ½ teaspoon baking soda, ½ teaspoon salt. Add 3 eggs which have been well beaten with 1 cup milk; 1 cup buttermilk. Stir just enough to mix. Preheat an electric skillet—with the cover on—to 460°. Add ¼ cup butter and, when melted, pour in the batter. Cook covered 20 to 25 minutes or until puffy and brown. Serve immediately from skillet or it will flatten. Add a scoop of butter to each serving.

INSTANT CAFÉ AU LAIT . . . Add instant coffee to hot milk. Serve in king-size cups or mugs.

VII. HOLIDAY HAM COLLÉE

Out of America's past comes inspiration for a festive but simple supper that begins with Mrs. George Washington's Crab Soup (a modern adaptation). The belle—or is it the Beau Brummel—of the table is a holiday ham, bought (if you are pressed for time) ready-baked, all set to serve, but mantled, regal-fashion, in a robe of green mayonnaise, shimmering with gelatin in the manner that is classically known as *Mayonnaise Collée*. Baby biscuits go along with the ham and the *tartines*, which is French for very thin slices of buttered bread.

Dessert, as in Old Virginia or Kentucky, might be a bowl of Ambrosia, snow-drifted deep in coconut, served with slices of fruit cake dewed with brandy.

Assorted Pickles and Relishes
Mrs. George Washington's Crab Soup, Adapted
Holiday Ham Collée
Asparagus Salad
Baby Biscuits
Tartines of Bread
Ambrosia in a Hurry   Sliced Fruit Cake

MRS. GEORGE WASHINGTON'S CRAB SOUP, ADAPTED . . . Mix 2 cans condensed cream of celery or cream of mushroom soup with 2 soup cans milk; ⅛ teaspoon mace; ½ teaspoon Worcestershire sauce; a few grains of cayenne pepper; the chopped whites of 4 hard-cooked eggs; 2 cups fresh-cooked, canned or frozen crab meat. Heat slowly 10 minutes, but do not boil hard. Crumble the hard-cooked yolks of the 4 eggs. Place a little of the yolks onto each of 4 or 6 soup bowls or mugs. Ladle the soup over the egg yolks. Garnish with slightly salted whipped cream tinted pink with a dash of paprika. Pass a small pitcher of warmed sherry and wisps of lemon peel which each person will twist and drop into his soup.

HOLIDAY HAM COLLÉE . . . Soften 2 tablespoons unflavored gelatin in ½ cup cold water 5 minutes. Dissolve over hot water. Add 2 cups mayonnaise greened with a few drops of food coloring. Frost the ham like a cake and decorate with flowers cut from pimientos. Wreathe with watercress studded with raw cranberries.

BABY BISCUITS . . . Use a mix and the package recipe for making drop biscuits. Drop by small teaspoonfuls onto the cookie sheet and serve too hot to handle.

TARTINES OF BREAD . . . Slice home-style close-textured white and whole wheat bread very thin. Remove crusts if you wish, although it is not strictly necessary. Spread smoothly with sweet whipped butter.

AMBROSIA IN A HURRY . . . To serve 6, you will need 3 large "eating" oranges or 3 cups canned mandarin orange sections, drained. Cut into bits. Combine in a bowl with 3 sliced bananas. Sprinkle with orange juice combined, if you like, with sherry, port or Madeira wine. Cover completely with Southern-style, moist-pack coconut or freshly grated coconut. Fleck lightly with bits of currant or guava jelly. Set in the freezer for 10 minutes or in the refrigerator for an hour or two.

VII. POLYNESIAN PUAA HOTU

Now is the time for those in the vanguard of hostesses to stage a *Tamaaraa*—Polynesian feast. The main dish is a *puaa*, pronounced poo-ah (which is pork), and *hotu*, pronounced hoh-too, meaning fruit. These individual bundles, in the South Sea islands, would be cooked in various exotic leaves. We use romaine lettuce. And to save time . . . excellent canned back ribs in barbecue sauce. These are now widely available, but a pound of lean pork cut into inch cubes will do. The cooking time would be longer—about 2 hours, instead of 15 minutes.

Curried Coconut Shrimp Soup
Puaa Hotu
Polynesian Rice
Fresh Tropical Fruits
(pineapples, bananas, oranges, mangoes, melons
and papayas)

CURRIED COCONUT SHRIMP SOUP . . . Melt 1 tablespoon butter or margarine in a saucepan. Stir in ¾ teaspoon curry powder. Add ½ cup flaked coconut. Mix well. Cook until lightly toasted, stirring frequently. Remove from heat and set aside. Combine two 10-ounce tins frozen condensed cream of shrimp soup, 2 soup cans milk. Heat, stirring now and then. Garnish with the curried coconut. Serves 4 to 6.

PUAA HOTU . . . For each person place 2 large leaves of romaine at right angles. Place on each ¼ can back ribs with barbecue sauce (heated), 6 pineapple chunks, 1 quarter of a sweet green pepper, ½ small tomato, quartered. Sprinkle each package with ¼ teaspoon powdered ginger or paprika. Fold leaves around the meat and vegetables to make a package. Fasten with toothpicks. Arrange in a shallow baking pan. Cover with foil and bake at 350° about 15 minutes or until sizzling hot. Serve packages individually.

POLYNESIAN RICE . . . Bring to a boil 2 cups water, 2 tablespoons chicken stock base, 2 tablespoons instant onion, ¼ cup soy sauce. Add 2 cups packaged pre-cooked rice. Remove from heat, cover and let stand about 5 minutes. Fluff with a fork.

IX. SPARERIBS AND SAUERKRAUT

Spareribs and sauerkraut are a favorite Saturday night supper at the new house that the Hamiltons, Dorothy and Edward, have bought in Hollis, Long Island. Dorothy is a lady who whips around town doing a variety of jobs. She had to learn the secret of achieving old-fashioned cooking in double-quick time. So the spareribs go into the pressure cooker. But hoe cake is often baked on the hearth, as it was in Richmond, Virginia, when she was a girl.

Spring Onions, Radishes and Picked Asparagus Spears
Spareribs and Sauerkraut
Boiled Potatoes
Hoe Cake
Hazelnut Pudding with Pears

SPARERIBS AND SAUERKRAUT . . . To serve four, cut 4 pounds of spareribs into serving pieces about 3 ribs apiece. Cover with boiling water; add 1 teaspoon salt, ¼ teaspoon pepper, 1 small onion cut in quarters, 1 stalk celery diced, 1 teaspoon caraway seed, 1 half bay leaf, 1 can sauerkraut. Cook in pressure cooker (at 15 pounds pressure) 15 minutes.

HOE CAKE . . . Mix 2 cups white cornmeal with 1 teaspoon salt and add about ¾ cup boiling water or enough to make a dough that is soft but not a batter. Heat a large, well-greased heavy iron pan and spread the dough on it in 1 cake, flattening it with your hand. Cook over medium heat or over embers until brown on one side, then turn with the aid of a wide spatula and your hand and brown until crusty on the other side. Serve hot.

HAZELNUT PUDDING WITH PEARS . . . Drain canned pears and place in sherbet glasses. Cover each serving with 2 or 3 spoonfuls of ready-to-serve hazelnut-flavored dessert pudding. Garnish with chopped hazelnuts or pecans.

X. TERRINE OF PARSLIED HAM

One of the wonders of the Burgundian table is a jellied *terrine* of ham so literally strewn with parsley that the pink ham seems to be cushioned in gleaming green grass. The aspic is marvelously scented with herbs. In the Burgundy wine country, the preparation of this dish is often started 3 days ahead of time. But here, with canned ham and chicken broth—and your freezer—hours and work are telescoped—to half an hour!

Our Fast Gourmet version of this Burgundian classic is featured in a menu that roams the world for inspiration, beginning with a Danish fruit soup contrived from a package of Danish fruit pudding mix. To adhere to the classic rule that there should be some hot foods served with a cold main course, we have potatoes hashed in cream. The green beans have a delicious lemony butter sauce. The dessert is Italian: cottage cheese entranced with a touch of rum and a dash of cinnamon.

> *Danish Fruit Soup, Chilled*
> *Terrine of Parslied Ham*
> *Potatoes Hashed in Cream*
> *Green Beans with Lemon Butter*
> *Crusty Bread*
> *Ricotta Condita   Heated Cinnamon Nut Loaf*

DANISH FRUIT SOUP, CHILLED . . . Make up according to directions 2 packages Danish Dessert mix (cherry-plum flavor); but add 2 more cups of water (or equal parts wine and water) than are called for in the recipe. Serve hot or cold in cups or soup plates. Garnish with slices of orange spiked with cloves. Serves 6.

TERRINE OF PARSLIED HAM . . . To serve 6, you will need 2 pounds of canned cooked ham. Drain off the juices and place in a saucepan with 2 cups dry white table wine or dry vermouth. Add 2 cups chicken broth or canned bouillon, 1 tablespoon dried tarragon leaves or 2 tablespoons fresh tarragon, 1 bay leaf, ½ teaspoon thyme, 2 small white onions, quartered, 1 clove garlic, crushed, 4 peppercorns. Bring to a boil. Cook about 10 minutes. Meanwhile cut the ham into dice. Place in serving bowl or casserole. Strain the stock, then add 2 envelopes unflavored gelatin which has been soaked in ¼ cup water for 5 minutes and dissolved in the warm broth. Stir in 2 tablespoons tarragon vinegar and a full cup of finely chopped parsley. Pour over the ham and allow to chill and jell. If you are in a hurry place in the freezer about 10 minutes. At serving time unmold if you wish or, as in France, serve directly from the terrine.

POTATOES HASHED IN CREAM . . . Use quick-frozen.

LEMON BUTTER . . . Melt 3 tablespoons sweet butter and add 1 tablespoon lemon juice, 1 tablespoon finely chopped chives.

RICOTTA CONDITA . . . To 2 cups Italian ricotta or creamed cottage cheese, add 2 tablespoons cream, 2 tablespoons sugar, 2 tablespoons rum. Blend or beat until very smooth. Serve in a chilled bowl. Sprinkle lightly with cinnamon. Serve with heated coffee cake or quick-frozen cinnamon nut loaf in thin slices.

XI. TURKEY HILL PORK CHOPS

Everything associated with the Tool Shed Herb Garden has charm . . . the name, the two lady herb farmers, the authentic old salt box house, the small formal flower and herb garden behind the low picket fence, herbs forming the hedges, growing in the fields, filling, spilling out of the little greenhouse. A hundred different herbs . . . and fragrances.

Ever since they escaped from the city eighteen years ago where Helen Whitman was a successful landscape gardener and Charlotte Lee an expert in mental health, these two have been growing herbs on Turkey Hill Road in North Salem, Connecticut.

After a full day's work there is not much time or zest for long elaborate cooking but the two know and love good food. So naturally they have developed a number of easy and unusual specialities. Herbs scent and flavor much of their cooking, but they warn against using too many or too much.

Turkey Hill Pork Chops in Sour Cream
Tarragon Potatoes
Salem Center Green Bean Salad
Dill Vinegar Dressing
Compote of Fruits Sweet Cicely

TURKEY HILL PORK CHOPS . . . For speed, when the hour grows late, they suggest that you use very thin pork chops or pound half-inch pork chops until they are only about ¼-inch thick. Sprinkle with salt and pepper. In a heavy skillet, brown lightly in a little pork fat or lard. Combine ½ cup hot water with ½ cup sour cream, 1 teaspoon fresh marjoram or ½ to ⅓ teaspoon dried marjoram. Pour over the pork chops, cover tightly and cook over low heat on top of the stove or in a moderate oven (350°) for 25 minutes or until very well done and tender. For half-inch thick pork chops, cook 50 to 60 minutes.

TARRAGON POTATOES . . . Same idea as parslied potatoes but more unusual and so delicious. Cook quick-frozen peeled potatoes only about 4 minutes instead of 7 as indicated on package. Roll in melted butter to which you have added a generous amount of chopped tarragon. If you use dry tarragon, allow the herb to seethe in the hot butter for 10 or 15 minutes.

GLAZED CARROTS . . . Cook smallish carrots in their skins. Peel and cut into halves, or drain canned baby carrots. Brush with melted butter. Sprinkle with salt, a very little cinnamon, brown sugar. Place in a heavy skillet over a low fire until well-glazed, basting from time to time with equal parts orange juice and melted butter.

SALEM CENTER SALAD . . . Serve lightly cooked or canned and well-drained green beans on Boston lettuce surrounded by quartered tomatoes and cover with a dressing made from equal parts peanut oil and dill vinegar, a little garlic; salt and pepper to taste.

DILL VINEGAR . . . To make dill (or any other herb vinegar) place ¼ cup of the fresh herb in the bottom of a quart-size crock. Pour over the herb ¼ cup boiling-hot wine or vinegar. Crush with pestle to bring out flavor. Fill the crock ¾ full of vinegar. Cover, cool and use immediately or allow to stand a week or two. Strain through cheese cloth and bottle. Herb vinegar made in this way retains its natural garden taste.

COMPOTE OF FRUITS . . . The herb-ladies like to serve combinations of fresh or cooked fruits with a sprinkle of sweet cicely which has a delightfully subtle licorice flavor. Lacking sweet cicely, you can, as in Mexico and Spain, use a dash of anisette liqueur.

VEAL IS SO YOUNG

❧⚜☙

VEAL

In France and Italy, veal is the most popular meat. In the United States, in most sections, it is the least popular, and appears seldom on American menus. Since veal is calf, a youthful type of beef, it is by nature tender and generally quite lean.

The best grades of veal are sometimes called milk-fed, for they are presumably from animals that are too young to be put out to pasture. This type of veal, obtainable in some of our larger cities, cooks up snowy white and marvelously tender.

To the hurried cook, veal chops, cutlets and steaks are sometimes a disappointment. For the meat, despite its youth, contains more connective tissue than beef and takes considerably longer to cook.

For broiling, you can buy veal loin chops, rib chops, shoulder chops, veal steaks and cutlets, sometimes known as French veal chops. When cut about a half inch thick, veal chops will require about twenty-five minutes cooking time to pan fry or braise.

To broil veal chops one or two inches thick takes eight to ten minutes on each side.

For very quick cooking, the veal should be cut thin and pounded even thinner. Often, as in Veal Scallopini, the thin slices are cut into smaller serving pieces, and this reduces the cooking time even further.

Vealburgers are delicious but, since the meat is generally lean, you should add at least an ounce of ground suet to each pound of chopped veal.

I. BLANQUETTE UNDER PRESSURE

For a long time, the pressure cooker has endured a reputation for producing quick, economical and nutritious but often dreadfully stodgy food. Lately, however, the picture has been changing. The pressure cooker has acquired new status. From gourmets yet!

It was in Paris that I discovered the most famous of classic white ragouts; a *blanquette* of veal prepared in the pressure cooker in less than one-fourth the usual time. Here in the States we've perfected a technique of adding a can of chicken gravy to the sauce instead of stopping to make a *veloute* sauce.

And why are we not all shouting from the housetops the news that the smoothest, silkiest, creamiest custards and their French relatives, the *pots de crème,* are being made nowadays without scalding the milk, without straining the mixture, without any fussing whatsoever in just 3 minutes in the pressure cooker.

Blanquette Under Pressure   Button Mushrooms
Baby Onions   Heart-Shaped Croutons
Watercress and Grated Carrot Salad
Coffee Pots de Crème   Macaroons and Ladyfingers

BLANQUETTE UNDER PRESSURE . . . To serve 6, have 3 pounds of veal cut into inch cubes. Place in a pressure cooker with enough hot water or chicken stock to cover the bottom of the pan about one inch deep. Add 1 onion stuffed with 2 cloves, 1 small carrot, sliced, 1 small piece celery. Cook according to manufacturer's instructions under pressure 12 minutes. Bring down pressure immediately. The meat should be tender, yet still firm. Add 1 can chicken gravy, two 6-ounce tins whole button mushrooms, 3 tablespoons lemon juice; salt and pepper to taste. Allow to simmer uncovered about 5 minutes longer. Add 1 can small white onions which have been drained and lightly tossed in butter. At serving time, place 2 slightly beaten egg yolks into a large warmed serving dish. Slowly, a little at a time, stir in some of the sauce before adding all the meat and gravy. Keep warm but do not allow to boil. Sprinkle with chopped parsley.

French chefs will tell you that a proper *blanquette* must always be garnished with heart-shaped croutons. So cut sliced white bread with a heart-shaped cookie cutter. Brown on both sides in foaming hot butter or margarine.

P.S.—Without a pressure cooker, veal must be cooked 45 to 60 minutes.

COFFEE POTS DE CRÈME . . . Beat, but only until evenly blended: 4 eggs, 1 cup heavy cream, 2 cups milk. Add 2 teaspoons instant coffee, ¼ teaspoon salt, 1 teaspoon vanilla, if desired. Butter 6 custard cups or French ramekins. Pour mixture into cups leaving at least ½ inch at the top. Cover cups with aluminum foil, pressing down edges firmly, and hold in place with rubber bands. Arrange cups on rack in pressure cooker. Add 1 cup boiling water to the cooker. Cook under pressure 3 minutes. Bring down pressure immediately and remove custard cups. Serve warm or cool.

II. CROWN ROAST AMORY

Cleveland Amory described himself once as "a not-so-gentle man of the Old School . . . who believes, among other things, in Boston."

"You know," says Martha, his New York-born wife, "you're always talking about Boston. But I notice your father didn't marry a Bostonian, your brother didn't marry a Bostonian and you didn't marry a Bostonian."

To which he answers, *"We can't . . .* we have to spread the culture!"

"Our household," says Martha, "is run, of course, around our master." Not only his Bostonian prejudices, but a string of allergies—real and fancied—make meal-planning hazardous. No nuts, for instance, are allowed. But she does sneak sliced water chestnuts (they're not really nuts) into his favorite Chinese pea pods. And her own crown roast of veal is speedily contrived by using broiled chops set crown-like around a mound of *polenta* —yellow cornmeal mush.

Crown of Veal Chops Amory   Polenta and Watercress
Frozen Chinese Pea Pods with Water Chestnuts
Boston Lettuce Salad with Genoa Toast
Bosc Pears with Bel Pease Cheese

CROWN ROAST AMORY . . . Have 6 or 8 tender veal chops cut 1½ inches thick. Trim the meat from the long bone leaving it bare for about an inch down. Wrap the bone-ends with aluminum foil. Brush meat fore and aft with salad oil or bacon drippings. Broil slowly about 8 minutes on each side. Season with salt and pepper. Stand the chops bone-side forward and pushed into a mound of *polenta*. Remove foil from the bone and replace with paper frills, spiced crabapples or large pitted olives. Garnish with nosegays of watercress.

POLENTA . . . In certain parts of Boston and certain other areas, this would have been known as cornmeal mush. To serve 6 to 8, cook 2 cups yellow cornmeal according to package directions for mush. When thickened, stir in 2 tablespoons butter. Mound into the center of a serving dish and surround with chops according to recipe above. Serve wedges of the *polenta* along with the chops.

FROZEN CHINESE PEA PODS WITH WATER CHESTNUTS . . . Cook 2 packages frozen pea pods according to package directions, adding at the last minute 6 or 8 drained canned water chestnuts cut into thin slices. If you can't find pea pods, use frozen peas.

BOSTON LETTUCE SALAD . . . Cleveland Amory won't touch it unless it is very crisp and well-chilled, torn rather than cut into bits and sprinkled with quantities (at least ½ cup) finely chopped parsley. Dressing must be made of 3 parts peanut oil, 1 part red wine vinegar, salt, pepper, a bit of English mustard—nothing more.

GENOA TOAST . . . A type of salty (rather than sweetened) zweiback that comes ready-to-serve in packets under various brand names. Martha Amory likes to serve it crisply warmed.

III. FILETS OF VEAL ROSEMARY

Not many years ago, any self-respecting chef would have committed hara-kiri before he would admit short cuts into his sacred precincts.

Now the restaurant cook has access to and uses even more ready and half-ready foods than the average housewife. Even in the most luxurious chef recipes (in practice if not in print) fresh, quick-frozen, dried and canned ingredients have become interchangeable.

On this interesting menu, certainly it would be ideal to have a spray of the freshest of rosemary and tarragon, broccoli and peaches fresh from the garden and bough.

Still, with the package, the freezer and the can, food can be beautiful—and swift and easy.

Filets of Veal Rosemary
Broccoli au Bearnaise
Rice Pilaf
Salad Caprice
Baked Peaches Piedmont

FILETS OF VEAL ROSEMARY . . . For each person, order a filet or cutlet of veal, preferably cut from the loin and only about ½ inch thick. Season with salt and pepper and roll in flour. Heat 4 tablespoons butter until it foams and sauté the veal first on one side, then the other until they have, as the chefs say, taken on a good color. Pour on 4 tablespoons hot consommé or white wine and add a small sprig of fresh rosemary or ½ teaspoon dried rosemary. Cover tightly and allow to cook slowly without boiling—about 10 minutes or until the meat is beautifully tender.

BROCCOLI AU BEARNAISE . . . Cook fresh or quick-frozen broccoli lightly so that it is still crisp. Drain and serve with Bearnaise sauce, made so: In a small frying pan, cook uncovered ¼ cup tarragon vinegar, ¼ cup water, 1 teaspoon finely chopped onion or shallot and 2 teaspoons fresh, or 1 teaspoon dried, tarragon. Boil until reduced to just about 2 tablespoonfuls. Stir into ¾ cup Hollandaise sauce which you can buy in a jar or make in seconds in an electric blender.

RICE PILAF . . . To serve 6, prepare 2 cups pre-cooked packaged rice with 2 cups chicken broth according to package directions, but add 2 extra tablespoons of butter.

SALAD CAPRICE . . . To a bowlful of tender young salad greens, add 2 sliced tomatoes, 12 black or green olives, pitted and quartered, ½ cup finely sliced celery. Dress the salad at the last minute with salt, pepper, 1 tablespoon red wine vinegar and 3 tablespoons olive oil.

BAKED PEACHES PIEDMONT . . . Peel and halve large yellow peaches, or use canned. Mash together 2 peach halves, ½ cup finely chopped macaroons, 1 tablespoon softened butter, 1 tablespoon sugar, 1 egg yolk. Add just enough peach syrup to moisten. Fill hollows with this mixture. Sprinkle with lemon juice and then with white or brown sugar. Bake in a shallow, buttered oven-proof dish 10 to 15 minutes at 350° or until peaches are tender and sugar has formed a pretty crust.

IV. MINCED VEAL EMMENTHAL

In New York, at a recent dinner party honoring the new Consul General of Switzerland, Dr. Hans Lacher, and his wife, the meal was not the usual formal hotel menu. It was so Swiss and so homelike that several of the guests, including the honored pair, were misty-eyed with joy and nostalgia.

The main course was the famous minced veal specialty in the style of Zurich, served with a Swiss version of home-fried potatoes—*Roesti*—quite like our own country-fried or hashed-brown potatoes, except that you begin with cooked rather than raw potatoes. The dessert . . . cooked apples and toast with more than a touch of glory!

Veal Emmenthal
Roesti
Fresh Steamed Zucchini with Nutmeg
Swiss Apple Toast

VEAL EMMENTHAL . . . Melt 4 tablespoons butter in a heavy skillet and add 2 pounds veal cutlets or loin of veal which has been cut into small thin slivers. Cook 2 to 3 minutes, remove meat and add ½ cup onion, finely chopped. Stir over low heat for 2 minutes longer. Add 3 tablespoons flour, 1½ teaspoons salt, ½ teaspoon freshly ground pepper, 1 cup dry white wine—preferably Swiss, of course, 1 cup chicken broth. Or, omit wine and use 2 cups chicken broth and 2 tablespoons lemon juice. When the sauce is slightly thickened, put the veal back into the gravy. Cook over low heat 15 minutes longer, stirring from time to time. Garnish with chopped parsley.

ROESTI . . . In Switlerland, they insist potatoes for *Roesti* should be cooked in their jackets, peeled at once. But we have had very good results with a package of pre-cooked sliced potatoes cooked according to directions. Heat 3 tablespoons butter, 3 tablespoons bacon drippings in a heavy skillet. When hot, add 3 cups thinly-sliced cooked potatoes. Press down into a smooth cake. Cover and cook over medium heat about 8 minutes. Remove cover, continue cooking 15 minutes longer or until a golden crust forms on the bottom. Serve brown side up.

FRESH STEAMED ZUCCHINI WITH NUTMEG . . . Cut tender, young *Zucchini* into long thin slices. Cover and cook in boiling salted water until barely tender. Drain. Dot with sweet butter, sprinkle with freshly ground black pepper; a few grains of nutmeg.

SWISS APPLE TOAST . . . A family dessert, but it made a great splurge at the Consul General's dinner party. Peel, quarter and slice thinly 4 to 6 medium apples. Place in a saucepan with ½ cup Swiss white wine or water, 4 tablespoons light brown sugar. Cook 5 minutes or until apples are tender but still firm. Drain. Cut 4 slices of raisin bread into 4 squares each. Heat 4 tablespoons butter in a large frying pan and brown the bread slowly on both sides, adding more butter if necessary. Add apples; fry together a few minutes longer or until bread is golden brown. Sprinkle with 2 tablespoons lemon juice or Swiss *kirsch,* 4 tablespoons cinnamon-sugar.

V. MOCK TURTLE STEAKS

On the bookshelf of a proud descendant, we found the book of Captain Joshua Slocum, *Sailing Alone Around the World.* He was the first to perform this feat and his book has been called the best of its kind.

One of his more curious tales concerns the Keeling Cross Islands, discovered in 1608. "Their first notable visitor," writes Captain Joshua, "was John Clunis-Ross, who returned two years later with his wife, family, mother-in-law and 8 sailor-artisans. Upon his return, he found one Alexander Hare who had meanwhile marked the little atoll as a sort of Eden for a seraglio of Malay women. The sailors began at once to take possession of the island—women and all. Hare had a hard time of it. He hung on to the atoll with his forty women until at last he found himself and his harem on the little island known to this day as Prison Island, where, like Bluebeard, he confined his wives in a castle. But the water was not deep and the 8 Scotch sailors wore long boots."

The lawless establishment was soon broken up by women deserting, even though Hare tried to bribe the sailors with rum and other luxuries. He wrote plaintively, "When I sent rum and roast pig to your sailors, I thought they would stay away from my flower garden."

Our Captain was a gourmet. He writes glowingly of dining on turtle steaks; cooking onions over a double lamp. He is in despair over a bad bag of potatoes and exults when he has sugar and cream for a dish of stewed pears.

Mock Turtle Steaks
Broiled Onion Rings
Carrots with Garlic Butter, Baked in Foil
Home Fried Potatoes
Captain Slocum's Stewed Pears with
Brown Sugar and Cream

MOCK TURTLE STEAKS . . . Lacking real turtle steak, one can make do with veal. To serve 4, have 1½ pounds of veal cutlets about ½ inch thick. Cut into serving pieces. Pound until ¼ inch thick. Sprinkle with salt and pepper. Sauté in 2 tablespoons butter in a heavy pan 5 minutes on each side. Add 1 tablespoon each: chopped onion and parsley, ¼ cup Madeira dry white wine or vermouth and ¼ cup hot water. Bring to a boil. Cover and simmer until veal is velvety-tender—about 15 minutes. Serve with lime or lemon sections for squeezing.

BROILED ONION RINGS . . . Slice a large Bermuda onion into half-inch-thick slices. Place on a well-buttered shallow pan or on foil. Brush with melted butter. Sprinkle with salt, pepper and oregano. Place under broiler about 5 minutes or until brown and tender. Broil only on 1 side.

CARROTS WITH GARLIC BUTTER, BAKED IN FOIL . . . To 2 cups thinly sliced, fresh or frozen carrots (thawed), add 2 tablespoons butter, ¼ teaspoon salt, 2 to 3 cloves garlic, crushed. Cook in foil over charcoal about 20 minutes, or in 350° oven, turning once.

HOME FRIED POTATOES . . . Use packaged dehydrated potatoes and follow directions.

CAPTAIN SLOCUM'S STEWED PEARS WITH BROWN SUGAR AND CREAM . . . (Modernized, we admit!) Drain 1 can pears. Melt 2 tablespoons butter in a large skillet. Sprinkle with 6 tablespoons brown sugar, 2 tablespoons rum or fruit juice. Allow to cook until syrupy. Add pears and cook until coated with syrup. Pour on ½ cup heavy cream and cook about 2 minutes, shaking the pan until the cream starts to thicken. Serve warm or chilled.

VI. NATURE SCHNITZEL, GARNI

One whole wall of the Chardas restaurant, far east on 79th street in New York, is a night-blue mural, painted on glass and lighted so that the windows gleam on the old castles and battlements; street lamps glimmer along the Bridge of St. Peter with its sensuous curve over the Danube linking the high town of Buda with the low town of Pest, forming Budapest.

Gypsy violins throb, an accordion murmurs, the cymbal trills and a curvy little blonde mezzo-soprano looks like a blend of all the Gabors.

The food, as well as the mood, is authentic Hungarian . . . with half a dozen different kinds of *gulyas* and paprikas on the menu. But, for the swift cook, perhaps the most interesting dish is a *schnitzel,* a thinner than thin veal cutlet that has no breading or coating. This veal *schnitzel* known as "nature" is ready to serve in less than 4 minutes. On the Chardas menu you will see it listed as Nature Schnitzel, Garni, which means that it is accompanied by a fried egg; the egg crisscrossed with two anchovy filets.

Marinated Herring Filets
Nature Schnitzel, Garni with
Fried Egg and Anchovy Filets
Poppy Seed Noodles
Green Salad
Warm Apple Strudel

This is a supper to evoke visions of old Budapest. Should be accompanied, whenever possible, by gypsy music on the Hi-Fi.

MARINATED HERRING FILETS . . . Thoroughly chill a jar of marinated herring filets. Arrange on lettuce leaves and garnish with paper-thin rings of red onion. Sprinkle liberally with chopped fresh dill or chives.

NATURE SCHNITZEL, GARNI . . . To achieve a proper *schnitzel,* a veal cutlet should be pounded so that it is scarcely a quarter-inch thick. Some obliging butchers will do this for you, but it is not at all difficult to manage yourself. Simply place each cutlet between 2 pieces of waxed paper and pound with a heavy rolling pin or a mallet until you have a piece about the size of a salad plate. Cut into 2-inch squares. Heat a skillet or electric fry pan to about 350°, melt 3 tablespoons butter and cook the pieces about 2 minutes on one side or until they are brown. Turn and cook another minute or two. Sprinkle with salt, pepper, a little paprika, if desired, and a few drops of lemon juice.

POPPY SEED NOODLES . . . To serve 4, cook half a pound of wide egg noodles in salted water until tender. Drain well; replace in pot. Add 1 tablespoon sugar, 3 tablespoons melted butter and 1 tablespoon poppy seeds. Shake pot until noodles are completely coated. Reheat before serving.

WARM APPLE STRUDEL . . . Heat frozen apple strudel or a strudel from the bake shop. Brush the strudel lightly with melted butter and sprinkle with cinnamon-sugar. Serve warm. Pass chilled cream, either sweet or sour.

VII. POJARSKI CUTLETS

In the elegant Nineties, imperial Polish cutlets of chopped veal, called Veal Cutlets *Pojarski,* appeared often as an entree for fashionable supper parties, or on elaborate buffet tables. Now these same cutlets have regained a measure of their old popularity, not only because they are so elegant, but also so quick, so simple to prepare and, at the same time, interestingly different.

The shin or shoulder meat of veal is considered most flavorsome for such cutlets. Since veal is naturally lean meat, a little suet is generally ground in with the veal—at least an ounce to the pound. If veal is unavailable, you can make mock *Pojarski* from beef.

Dessert might be miniature tarts filled with a prepared caramel nut pudding that has a rich, old-fashioned flavor and a crunchy nut texture. It requires only one minute of beating and no cooking.

Celery and Olives
Pojarski Cutlets of Veal
Mashed Potatoes   Harvard Beets
Broiled Eggplant
Caramel Nut Tartelettes

POJARSKI CUTLETS OF VEAL . . . Combine 2 pounds chopped veal with 2 ounces chopped suet or have the suet ground with the meat by the butcher. Season the meat with 2 teaspoons salt, 2 tablespoons finely chopped onion, 1 egg, ½ teaspoon freshly ground black pepper and ¼ teaspoon ground allspice. Form into six large or twelve small oval-shaped patties. Heat 2 tablespoons butter in a heavy skillet. When it sizzles, pan-broil the patties, first on one side and then on the other, about 10 to 15 minutes, or until cooked through.

Sprinkle the patties with 1 tablespoon paprika if desired. Remove from the pan; keep warm. Then stir into the pan juices, 1 cup commercial sour cream. Blend over the heat, but do not allow to boil. Pour sauce over cutlets.

HARVARD BEETS . . . These can be bought in cans or frozen, complete with the Harvard sauce.

BROILED EGGPLANT . . . Cut eggplant into ½-inch thick slices, either crosswise or lengthwise, depending upon the size of the eggplant. Do not peel. Brush first with lemon juice, then with olive oil on both sides and sprinkle with salt and pepper. Place in a shallow, buttered or oiled, serving dish and broil only on the top side until brown and tender. Garnish with chopped chives and serve from the same dish.

CARAMEL NUT TARTELETTES . . . Make or buy a dozen small tart shells, or use the packaged variety generally sold for canapés. Fill with the caramel nut packaged pudding (it is new and instant). You may want to add ¼ teaspoon cinnamon or 1 tablespoon rum.

VIII. SALTIMBOCCA OR LEAP IN THE MOUTH

In the last few years, a tidal wave of tourism has swept across the paradise island of Jamaica. The tourist industry is the third largest there, surpassed only by bauxite and sugar. But this great wave of the future has swept away many of the gracious remnants of the past.

Perhaps it is partly nostalgia for the Jamaica of another age which has made the Terra Nova (restaurant and hotel), the most quietly chic in the Kingston area, for the place retains the look and the charm of a Jamaica Great House, which indeed it is. As we were told, "Lady Barker's father bought it as a wedding present for her in 1916. She lived there 35 years and sold it to Sir William Coker, who sold it to Percy Lindo of the famous Lindo family of Jamaica. It was 'Uncle Percy's house' to everyone until three years ago."

The Terra Nova is the expression of one dynamic man—Roc Pavesi—originally of Milan. The food often has a suave Italian accent.

Onion Soup with Croutons and Grated Parmesan Cheese
Saltimbocca
Rice
Peas with Mushrooms
Cos Salad with Anchovy Dressing
Crêpes Suzette

ONION SOUP . . . Use one of the excellent dehydrated onion soups and, just before serving, add a couple of tablespoons of Cognac. Serve with sliced French rolls, grated Parmesan cheese.

SALTIMBOCCA . . . A little treasure for the gourmet who cooks in a hurry. This leaps in the mouth because it is so good, so quick.

To serve 4, get 8 very thin slices of veal, each about 4 or 5 inches wide, also 8 slices of cooked ham the same size. Italian *prosciutto* is best, but you can use baked Virginia ham or Westphalian. Sprinkle veal slices lightly with powdered sage or oregano and a little pepper, but no salt, for this is supplied by the ham. Cover the veal with ham, secure with toothpicks (like a darning stitch), then sauté gently in butter 5 to 6 minutes on each side. Serve immediately with sections of lime or lemon. Two to a person.

PEAS WITH MUSHROOMS . . . A quick-frozen specialty.

COS SALAD it is called in Jamaica . . . We say romaine. Serve with simple dressing made of 1 part lemon or lime juice, 3 parts light olive oil or salad oil, a little pepper and a dab of anchovy paste for saltiness. Garlic if desired.

CRÊPES SUZETTE . . . Don't whisper it, but you can get *fine Crêpes Suzette* in tins or jars. Those that come folded into quarters look more authentic than the kind that are rolled. Simply heat in their own sauce. A sure-flame method to flambé: Warm half a cup of Cognac very slightly over a candle flame, in a ramekin. Set a match to the spirit and pour while flaming over the *crêpes*. Serve 3 or 4 per person on warmed plates.

IX. VEAL BOLOGNESE

The city of Bologna and, in fact, the whole province of Tuscany in northern Italy, has been called the birthplace of modern *haute cuisine*. For it was from here that Marie de Medici took to the court of Louis the inspiration, and many of the fundamental principles, that later produced the greatest cooking of the western world.

These collops of *Veal Bolognese* have the classic simplicity of the region. To the food scholar it would be obvious that the recipe belongs to the land where the olive oil and butter civilizations meet, for it calls for browning the meat in 2 tablespoons butter. Of course, you may, if you wish, substitute 4 tablespoons of either olive oil or butter. Or you could use shortening.

Antipasto Salad Platter
Veal Bolognese
Quick Risotto
Spumoni
Instant Coffee Mazagran

ANTIPASTO SALAD PLATTER . . . To be served along with the meat course. Drain canned or cooked lima or *ceci* beans and sliced carrots. Cover with Italian dressing. Arrange in separate mounds on a platter. Garnish with drained canned pimientos and hearts of celery or *finocchio* and olives. Serve chilled.

VEAL BOLOGNESE . . . To serve 4, provide 8 small thin veal steaks or cutlets weighing about 3 ounces apiece. Sprinkle with salt and pepper. Dust with flour. Lightly grease a very hot frying pan, quickly pan-broil the veal steaks, reduce the heat to medium. Meanwhile, combine 2 tablespoons melted butter, 2 tablespoons olive oil and sauté, until lightly brown, 1 large onion finely chopped, 1 clove garlic crushed. Add one 8-ounce can tomato sauce, ¼ teaspoon dried basil. Simmer 10 minutes, add the meat to sauce. Sprinkle with ½ cup grated Parmesan cheese. Set under the broiler to melt the cheese. Serve from the same dish.

QUICK RISOTTO . . . Heat 2 tablespoons olive oil, add 2 cups quick-cooking rice and heat while stirring until the grains of rice are lightly gilded. Add 2½ cups heated chicken broth and ¼ teaspoon saffron or curry powder. Cover and allow to cook gently for about 5 minutes. *Risotto* should be a little softer and less dry than American rice dishes.

INSTANT COFFEE MAZAGRAN . . . Make instant espresso coffee according to directions and serve in a glass with a twist of lemon peel. To keep the glass from breaking, place a silver spoon in the glass and pour the hot coffee against the silver spoon.

X. VEAL CHOPS GRAND-MÈRE

Chiquita Banana was, to all appearances, the honored guest at a resplendent press luncheon at The Four Seasons restaurant in New York. Home economist Deborah Hale came down from Boston for several confabs with the restaurant's dashing director, Stuart Levin, and their chef of chefs, Albert Stockli.

"A triumph of simplicity and grace!" raved the gathered gourmets.

There were double-thick veal chops, broiled to a rosy-bronze turn and served with tiny browned onions, baby carrots and mushrooms. This is known as *Garniture Grand-mère*. Whose grandmother, we often wondered. Not that it matters!

Lodestar of the lunch was a banana dessert invented especially for the occasion and shown that day for the first time to the waiting world.

So is gastronomic history made!

Consommé Celestine
Broiled Veal Chops

Garniture Grand-mère
Tarragon Salad
Four Seasons Banana Dessert

CONSOMMÉ CELESTINE . . . This is a classic combination . . . consommé garnished with thin-as-thin French pancakes cut into narrow ribbons. The easiest way to achieve this delicate soup—outside of The Four Seasons—is to buy it (garnish and all) in a package. Comes dehydrated. Ask for *Consommé Celestine*.

BROILED VEAL CHOPS . . . Have young tender veal chops cut about 1½ inches thick. Brush with salad oil, pork or bacon drippings. Sprinkle with salt and broil 10 minutes on one side. Turn and brush with more oil or drippings and cook until thoroughly done.

GARNITURE GRAND-MÈRE . . . Cut 2 strips of salt pork or bacon into small dice and cook until brown and crisp. Remove the bits and, in the fat, brown 1 dozen small, peeled, fresh silverskin onions. Add 1 can drained Belgium baby carrots and one 6-ounce tin small, whole mushrooms (drained). When vegetables are lightly browned, add the liquid from the mushrooms and 1 teaspoon beef extract. Return browned bacon or pork bits to pan. Boil up once. Serve around the broiled veal chops. Serves 4.

TARRAGON SALAD . . . Toss a green salad at the table with a dressing made of 6 parts olive oil or peanut oil, 1 part plain wine vinegar and 1 part tarragon vinegar. The salad may be sprinkled with coarsely chopped fresh tarragon leaves—if you have them. Dried tarragon doesn't do much for a salad.

FOUR SEASONS BANANA DESSERT . . . These might have been called glazed bananas on the half-shell. To make 4 servings, you will need 2 large bananas. Do not peel them but cut in half, lengthwise. Carefully now, remove the bananas from their natural casings. Take care that the skins do not split. Reserve two of the halves. Brush them lightly with lemon juice to prevent darkening. Cut the two remaining pieces into bits. Mash with a fork, then beat until smooth and creamy. Add 2 tablespoons sugar, ½ cup heavy cream, ½ teaspoon almond extract. Beat until firm. Spoon this mixture into the 4 banana skin shells. Cut the reserved halves once again in halves, lengthwise. Place each strip on top of the banana mixture.

Make a glaze by adding 1 tablespoon hot water to ¼ cup apricot preserves. Use just enough water to thin the preserves slightly. Then spoon preserves on top of the banana strips. Sprinkle with candied cherries and toasted slivered almonds.

OLD-FASHIONED COOKING—NEW WAY

Neither wild woodland mushrooms flown from California nor sea urchins fished from the Mediterranean the night before, have, in our house, proved more impressive than homemade bread and butter. No scent on earth makes so thrilling an overture as newborn loaves.

The butter takes less than three minutes in a blender. The loaves may, if you wish, require nothing more than a package of hot roll mix.

Blender-Made Butter

To make the butter: Place a half pint of heavy (forty per cent) whipping cream in the glass container of an electric blender (a beater will not do). Whir until the cream is stiff: this should take just a few seconds. Add one-half cup of ice water (complete with bits of ice, if you choose) and allow the blender to go on working until you hear a hoarse, complaining *garumph*. The butter's moment of truth comes when globules appear along with a watery *petit lait*—"the little milk" of France. Then you have only to pour the new butter into a sieve, hold it under the cold water faucet to wash it slightly. This daffodil-pale butter, newborn, may be served immediately —most poetically, I think, in a small crock, and always at room temperature (chilling robs it of its proper and salubrious quality). Ounce for ounce, this homemade butter costs about twice as much as the mass-produced. How or where else can you find gastronomic ecstasy for so little?

Your Own Bread

The directions for making bread from a hot roll mix are

inside the package. Since charm rather than practicality is your motive, you will mould the living dough not into one utilitarian large loaf but into two or three small loaves to be presented whole, we hope, on a board at the table. Miniature straight-sided bread pans are available. For a highly professional look, glaze the loaves before baking with milk or cream or a beaten egg—or, as in Paris, with equal amounts of egg yolk and melted butter stirred together. If, by chance, you should be able to retrieve a loaf for the freezer, be sure to slice it first and tie it up in a plastic bag (loaves have a tendency to crumble when they are thawed and then sliced, and it is a convenience to thaw or toast slices as needed).

Making Your Own Stock Fast

Even though the great Escoffier, and probably hundreds before and after him, have agreed that the basis of all fine cooking lies in a rich stock, the stock pot is long gone from the back of the range. There are, of course, excellent canned consommés, bouillons and broths, as well as cubes and dehydrated mixes that produce passable substitutes. Many, however, are overly seasoned, heavy-handedly salted. And none provides the variety you can achieve for yourself—quite easily in these days of the electric pressure cooker and the freezer. Actually, all you have to do is to cook the broth down, making it double or triple strength.

Then comes the New Wave. Pour the reduced stock into plastic refrigerator trays (regular ice cube trays should be filled with cold water only; hot water or other liquids impair the lining which keeps cubes from sticking) and freeze into cubes. No need to skim or remove the fat. Bits and pieces, as well as fat, cling to the surface, and can be easily scraped away before the cubes are emptied into plastic bags, tagged and stored in the freezer to create an instant stockpile.

Not only beef and chicken but veal stock can be yours, or an essence of mushrooms, or a very special *fumet* of fish or seafood made from bones, scrapes and peelings. For the best and richest flavors I insist that the stock, even though you cook it in a pressure cooker, should simmer for a little while afterwards, uncovered, on top of the stove, so that the air and the oxygen can work their peculiar magic. Be extra chary with the seasonings. Most herbs, even onions, undergo a curious ice change in the freezer—a change discernible in a few weeks, obnoxiously noticeable in a couple of months.

See Recipe Broth from Bones (page 237).

A TASTY MISCELLANY

I. STARRING FRENCH CRÊPES

❦

"If only I could make *crêpes*, or *Crêpes Suzette*," one woman sighed, "I would feel that I had really arrived as a gourmet cook!"

If the truth were told and it rarely is . . . the making of French *crêpes*, those thin-as-thin pancakes, requires no particular magic, not much skill and comparatively little effort or time.

As for the Suzette Sauce, we fly in the face of tradition. Our fast-as-fast version is whisked together with no more effort than it takes to combine melted butter, orange marmalade and brandy in equal parts.

Smoked Salmon with Trimmings
Pumpernickel Fingers "21" Style
Broiled Double Lamb Chops
Broccoli
French Crêpes   Suzette Sauce

SMOKED SALMON WITH TRIMMINGS . . . Arrange salmon on lettuce leaves on a small platter or individual plates. Sprinkle with capers. Provide coarsely cracked black peppercorns and a tiny cruet of the best olive oil. Each person adds pepper and olive oil to taste.

PUMPERNICKEL FINGERS "21" STYLE . . . Use very thin, very dark pumpernickel; the kind that comes in cans is fine. Put 2 slices together with plenty of whipped sweet butter between and cut into fingers about an inch wide.

BROILED DOUBLE LAMB CHOPS . . . Young mutton has a mild, delicious flavor and may be as tender as lamb. The taste of shoulder lamb chops is fairly close to that of young mutton. Have the shoulder lamb chops about 1½ inches thick. Rub with dry English mustard. Sprinkle with garlic salt. Brush with vegetable oil. Broil rare.

FRENCH CRÊPES . . . Place into a blender (if you have one) 1 cup water, 1 cup milk, 4 eggs, ½ teaspoon salt, 2 cups all-purpose flour, 4 tablespoons melted butter or salad oil. Blend at top speed one minute. If you have no blender, put the flour into a bowl, make a well in the center, break the eggs into the well. Stir them in, gradually adding the liquid and melted butter. If there are any lumps, strain the batter. Allow to stand 2 hours in the refrigerator if possible, although it is not absolutely necessary. The batter should be like coffee cream, "just thick enough to coat a wooden spoon." If it seems too heavy, add a little water a spoonful at a time.

You will need a small *crêpe* pan or iron skillet 6 or 7 inches in diameter. Brush lightly with a *few drops* of salad oil. Heat until pan "begins to smoke" or reaches 370°. Remove from heat. Pour a scant quarter cup of batter into middle of pan. Quickly tilt in all directions so bottom is covered with a thin film. Pour back into bowl any batter that doesn't adhere. This operation takes 2 seconds. Return pan to heat just a few seconds until *crêpe* looks dry and a fine line of golden brown shows at the edges. Turn and cook a few seconds on the other side.

SUZETTE SAUCE . . . There are many classic recipes involving much ceremony, but try this one: first fold the *crêpes* into quarters and, at the table, heat them in this bubbling sauce: Melt ½ cup sweet butter, stirring in ½ cup shredded orange marmalade. Then warm and set ablaze ½ cup brandy. Pour over *crêpes* and serve flaming on heated plates, 2 or 3 to each person. A squeeze of lemon juice is a pretty gesture, adds a fine taste.

II. CALVES LIVER ON SKEWERS

The spirit of Shakespeare holds sway over the Mermaid Tavern at Stratford, Connecticut. One of the summertime joys of the neighborhood is to dine at the Mermaid, then proceed to the play in the theater—a large air-conditioned and very elegant version of the one where the Bard was among the players.

The food, as well as the menu, at the Mermaid Tavern

has an Elizabethan quality. Dinner will start with a War-ner. There are entrees from Grate and Gridiron, Salletts, Pyes. An apple becomes a Pippin. And since the s's are f's, as in the old fashion, the Pippin is served with Cheefe.

Warner of Tiny Shrimp
Calves Liver and Bacon with Tiny Onions and Mushrooms
Grilled on a Skewer
Whipt Taters
Sallett of Greens Toffed wyth a Country Dreffing
Snow Topped Ice Creame Pye

WARNER OF TINY SHRIMP . . . Drain the small canned shrimp or cut ordinary cooked shrimp into small pieces. To 2 cups shrimp add ½ cup canned pineapple nuggets. Pieces should not be more than ½ dice. Mix with dress-ing made by combining ½ cup mayonnaise, ½ cup cream, 2 tablespoons ketchup. Serve on a lettuce leaf or a scal-lop shell, the kind that is used for baking.

CALVES LIVER AND BACON WITH TINY ONIONS AND MUSHROOMS GRILLED ON A SKEWER . . . To serve 4, you will need a pound of calves liver sliced ½-inch thick and then cut into inch squares. Have ready 4 slices bacon, a dozen small white onions parboiled or canned, a dozen button mushrooms, fresh or canned. Place first on the skewer a long slice of bacon and then one or two pieces of liver. Then put the skewer through the bacon again. Add an onion, a mushroom, 2 more pieces of liver. Continue until the skewer is filled with pieces of liver, mushrooms and onions; the bacon like a ribbon between them. On the tip of the skewer, a mushroom. Brush with equal parts lemon juice and butter and broil just about 5 minutes. Turn often and brush with more lemon juice and butter. Be careful not to overcook. At serving time, sprinkle with chopped parsley. Serve with a wedge of lemon and a bouquet of watercress.

WHIPT TATERS . . . Use packaged mashed potatoes, beating in at the last an extra ½ cup hot milk.

COUNTRY DREFFING . . . Beat with a whisk or fork ½ cup thick sweet or sour cream. Add to it slowly 1 table-spoon chopped chives or tarragon, 3 tablespoons vinegar or lemon juice, ¼ teaspoon salt, ⅛ teaspoon white pepper. Makes 1¼ cups.

SNOW-TOPPED ICE CREAME PYE . . . Have ready a baked pie shell or crumb crust. Fill with one quart ice cream . . . strawberry, peach or whatever. Keep in freezer until serving time. Then cover with Snow made by whipping 2 egg whites along with 1 tablespoon lemon juice, 1 tablespoon sugar. Sprinkle with crumbs or finely chopped nuts. Serves 6.

III. DAME BLANCHE GLACÉ

Among international gourmets, there is general agreement that some of the most enjoyable meals in Paris are those you get when you call Room Service at certain hotels like the Plaza Athenae.

The same sort of acclaim should be given to the excellent cuisine served in the rooms at the Queen Elizabeth in Montreal. This menu is a delightful sample that lends itself happily to reproduction even in the smallest kitchen.

For the main dish, romantically billed as *Dame Blanche* or *White Lady*, you could use leftovers or buy slices of ham and turkey meat from the nearest delicatessen.

Where in the world could you find a hot ham and turkey sandwich so beautifully caparisoned?

Jellied Madrilene with Lime
Dame Blanche Glacé (Hot Ham and Turkey Sandwich)
White Asparagus
Spiced Crab Apples
Bouquet of Watercress and Carrot Curls
Supreme of Tropical Fruits with Coconut

JELLIED MADRILENE WITH LIME . . . Chill in the tin. Spoon into chilled cups or champagne saucers and sprinkle with fresh lime juice. Garnish with slices of lime.

DAME BLANCHE GLACÉ . . . Butter a copper pan or any attractive shallow bake-and-serve dish. Remove crusts from 4 slices of white bread and cut slices in halves. Place in bottom of dish. Cover bread with thin slices of baked or boiled ham and then with 2 layers of thinly sliced white turkey meat. Arrange in groups of 3, canned white asparagus (what but white for a White Lady) using 6, 9 or 12 stalks. Cover the whole thing with a sauce made by adding to one can chicken gravy, 1 tablespoon lemon juice, 1 beaten egg yolk. Mix thoroughly, then fold in the stiffly beaten white of one egg. Sprinkle with (and this is the subtle touch of genius) the merest suspicion—a scant teaspoonful—white sugar. Set in a moderate oven (325°) just long enough to heat thoroughly, and brown delicately . . . about 10 minutes. Serve immediately to 2, 3 or 4 happy people. (How hungry are they?)

SPICED CRAB APPLES . . . Right from a jar.

BOUQUET OF WATERCRESS AND CARROT CURLS . . . Arrange crisp chilled watercress in a shallow bowl and intersperse with chilled carrot curls or sticks.

SUPREME OF TROPICAL FRUITS WITH COCONUT . . . Combine 1 package frozen grapefruit sections, 1 small tin canned, drained, mandarin oranges and 1 tin frozen pineapple chunks. Sprinkle with grated coconut. Fruit tastes best if it is just a shade this side of thaw.

IV. FRENCH FRIED MUSHROOMS, NEW ART

A different main dish is a vegetable platter planned around whole fresh mushrooms complete with stems, beautifully encrusted and deeply fried. According to a startling new technique, the vegetable oil is not preheated but starts out cold. Never spatters, never smells, never smokes! This is the easiest of all ways to fry a fritter.

A great variety of raw vegetables may be prepared in this fashion, such as parsnips or carrots quartered lengthwise, whole small white onions or quartered onions, cubes of eggplant, spears of asparagus or Brussels sprouts.

French Fried Mushrooms, New Art
Leaf Spinach with Pine Nuts and Raisins, Italian Style
Grilled Tomatoes
Baked Stuffed Potato
Deep Dish Peach Pie with Cheddar Cheese

FRENCH FRIED MUSHROOMS, NEW ART . . . Trim a pound of fresh mushrooms. Do not peel or even wash unless the mushrooms are really sandy or blemished.

Simply wipe with a damp cloth. The mushroom should be as close to one size as possible. If they are not, cut into uniform pieces. Leave the stems intact. Dip into slightly beaten egg to which you have added 2 tablespoons slightly warm water. Shake off any excess moisture and roll the pieces in well-seasoned, dry breadcrumbs.

For cold-start fritter frying, pour vegetable oil, which is at room temperature, ½ inch deep in a large skillet. Gently place the coated mushrooms into the oil so as not to disturb the egg-crumb coating. Then place skillet over medium heat or turn skillet heat control to medium high (350°). Fry until golden brown, turning once after 7 minutes. (After the first 5 minutes slip a spatula under the mushrooms to keep them from sticking.) Fritters should be done in 15 minutes. Turn off the heat. Remove with a slotted spoon. Drain on paper towels.

LEAF SPINACH WITH PINE NUTS AND RAISINS, ITALIAN STYLE . . . Heat 2 tablespoons olive oil in a frying pan; add 2 tablespoons pine nuts (*pignoli*) or, if these are not available, use salted pistachio nuts; add 1 package frozen leaf spinach cooked according to directions and drained; add ½ cup seedless raisins, 1 clove garlic crushed. Cook gently about 5 minutes. Makes 4 small servings.

BAKED STUFFED POTATO . . . Use frozen or packaged baked stuffed potato. Prepare according to directions.

DEEP DISH PEACH PIE . . . Place 2 packages frozen sliced peaches into a shallow buttered baking dish. Sprinkle with 1 tablespoon lemon juice, ¼ teaspoon nutmeg. Dot with 1 tablespoon butter. Cover with pie pastry, anchoring the pastry securely to the sides of the dish. Bake in a moderately hot oven (375°) 15 to 20 minutes or until the peaches are bubbly hot and the crust is deliciously browned. Serve warm with cheddar cheese or cream, plain, whipped or ice.

V. GODMOTHER'S QUICK QUICHE

The overseas operator had a fairly desperate call from New York City: "But I must get in touch with my godmother," wailed an obviously young voice. "I'm having people to lunch tomorrow and she always tells me what to serve and how to do it."

Despite its rapidly growing international renown Charlotte Amalie is still a small town. So it was not too difficult for an obliging telephone operator to locate the godmother, Olga Schwartz, who hails originally from Budapest but has, in her own words, "lived, cooked and baked in practically every part of the world except, maybe, Scandinavia and South America—outside Venezuela, that is."

In the menu transmitted by long distance she suggested for the main course, a quick *Quiche Lorraine* (cheese and ham custard pie) that could be baked—believe it or not—in just 15 minutes.

> *Melon with Salami*
> *Godmother's Quick Quiche*
> *Dandelion Salad*
> *Ambrosia*
> *Capri Cookies*

MELON WITH SALAMI . . . The idea is the same as the more usual melon with prosciutto ham but salami is somewhat easier to find. Almost any sort of melon may be used . . . honeydew, cantaloupe, papaya. Melon should be cut loose from the rind, the salami sliced tissue-paper-thin. Pass a pepper grinder.

GODMOTHER'S QUICK QUICHE . . . For speed in cooking and ease in serving, these pies are baked individually in pans about 5 inches in diameter. Line the pans with an extra thin layer of pie pastry which you can, if you are unsure of yourself, buy already frozen or make from a mix. Over the pastry in the bottom of the pan lay a thin slice of Swiss cheese; over the cheese a scatter of crumbled crisply cooked bacon using 1 or 2 slices of bacon to each pie. Then add 1 egg, slightly beaten with 1 tablespoon heavy cream, a little white pepper and a few grains nutmeg. On top of everything . . . some coarsely chopped cooked ham, 2 to 3 tablespoons. Bake in a fairly hot oven (375°) about 15 minutes or until the custard is set, the pastry delicately crisp and browned.

AMBROSIA . . . If you can't be bothered peeling and slicing oranges, use canned, drained mandarin orange sections. Arrange in layers in a pretty glass bowl . . . a layer of oranges, a layer of coconut, more oranges. Top layer should be coconut. Sprinkle with a little Cointreau.

CAPRI COOKIES . . . A new packaged variety . . . delicious chocolate-flavored wafers held together with a rich, delicately flavored, creamy white filling.

VI. JOSEPHINE BAKER'S SOUPE LA MIQUE

The fabulous, dazzling, stupendous Josephine Baker loves to cook, particularly for her eleven children, ranging in age from four to twelve and a half. She found them all over the world—in Korea, Japan, Colombia, Israel, Algeria, the Ivory Coast, Venezuela and France. And they all live together in a small chateau near Bordeaux, France, in the region famous for its wines and cooking *à la Bordelaise*.

Her favorite menu begins with the local *Soupe La Mique,* where a large dumpling bobs in the pot and is served in slices in the broth. Afterwards there must be *cèpes,* the great orange-colored mushrooms of the area, served perhaps with an omelet and a salad which the children call *à la Maman Josephine.* For dessert . . . *Purée des Pommes* (that's applesauce) under a cloud of meringue.

> *Josephine Baker's Soupe La Mique*
> *Cèpes or Mushrooms Bordelaise*
> *Omelet*
> *Salade à la Maman Josephine*
> *Applesauce au Meringue*

SOUPE LA MIQUE . . . To serve 6, use at least 2 quarts of good, rich chicken broth or consommé. To make the great dumpling known as *La Mique,* Josephine Baker uses the soft inside of a large loaf of crusty bread or a loaf of any plain white bread with crust removed. Crumble and add 6 tablespoons lukewarm water, 3 egg yolks well beaten, ½ teaspoon salt, ⅛ teaspoon pepper, 2 tablespoons parsley, 2 tablespoons finely chopped onion. Form into a large ball. To shorten the cooking time, make into two smaller balls. Drop into furiously boiling broth; cover. When it begins to foam, turn down the heat, cover and cook gently until the dumpling rises and floats. For smaller balls, this would take about 20 to 25 minutes. For the large one, perhaps 40 minutes.

At serving time, remove dumpling, cut into ½-inch slices. Serve 1 or 2 slices in each soup bowl. There is a special wine country custom: When the bowl is almost empty, add a little red wine, tip up the bowl and drink the wine.

CÈPES OR MUSHROOMS BORDELAISE . . . The true French *cèpes* can be found in cans or you may substitute any other flavorsome mushrooms. Drain a 6- or 8-ounce can, brown lightly in 2 tablespoons olive oil. Add 1 clove garlic, crushed or very finely chopped, 1 teaspoon chopped parsley and 2 heaping tablespoons of bread crumbs. Heat a minute or two longer.

SALADE À LA MAMAN JOSEPHINE . . . In a china bowl rubbed with garlic place fresh crisp greens, almost anything except iceberg lettuce. Sprinkle generously with 2 finely chopped hard-cooked eggs and 2 tablespoons finely chopped chives. Toss with French dressing.

APPLESAUCE AU MERINGUE . . . To serve 6, put 3 cups raspberry-flavored, chunky applesauce into a shallow baking dish. Top with meringue made by whipping the whites of 3 eggs with ¼ teaspoon cream of tartar (optional) until light and frothy. Add gradually 6 tablespoons superfine sugar. Pile in peaks over the applesauce. Set in a hot oven (450°) about 4 minutes or until the meringue is lightly tinged with gold.

VII. LUCHOW'S GERMAN PANCAKE

Undisputed monarch of pancakes must certainly be the one that is served at Luchow's Restaurant, that temple of gusty eating on East 14th Street in New York.

There, an order for the German pancake calls for a spectacular performance on the part of the chef and the waiter or captain. Borne from the kitchen, the pancake measures full 18 inches in diameter. At home you might have to settle for a lesser size. All depends on the pan that you can muster.

Filled with sliced cooked apples or applesauce, or slathered deeply in jam, Luchow's German pancake is theoretically a dessert. Wisdom suggests, however, that you treat it deferentially as the star of the supper.

Herring Tidbits in Sour Cream
Paper-Thin Rye Bread Sandwiches
Split Pea Soup Farmer Fashion
Belgian Endive with Pimiento Strips
Luchow's German Pancake

HERRING TIDBITS . . . They come in a jar. Chill well.

SPLIT PEA SOUP FARMER FASHION . . . Make up a package of dehydrated split pea soup according to directions. Combine with 1 can condensed tomato soup diluted with 1 soup can water. Add ½ small onion finely chopped and ¼ teaspoon sage. Simmer 5 minutes. Meanwhile cut crusty French bread into slices about 1 inch thick. Brush with olive oil. Sprinkle with garlic salt, set in a hot oven (450°) about 5 minutes. Bring soup to the table in a large bowl. Have the toasted bread ready. Place a slice in each plate or bowl, ladle soup over the bread and sprinkle lavishly with chopped parsley. Slices of hot dog, frankfurter or sausage may be added if desired.

LUCHOW'S GERMAN PANCAKE . . . To 6 eggs lightly beaten add 1½ cups sifted flour, ¼ teaspoon salt, 1 tablespoon sugar, 2 cups milk. Beat 5 minutes with a rotary beater or whir in an electric blender 1 full minute. The batter should be thin and smooth.

In the widest frying pan you can find melt 2 or 3 tablespoons butter. There should be enough butter to coat the bottom and the sides of the pan. When the butter is good and hot, pour into the center of the pan 4 to 5 tablespoons of pancake batter. Turn and slant the pan from side to side, so that the batter spreads to form a large, thin pancake. Cook over high heat until the pancake looks dry on top. Turn and bake the other side. Slip onto a hot plate.

At the table, sprinkle the top of the pancake thickly with sugar and cinnamon. Squeeze the juice of ½ lemon over the pancake, cover with sweetened, sliced, canned, cooked apples (the kind you buy for pie) or with applesauce or jam. Roll like a jelly roll. Then, if there is drama in your soul, slightly warm in a small metal cup or ramekin 4 tablespoons rum, set a match to the rum and, as it blazes up, pour over the pancake. Serve immediately on heated plates. This recipe makes 4 to 6 pancakes.

VIII. MAMA LAURA'S HOMEMADE FETTUCINI

The new generation of gourmet cooks is unpredictable. A few days ago we were startled to come upon one of the Bright Young Marrieds in the act of kneading her own noodles.

"No, I am not going into competition with the Original Alfredo's of Rome," she laughed. "But I couldn't resist, for Mama Laura told me exactly how she makes *fettucini*. And, if I remember correctly, it was you who wrote that Mama Laura's *fettucini* are just as good and sometimes even better than Alfredo's."

The real inside secret of Mama Laura's *fettucini* lies not in the sauce or in the mixing but in her homemade, handmade, handkneaded pasta. All things considered, it is not such a chore to do yourself, although the dough needs at least 10 minutes of kneading to give it the proper satiny sheen and tenderness. All told, the whole process can be accomplished in half an hour.

Carlo's Favorite Antipasto
Mama Laura's Homemade Fettucini
with Alfredo's Sauce
Sautéed Calves Liver
Buttered Broccoli
Strawberries alla Mama

CARLO'S FAVORITE ANTIPASTO . . . Carlo is Mama Laura's tall and handsome son, and also the *maître d'hôtel*. When the selection of antipasto is left to him, almost certainly it will include cole slaw, pickled beets with onion rings, sardines and a most appetizing appetizer salad of cooked chick peas with a dressing made of equal parts wine vinegar and olive oil plus chopped onion, chopped pimiento and chopped parsley.

MAMA LAURA'S HOMEMADE FETTUCINI . . . Interviewed at the homey but ever so elegant Mama Laura's Restaurant far east on 58th Street in New York, the tiny, bright-eyed, white-haired chatelaine gave these directions: "For 4 people, use 3 eggs," we quote exactly. "Cup your hands together and fill them with this much flour." Translated, "this much" means just about 3 cupfuls, a little more or less, depending upon the size of the eggs. "Put the flour through a strainer to make it fluffier." Spread onto a board, making a circle with a depression in the middle. Into the hole, crack open the 3 eggs, beat slightly with a fork and mix with the flour. "When the eggs are thoroughly absorbed, mix with your hands to a smooth dough, kneading until the dough looks satiny and has little bubbles." Form into a ball, roll out like a thin pancake. Let dry at least 5 minutes. Fold like a jelly roll. Cut into strips about ½-inch wide. Cook immediately or separate the strands and allow to dry for half an hour. Drop by handfuls into 3 quarts boiling water with 1 tablespoon salt, 1 tablespoon olive oil. Cook just about 4 minutes or until tender but still firm.

ALFREDO'S SAUCE . . . At the table in a chafing dish or electric skillet place ¼ pound butter cut into bits, 2 tablespoons heavy cream. Still together until light and frothy. Add drained, cooked *fettucini*. Sprinkle with 1 cup freshly grated Parmesan cheese. Toss lightly with 2 forks until strands glisten. Sprinkle with coarsely ground black pepper.

STRAWBERRIES ALLA MAMA . . . To serve 4, slice 1 pint fresh strawberries lengthwise in fourths; sprinkle with 1 or 2 tablespoons sugar, depending on the berries and your own taste. Add 1 tablespoon sherry wine, 2 tablespoons white wine or orange juice, 1 teaspoon grated lemon peel, 1 teaspoon grated orange peel. Allow to stand 15 minutes or longer. Serve over vanilla ice cream.

IX. MR. OMELET'S BASIC OMELET

Once a year Mr. Omelet, whose real name is Rudolph Stanish, helps to swell the camp funds for the Church of the Ascension in New York with an omelet luncheon. Provided with a battery of portable little stoves brought into the parish house on Sunday after the services, he turns out omelets at the rate of four a minute. Each a little golden poem!

Aside from caviar, which is eaten raw, the omelet is the fastest of all gourmet specialties. Rudolph Stanish is the acknowledged king of omelet makers. To be treasured is his own description of the way to make a basic omelet. The pan, he feels, is most important. He favors sturdy aluminum 9 or 10 inches in diameter with rounded sloping shoulders. In his opinion omelet pans should be used for omelets and nothing else.

Tomato Juice Bracer   *Giant-Sized Pretzels*
Herb and Ham Omelet
Crisp Relishes   *French Bread*
"The Big Sweet"

TOMATO JUICE BRACER . . . An exceptionally zesty tomato juice cocktail made by adding to 2 cups tomato juice, ½ cup bottled lemon juice, 1 teaspoon Worcestershire sauce, ½ teaspoon sugar, dash of celery salt, salt and pepper to taste.

MR. OMELET'S BASIC OMELET . . . For one or two— break 3 eggs into a bowl, add 1 tablespoon cold water, ¼ teaspoon salt, a dash of Tabasco . . . "to bring out flavor and develop tenderness." Beat until light and foamy. Heat omelet pan until a few drops of water dropped on the pan will dance about and disappear almost instantly. Add 1 tablespoon butter. Swirl it about. Pour in eggs. Move pan back and forth with your left hand while, with a fork in your right hand, you keep stirring with a circular motion, holding the flat part of the fork on the flat part of the pan. The back and forth motion keeps the omelet from sticking; the stirring gives lightness.

When eggs are set on the bottom but still moist, loosen omelet with a fork and roll it over on itself so that it looks rather like a pillow.

HAM AND HERB OMELET . . . Dice two ¼-inch thick slices lean cooked ham. Mix with 1 tablespoon dry sherry, 2 teaspoons chopped chives. Stir into basic omelet. Cook according to Basic Omelet recipe above. Serve immediately with a little sweet butter spread on top and a sprinkle of freshly ground pepper and chopped parsley.

"THE BIG SWEET" . . . Practical solution to the problem of providing an inexpensive, easy dessert for a crowd . . . a new triple-decker chocolate bar. To dress it up further when you serve it at home you might add a garnish of whipped cream, whipped topping or serve with ice cream.

X. NASI GORENG WITH SHRIMP

A friend telephoned excitedly. "The McCanns," she told me, "Dora and Al—they're looking for you. They just said so on the radio."

"That's odd," I said. "They know where to find me." I tuned in on the program. They were not looking for me—personally—but for one of my recipes. It seems a doctor in New Jersey had expressed a great yearning to make *Nasi Goreng*—a dish that hails originally from Indonesia but has become exceptionally popular in Holland.

Most recipes for *Nasi Goreng* are wildly complicated. But some years ago, as the McCanns remembered, we had become enamored of the dish after a visit to Amsterdam and had been able to put together a quick and simple version. Made with instant rice and peanut butter this *Nasi Goreng* recipe—a most impressive buffet party dish—can be prepared in less than 15 minutes.

Rather like a curry, *Nasi Goreng* is served with chutney and a variety of relishes, most of them very hot. Often it is topped with fried eggs. The eggs may be omitted but they are tastier than you would think.

> *Pagoda of Crisp Raw Vegetables*
> *Nasi Goreng with Shrimp*
> *Fried Eggs* (optional)   *Sautéed Banana Strips*
> *Indonesian Fruit Compote with Cucumbers*
> *Lemon Ice   Almond Cookies*

PAGODA OF CRISP RAW VEGETABLES . . . Over a packed mound of crushed ice, make an interesting arrangement of celery sticks, radish roses, tender raw green beans, small wedges of cabbage, carrot curls.

NASI GORENG WITH SHRIMP . . . To serve 6, add 3 cups clam broth, rich chicken stock or consommé to 3 cups packaged pre-cooked rice. Add 1 teaspoon ground cumin seed, 1 teaspoon ground coriander seed, ½ teaspoon chili powder, ¼ teaspoon mace, 4 tablespoons peanut butter. Bring to a boil, cover and set aside in a warm place 10 minutes. Meanwhile heat ⅓ cup peanut oil to

370°. Cook until lightly browned 2 cups frozen chopped onions, 2 cloves garlic, crushed. Stir frequently to avoid burning. Add to cooked rice. Taste and add salt and pepper if needed. Pile onto a heatproof platter. Garnish with 2 to 3 cups cooked shrimp and 6 fried eggs, if desired. Surround with sautéed banana strips. Pass chutney and tiny bowls of very hot pepper sauce or barbecue sauce or *Tabasco*, to be added at will.

SAUTÉED BANANA STRIPS . . . Cut 6 small bananas into quarters, lengthwise. Brown lightly in butter. Sprinkle with lemon or lime juice.

INDONESIAN FRUIT COMPOTE WITH CUCUMBERS . . . To serve 6, combine 2 cups water with 1 cup dark brown sugar. Add ½ teaspoon crushed red hot chili peppers or ¼ teaspoon *Tabasco*, 3 tablespoons lemon juice. Cook until you have a clear syrup—about 5 minutes. Add 1 can grapefruit sections, 2 small cans mandarin oranges with their syrup, 1 peeled lemon cut in eighths, 2 tart well-flavored apples cut into wedges (apples may be pared or not as desired). Lastly, add 1 good-sized, unpeeled cucumber cut into thin slices. Serve warm or chilled as an accompaniment to the *Nasi Goreng*.

XI. A NOBLEMAN'S PANCAKE

The original recipe for this pancake was given to me years ago in Helsinborg in the south of Sweden by the sister of a nobleman who had come to live in the United States. He loved practically everything about his new country except "the blueberry so-called pancakes, speckled," he said, "with a few lonely berries." How he had longed for the great gold fruit-filled, cinnamon-scented discs that he remembered from his childhood.

Onion Soup with Croutons Melba
A Nobleman's Pancake
Cold Baked Ham
Sliced Tomatoes
Celery and Carrot Sticks
Quick Hearts of Cream   Ginger Marmalade
Heated Crackers

ONION SOUP WITH CROUTONS MELBA . . . Make up

your favorite canned or dehydrated onion soup but, at the last moment, add a tablespoon of wine or cider vinegar. Gives a lovely tingle!

A NOBLEMAN'S PANCAKE . . . To make a main dish pancake for two or four (depending upon one's appetite and degree of devotion to this pancake) stir together until smooth ½ cup flour, ¾ cup milk, 1 teaspoon sugar, ½ teaspoon salt. Beat in, one at a time, 2 egg yolks. Beat 3 egg whites, adding, after they are slightly stiffened, 1 tablespoon sugar, and continue to beat until they stand in peaks. Fold into the batter.

Heat in a large heavy skillet 1 tablespoon butter and 1 tablespoon salad oil. Pour in half the batter. Cover with a single layer of fresh or frozen blueberries or diced, canned, sliced apples, or tart green apples very thinly sliced. Sprinkle with 2 tablespoons brown sugar, ¾ teaspoon cinnamon. Add the rest of the batter. Cook over high heat until the bottom is nice and brown. This you can judge by peeking or by noting the presence of a rim of golden brown around the edges. Place the skillet under a pre-heated broiler, watching carefully until the top is cooked, puffy and delicately browned. Serve instantly, cutting the pancake into 4 sections. Some say that maple syrup is the only worthy accompaniment. Others insist upon sugar and cinnamon and a wedge of lemon to squeeze.

QUICK HEARTS OF CREAM . . . Dear to the hearts of epicures everywhere, are the French *Coeurs à la Crème* . . . the creamiest of cream cheeses pressed into heart-shaped baskets. Now there is a new way. Simply cut a 3-ounce package cream cheese with a heart-shaped cookie cutter. Frost lightly with sour cream or whipped cream, being careful not to obscure the shape. To serve 4, surround 2 such hearts with crisp heated crackers. Provide ginger marmalade or, if ginger marmalade is hard to find, add ¼ cup preserved or crystallized ginger, finely diced, to 1 cup orange marmalade.

XII. PAELLA OF VALENCIA

Most famous of all the specialties of Spain is the *Paella*. And the most esteemed of all the *Paellas* is that of Valencia which can become, in its native land, a most elaborate production, produced in a certain way in a certain special shallow pan with a flaring edge. On its native hearth, according to the experts, a proper *Paella* can be produced only when it is cooked outdoors over a fire of orange or olive wood.

All of this may be absolute gospel, nevertheless we dare to suggest that a fine *Paella* like this one may be achieved in an electric skillet.

"The body of a *Paella*," they will tell you when you visit in Spain, "is the rice. The heart is seafood and the soul is meat." Furthermore, no self-respecting *Paella* is possible unless you use Spanish olive oil now widely available in this country. A touch of saffron is indicated, but not absolutely necessary. Otherwise there are endless opportunities for improvising.

Paella of Valencia
Carrot Salad
Andalusian Tomatoes
Crusty Whole Grain Bread
Pineapple Dolce

PAELLA OF VALENCIA . . . In a heavy skillet, heat 2 peeled cloves of garlic in 4 tablespoons Spanish olive oil until brown. Then remove and toss away the garlic. Add ¼ pound lean pork, diced, or 1 uncooked chicken breast, boned and cut into 1-inch pieces. Cook until lightly browned. Push to one side. Add 1 pimiento, diced, and ½ cup chopped onion. Cook until onion is soft. Add 1 cup rice; stir to coat the rice with oil. Add ½ teaspoon saffron, 1 teaspoon salt, 2½ cups rapidly boiling water. Bring once more to a boil. Then add small (7- or 8-ounce) tin minced clams with juice, one 10-ounce package frozen cut green beans, 1 cup cooked shrimp. Slowly allow once more to come to a boil, then lower heat and cook uncovered 15 minutes, or until the rice is done. Sprinkle with minced parsley. Cover; allow to stand in a warm place or a slow oven (250°) about 10 minutes or until all the liquid has been absorbed. A fine and hearty one-dish meal for four.

CARROT SALAD . . . Cook carrots until just tender, or drain canned carrots and cover with a dressing made of 3 parts olive oil, 1 part wine vinegar, 1 tablespoon chopped chives or finely grated onion and a generous amount of chopped parsley. Add salt and pepper to taste. Serve very cold, garnished with escarole.

ANDALUSIAN TOMATOES . . . Slice 4 ripe garden-fresh tomatoes and 1 large sweet Bermuda onion very thin. Cover with the same dressing as for the carrots, above. Chill thoroughly and garnish with anchovy filets and pimiento-stuffed olives.

PINEAPPLE DOLCE . . . This dessert is perhaps more Caribbean, than Spain-Spanish. Delectable, fast and easy. To 2 good-sized ripe bananas, sliced, add 2 tablespoons brown sugar, 1 cup crushed, drained, canned pineapple, 1 cup sour cream. Serve with a topping of toasted grated coconut.

XIII. QUICK TAMALE PIE

Everyone comes back from Italy talking about the little taverns, the country inns, the *trattorie* on the little side streets. But only a few have a word to say about Italian beergardens—among the most leisurely, ingratiating and hospitable eating places on the continent.

There was, for example, a few years ago, in the city of Turin in the northern province of Piedmont, a *Birreria* that nobody forgets . . . the *Birreria* of the Bronze Horse. Most famous not for beer, but for bananas cooked in a special way.

So dramatic, so different, the Bananas of the Bronze Horse can transform the most impromptu supper into a memorable occasion. Here it follows a lightning-swift *Tamale* Pie in which the ingredients are heated separately on top of the stove and grilled under the broiler.

Quick Tamale Pie
Ring of Tomato Aspic Filled with Cole Slaw
Belgian Endive
Bananas of the Bronze Horse

QUICK TAMALE PIE . . . Heat together 2 cans of *chili con carne*, 1 small can whole kernel corn, ½ teaspoon cumin seed, 1 clove garlic, crushed. At the same time heat and drain a can of *tamales*. Place the chili and corn in a shallow heat-proof dish. Sprinkle with 1 cup sliced, pimiento-stuffed olives. Cover with heated *tamales* (husks removed, of course). Sprinkle with ½ cup grated sharp cheese. Set under the broiler just long enough to melt the cheese.

RING OF TOMATO ASPIC FILLED WITH COLE SLAW . . . Tomato aspic already jellied, ready-to-slice and serve, comes in convenient tins. But if you want to have a mold of aspic, you have only to warm it slightly. Add a little extra seasoning, i.e., 1 teaspoon *Worcestershire,* ¼ teaspoon dried basil or oregano. Pour into a mold. It will set at room temperature, but will taste better if allowed to chill for a few minutes in the refrigerator. Unmold and surround with cole slaw. Garnish with fingers of Belgian endive.

BANANAS OF THE BRONZE HORSE . . . In an electric skillet or wide frying pan, melt 4 tablespoons butter. Add ½ cup sugar, ¼ cup water, 4 thin strips lemon rind, 1 dozen pitted dates, cut in quarters. Cook until mixture takes on the pale hue and look of caramel syrup. Add 6 good-sized bananas cut into inch chunks. Carefully turn the pieces from time to time so that all are well and evenly cooked, but not soft. Serve plain or with whipped cream.

XIV. SENEGALESE RICE

With the learned curator of the museum in Abijan, I talked at length about the influence of West African art upon the 13th Century sculpture of Medieval Europe, which is remarkably similar to that of the Ivory Coast in its spare, elongated forms. Also, we talked about the anthropology of food and how certain dishes, probably born in Africa, have been adopted and transformed in modern times. He mentioned especially a popular dish in the Ivory Coast called Senegalese Rice. In many other parts of West Africa it is known as Jollof Rice, named after the particular tribe in Senegal that is supposed to have invented it. Practically the same dish reappears as a *paella* in Spain and Corsica. In New Orleans, it becomes *Jambalaya.* All over the United States, various versions are known as Spanish Rice.

All kinds of meat, fish and chicken, alone or in combinations, can go into Senegalese Rice. We had it done to perfection in a restaurant outside of Abijan where we sat on a porch set on piles, like a wharf jutting into the sparkling, shiny-black tropical sea; the stars hanging big and low like fire balls over our heads.

"Small Chop" of Sweet Red Pepper
Senegalese Rice
Chef's Salad
Peach or Mango Whip   Coconut Macaroons

"SMALL CHOP" OF SWEET RED PEPPER . . . "Small Chop" is a West African term for any sort of appetizer or tidbit. Fresh, sweet, red peppers may be used for this dish or a 4-ounce can of pimientos. Either should be cut into long strips. Arrange on a plate alternating strips of sweet red peppers or pimientos and anchovy filets. Blend the oil from the anchovy tin with 2 tablespoons olive oil. Add 1 tablespoon wine vinegar and pour over the peppers and anchovies. Garnish with parsley or capers. Serve with crusty bread. Bread must, of course, be dunked!

SENEGALESE RICE . . . To 2 cans of Spanish Rice, add one 8-ounce tin tomato sauce or 1 cup condensed undiluted tomato soup, 1 or 2 cloves garlic, crushed, ¼ teaspoon thyme, 1 tablespoon *Worcestershire* sauce, ¼ teaspoon hot pepper sauce or *Tabasco*. Heat thoroughly. Meanwhile, cut into inch-thick slices 1 package of brown 'n serve sausages and crisp them in 2 tablespoons olive oil. Have ready 1 cup diced cooked ham. At the last minute, brown the ham ever so slightly by tossing in the same frying pan.

At serving time, pile the rice into a heated serving dish. Cover with the meats and garnish around the edge with sliced tomatoes and sliced hard-cooked eggs. The eggs are a very African touch. Serves 4 generously. For true authenticity, provide hot pepper sauce or *Tabasco* for extra sprinkling at the table. Africans like it tingling, sizzling *hot*.

PEACH OR MANGO WHIP . . . Whip 1 cup heavy cream. Fold in about 1 cup (or a 7¾-ounce jar junior food) of mashed peaches or mangoes. Add 2 teaspoons lemon juice. Top with fresh or frozen sliced peaches, mangoes or berries.

XV. SICILIAN SANDWICHES GUASTIEDDE

The busy pizzerias of New York City and the myriad little shops that do a fine business selling Heroes—hot and cold —report that the Hero is being challenged by a newcomer fresh from Sicily.

Not too well known in this country up to now, the invader is a Sicilian sandwich roll that has the affectionate nickname of *Guastiedde*—a jolly good fellow.

Essentially the *Guastiedde* is a hot sausage and melted cheese sandwich served in a large soft roll like an oversize hamburger bun. The principal ingredients are peppery sausages fried and cut into slices, combined with a layer of Italian *ricotta* (or creamed cottage cheese) and slices of mozzarella cheese which might be replaced by a mild Muenster or Monterey Jack cheese.

For an easy and savory supper planned to star those Jolly Good Fellows, you might follow the traditional Sicilian custom and serve a Salad for Strength (*insalata rinforza*) and a *Zuppa Inglese*. The name means English soup though it isn't a soup at all, but a kind of dessert somewhat similar to an English trifle. In this case, however, there is no custard, but only fruit cocktail (canned or frozen) and a lovely *obliggato* of rum.

Mugs of Minestrone with Spinach
Sicilian Sandwiches Guastiedde
Insalata Rinforza (The Salad for Strength)
Zuppa Inglese can Frutta

MINESTRONE WITH SPINACH . . . For 6 servings, add 1 package frozen leaf spinach to 2 cans condensed minestrone, 1 soup can vegetable juice cocktail, 1 soup can water. Bring to a boil. Simmer together 5 minutes.

SICILIAN SANDWICHES GUASTIEDDE . . . To serve 6, fry 1½ pounds of Italian sausage until well cooked and lightly browned. Remove from pan. Drain and cut into slices about ¼ inch thick. Cut 6 large hamburger-type buns in half crosswise. Cover the bottom half with a layer of sliced fried sausage, a layer of *ricotta* or creamy cottage cheese. The layer should be about ¼ inch thick. Cover the *ricotta* with a layer of mozzarella cheese or Muenster or Monterey Jack, also cut ¼ inch thick. Sprinkle with 1 teaspoon of the sausage drippings. Replace top on the roll; wrap each one separately in foil. Place in a moderately hot oven (375°) 10 to 12 minutes or until the bread is thoroughly warmed and the cheese lusciously melted. Serve in the foil.

INSALATA RINFORZA . . . To serve 6, rub salad bowl with garlic. Line with crisp lettuce, romaine or escarole. Pile into the center of the bowl 2 packages frozen cauliflowerettes cooked according to directions, drained and chilled. Cover the cauliflowerettes with 1 cup sliced or quartered black olives. Garnish with filets of anchovies or drained capers and pickled peppers. Toss with Italian dressing.

ZUPPA INGLESE CON FRUTTA . . . Cut a layer of sponge cake in half crosswise. Sprinkle the cut sides with rum, using about ½ cup. Drain canned fruit cocktail or frozen fruit cocktail or salad (thawed but not mushy). Place fruit between slices and on top of cake. Cut into squares or wedges and serve with or without a spoonful of ice cream. May be used immediately, but is even better when allowed to stand in the refrigerator several hours.

XVI. SPAGHETTI ALLA CARBONARA

Here is spaghetti with a difference and a legend! No tomato sauce or meatballs. This type of spaghetti, according to olden stories, was enjoyed by men who went off to the forests in Italy to gather and burn wood for the making of charcoal. They carried the makings with them in knapsacks.

Tray of Antipasto
Woodmen's Spaghetti (Spaghetti alla Carbonara)
Chef's Salad   Italian Hearth Bread
Fresh Pears with Gorgonzola or Blue Cheese
Café Espresso with Lemon Peel

SPAGHETTI ALLA CARBONARA . . . To serve 4 to 6, cook and drain 1 pound of spaghetti. Just before serving (perhaps at the table) fry 4 slices of bacon until crisp. Then add ¼ cup Italian *prosciutto* ham or any raw smoked ham or smoked shoulder which has been cut into julienne strips. Heat together 1 or 2 minutes. Meanwhile, in a small bowl beat 2 eggs slightly with a fork. Stir into the eggs ½ cup grated Parmesan cheese. Toss the hot spaghetti with the bacon and ham mixture. Then immediately, before it has a chance to cool, add the egg and cheese mixture. Serve quickly. Sprinkle generously with more grated Parmesan cheese and coarsely ground black pepper.

XVII. SWEETBREADS ORIELS

In the gay-blade days of King Edward, there was much ado about sweetbreads. Now they are widely neglected and have an undeserved reputation for being exotic and expensive.

Robert Misch, one of our country's leading wine and food experts, discovered the local butcher in the small Adirondack village of Schroon Lake a reliable source for sweetbreads. "In almost any town," he says, "butchers are delighted to save them for you. In many places they can be procured quick-frozen."

Although veal sweetbreads are most prized by epicures, Bob Misch says that beef or lamb sweetbreads are excellent too, tender and delicate as chicken. Sweetbreads cooked in the Misch manner are named Sweetbreads Oriels, after The Oriels, their old house on the lake. (An oriel by the way is not a bird, but a bay window.)

Corn on the Cob (Served as a First Course)
Sweetbreads Oriels on Toast
Baby Squashes
Pineapple Mandarin

CORN ON THE COB . . . There is no better rule than the old one—a big kettle of water should be a-boiling on the stove before you go out to pick the corn. If this is impossible, keep the corn in the refrigerator; do not shuck a moment too soon. Do not add salt to the cooking water, for it tends to harden the kernels. A little milk, sugar or honey added to the cooking water is favored by many connoisseurs.

SWEETBREADS ORIELS ON TOAST . . . Cover a pound of sweetbreads with a quart of water which has been boiled five minutes with 1 teaspoon salt, 1 tablespoon lemon

juice, a sprig of thyme, a small bay leaf, a sprig of marjoram, 2 or 3 sprigs of parsley, 1 thin slice of onion or a
crushed shallot. Cook sweetbreads gently about 5 minutes; cool, remove skin and gristle. Cut into inch-size
pieces. To a 10½-ounce can cream sauce or chicken
gravy, heated (or 1¼ cups homemade cream sauce), add
¼ cup dry sherry. Then add the sweetbreads and serve
on hot buttered toast. Serves 4.

BABY SQUASHES . . . Look for the most infant squashes
available. Do not peel, but cut into slices or dice. Squash
may be steamed or, if you are really rushed, you can cook
it beautifully and speedily by putting a half-inch of boiling water into a wide skillet. Then add a single layer of
squash. Cover and cook only 3 or 4 minutes. Add a little
butter or sour cream, chopped chives and freshly ground
black pepper.

PINEAPPLE MANDARIN . . . Cut a pineapple lengthwise
and scoop out the flesh. Cut into dice. Combine with
drained, canned mandarin orange sections. Sprinkle with
orange juice or orange-flavored liqueur such as Cointreau, Triple Sec or Mandarino. Serve in shells.

XVIII. COLD TONGUE WITH HOT CUMBERLAND SAUCE

"Cold tongue," according to Laura Bunyard writing in the
Epicure's Companion a generation ago, "appeals to the
palate by certain very subtle suggestions rather than definite tastes."

A friend from London suggests that the subtlety is
greatly enhanced when the tongue is cold and the sauce is
hot. She sends along a recipe attributed to Elsie de Wolfe,
better known as Lady Mendl . . . a recipe refurbished and
modernized somewhat by England's famous food writer
Elizabeth David.

"This," she says, "is a particularly *dashing* Cumberland sauce!"

If you have time and want to make the effort, you may,
of course, soak a smoked beef tongue for 24 hours and
simmer it ever-so-gently 2 or 3 hours longer according to
size.

More realistically, you might provide yourself with
some sliced cooked tongue from the delicatessen or from

a can or jar. The slices should be about ¼ inch thick—somewhat heftier than for sandwiches. Serve 3 or 4 per person; very thin slices, 6 to 8 per person.

Cold Tongue with Hot Cumberland Sauce
Rice with Currants
Spinach en Branche
Heated Parker House Rolls
Instant Chocolate Frosted Bombe

COLD TONGUE WITH HOT CUMBERLAND SAUCE . . . With one of those handy five-and-dime store potato peelers, cut the rind from 2 California oranges and slice into julienne strips. Cover with boiling hot water. Cook 5 minutes and drain. Place the orange rind strips in a bowl with 4 tablespoons red currant jelly, 2 teaspoons prepared yellow mustard, ¼ teaspoon pepper, a dash of salt. Heat over hot water until the jelly is melted. Add ¼ cup port wine or orange juice. Stir and cook 5 minutes longer. Very good, too, when served with ham. Serves 4.

RICE WITH CURRANTS . . . Cover ½ cup seedless currants or small raisins with warm water. Simmer gently 5 minutes or until plump and soft. Fork lightly into 2 cups fluffy cooked rice.

SPINACH EN BRANCHE . . . This is nothing more or less than leaf spinach. Use frozen spinach. Prepare according to package directions. Garnish with squeezable lemon sections.

INSTANT CHOCOLATE FROSTED BOMBE . . . This elaborate-looking and beautiful-tasting *bombe* was inspired by a new product; a luscious, creamy chocolate frosting that comes ready to spread in a tin. Particularly effective when used lavishly over a brick or mold of ice cream! The ice cream may be chocolate-frosted immediately before serving or done ahead of time and kept in the freezer until ten minutes before serving. Fudge-frosting made from a mix may be substituted if desired.

WEEKEND SUPPERS

❧§❧

I. CHOWDER SUPPER

❦

Back Bay is being shaken, as if the earth trembled. Some modern, busy Bostonian ladies, otherwise unassailable, are taking liberties with chowder. Instead of cooking the heads and bones of fish to make the stock, they are using bottled clam broth . . . and butter instead of salt pork. Some even resort to canned, frozen chowder and add extra fish. A fine thought for a quick and sturdy Saturday night supper.

New Back Bay Fish Chowder
Sea Biscuits and Common Crackers
Mammoth Salad Bowl
Sailor's Duff

NEW BACK BAY FISH CHOWDER . . . To serve 4, cut a pound of fish filets (cod, halibut, or haddock) into strips. Cover with hot water. Add ½ bay leaf, the merest flick of thyme, ½ teaspoon salt, ¼ teaspoon pepper. Poach gently until the fish flakes easily. Add two 10-ounce cans frozen, condensed fish chowder, one 8-ounce bottle clam broth, ½ cup light cream or evaporated milk. Simmer 5 minutes longer.

SAILOR'S DUFF . . . Combine 1 well-beaten egg with 2 tablespoons sugar, 2 tablespoons butter, 2 cups molasses. Sift together 1½ cups flour, 1 teaspoon baking soda, ½ teaspoon each: cinnamon, nutmeg and ginger. Add to the egg mixture. Then stir in ½ cup boiling water. Mix thoroughly. Pour into a bowl or pudding mold. Cover with aluminum foil tied on securely with a string. Cook in a pressure cooker 15 minutes or steam 1 hour. Serve with . . .

SCIHONCEST SAUCE . . . Beat 2 egg yolks until very light and pale in color, gradually adding 1 cup sugar and

1 teaspoon each lemon juice and grated lemon rind. Fold in gently 1 cup heavy cream, whipped till stiff.

II. BOURBON BAKED BEANS

A Detroit friend wrote that she was about to hostess a buffet party and would like to serve our recipe for baked beans with pineapple and Bourbon. This recipe, it seemed, had disappeared. Whoops! It wasn't our recipe, but it did sound like a fine idea. So we experimented and herewith is the recipe for Bourbon Baked Beans and a menu suggestion for a Saturday night buffet.

Baked Ham
Bourbon Baked Beans
Big Salad Bowl of Lettuce, Cucumbers
Radishes and Chopped Green Peppers
Italian Dressing
Heated Rolls
Lemon Meringue Pudding with Fresh Blueberries
Nut Wafers

BOURBON BAKED BEANS . . . To serve 6, place in a casserole 2 large cans Boston style baked beans with pork and molasses. Cover the top of the casserole with slices or wedges of pineapple. Combine ¼ cup Bourbon, ¼ cup honey, ¼ cup soy sauce and a clove of garlic, crushed. Stir and pour over beans. Bake in a hot oven (400°) about 30 minutes or until the pineapple is browned and the beans hot and bubbly.

ITALIAN DRESSING . . . From the bottle.

LEMON MERINGUE PUDDING WITH FRESH BLUEBERRIES . . . Make up 2 packages lemon pie filling according to directions for lemon pudding. Allow to cook a little. Fold in 1 cup heavy cream, whipped. Pile into an attractive china or glass bowl. Chill in refrigerator (or in freezer 10 minutes). At serving time cover with fresh blueberries and sprinkle with powdered sugar. Serves 6.

III. COUNTRY EMPORIUM CHILI

This menu for a *chili con carne* picnic supper is based on one that was served by theatrical producer Jean Dalrymple to fifty friends on a recent Saturday night. Food was supplied by the Country Emporium, a gourmet grocery shop in West Redding, Connecticut, our home town.

SATURDAY NIGHT PICNIC
Country Emporium Chili
Parslied Rice
Michael Tree's Cucumbers   *Celery*   *Radishes*
Dill Pickles
Scallions
Raw Cauliflowerettes   *Sliced Tomatoes*
Apple Pie with Store Cheese   *Coffee in Mugs*

COUNTRY EMPORIUM CHILI . . . The Country Emporium makes their own *chili* from a secret recipe! A creditable facsimile thereof may be produced by adding to 2 cans *chili con carne* with beans, 2 cloves garlic crushed, 1 teaspoon cumin seed, 1 tablespoon paprika. Heat, stirring occasionally. Serves 3 to 4.

PARSLIED RICE . . . Add ¼ cup chopped parsley to 2 tablespoons melted butter and stir into 2 cups hot cooked rice.

MICHAEL TREE'S CUCUMBERS . . . Slice a cucumber very thin. Do not peel unless skin is tough. Place cucumber in glass or pottery bowl. Sprinkle with "lots of salt"—about 2 tablespoons. Cover with ice cubes. Allow to stand 2 hours. If too salty, wash off some of the salt. Squeeze cucumbers to remove most of the water. Dress with sour cream to which you have added a little tarragon vinegar. Sprinkle with cracked pepper. Serves 4. These cucumbers are marvelously crisp and tasty. Will stay crisp for a week in the refrigerator.

IV. FIRESIDE PICNIC

When you gather round the glowing hearth—or around the cosy broiler, regale yourselves with a fireside picnic where the steak is gloriously seasoned in seconds under blue flames of Bourbon whiskey. Let your sundae, too, be blessed with fire.

Shrimps on Horseback
Bourbon-Broiled Steak

Tossed Vegetable Salad   Oil and Vinegar Dressing
Crusty French Rolls
Firelit Sundae

SHRIMPS ON HORSEBACK . . . Drop medium-size frozen or fresh shrimp into boiling water flavored with salt, pepper and lemon juice. Cook just about 3 minutes when frozen shrimp should be thawed; fresh shrimp will have turned pink. Drain; dry. Wrap each shrimp in half a slice of bacon and broil. Serve as an appetizer with soy sauce for dipping.

BOURBON-BROILED STEAK . . . Slightly warm ½ cup Bourbon whiskey. Set a match to the whiskey and pour it while flaming over a 2-inch-thick sirloin steak. Gash the fat in several places so that it will not curl. Broil over charcoal or in an open broiler 14 to 20 minutes or until done to suit your taste. Season each side after it is cooked with salt and pepper.

TOSSED VEGETABLE SALAD . . . Scatter drained, canned vegetables over a bowl of mixed greens. Garnish with anchovy filets. Toss at the table with oil and vinegar dressing.

FIRELIT SUNDAE . . . Place a marshmallow on top of each sundae. Into the marshmallow press a rectangular lump of sugar that has been dipped for a second into lemon extract. Set fire to the sugar which in turn will toast the marshmallow.

V. GASPACHO

Gaspacho! Some people spell it *Gazpacho*. Either spelling seems to be right. And there are no absolutely set and unalterable recipes for making it. One thing is certain: *Gaspacho* is one of the glories of Spanish cuisine, a liquid, salad-like soup, or, if you prefer, a soup-like salad. It is the best of all possible summertime dishes—especially in the season of garden tomatoes.

Hot house tomatoes are not right for *Gaspacho*; neither are those that are picked green. Essentially a dish of the land, it is said that the women in olden days used to carry it to their men as they worked in the fields and the olive groves. Although *Gaspacho* is often a puree, the vegetables can be finely diced. A few hours of mellowing in the icebox does wonders for this soup. There should by rights, when it is served, be an ice cube or two in the plate or the bowl to make a tiny, cooling clatter. For a summer supper, nothing could be finer than *Gaspacho,* served along with crusty bread and a platter of cold meats and cheese.

Punch Bowl of Gaspacho
Hot French Bread
Platter of Cold Meats and Your Favorite Cheeses
Pecan Pie with Ice Cream Sauce

PUNCH BOWL OF GASPACHO . . . To serve six, use 6 large native tomatoes cut into small dice or placed in the blender along with 1 small tin (about 4) pimientos. Add 2 onions finely diced, 2 small peeled cucumbers, coarsely chopped or finely diced, 1 clove garlic, crushed, ¾ cup olive oil, 3 tablespoons red wine vinegar, 1 can tomato juice, 1 tray ice cubes. Season to taste with salt and pepper. Serve very cold with chopped parsley, chives, or other herbs, and croutons of toasted bread, or crumbled breadsticks to be scattered over the top.

PECAN PIE . . . Thaw a quick-frozen pecan pie and warm slightly in the oven or under the broiler.

ICE CREAM SAUCE . . . With a fork, soften a half pint of vanilla ice cream and stir in 2 tablespoons of *Crème de Cacao* liqueur.

VI. LAURENTIAN BEANS

Years ago in Quebec, as in New England, beans were soaked on Thursday night, boiled on Friday, carried on Saturday morning to the baker. Then and now, they were and are, the best of all possible Saturday night suppers. Now amazingly easy when you begin with canned beans of the Boston type and add typical Laurentian accents.

Laurentian Beans
Pickled Gherkins   Pickled Onions
Baby Lettuce with Egg and Vinegar Dressing
Warmed Date-Nut or Banana Bread
Blueberry Pie with Sugarbush Topping

LAURENTIAN BEANS . . . Place 2 cans Boston baked beans with pork and molasses in a beanpot or casserole along with 1 peeled and quartered red onion that has been rolled in 1 teaspoon dry mustard. Add ½ cup dark molasses or maple syrup. Cover with sliced bacon or salt pork. Bake in a moderately hot oven 375° 25 minutes or until beans are piping hot, and pork, crispy brown. Serves 6.

BABY LETTUCE WITH VINEGAR DRESSING . . . Sprinkle baby lettuce with chopped hard-cooked egg, and just before serving, toss with dressing made by adding 1 tablespoon water to 4 tablespoons cider vinegar. Season with salt, pepper and about ½ teaspoon sugar.

DATE-NUT OR BANANA BREAD . . . Buy or make from a mix or settle for canned brown bread.

BLUEBERRY PIE WITH SUGARBUSH TOPPING . . . Brush the top of a ready-baked blueberry pie with cream. Cover with maple sugar. Sprinkle with lemon juice and heat till the pie is warm and the sugar melted. (Sugarbush refers, of course, to maple sugar.)

VII. MANDARIN'S SATURDAY NIGHT

Inspired by the full selection of Chinese vegetables, sauces and noodles now available in cans at almost any market, we have planned a Mandarin's Saturday Night with quick versions of ancient dishes for which we have retained the authentic old poetical names.

Golden Moons in a Silver Sea
Famous Scholars' Abandon
Jade Growing out of Coral
Pekin Peaches under Velvet Dust

GOLDEN MOONS IN A SILVER SEA . . . (Hard-cooked eggs in broth) . . . In ancient China they used pigeon eggs. We will settle for a hard-cooked egg yolk for each person, cut in halves and placed in a cup of clear chicken broth. Garnish with shredded lettuce.

FAMOUS SCHOLARS' ABANDON (not unlike Chop Suey!) . . . Prepare 2 packages frozen Chicken Chop Suey according to directions, adding, at the last, 3 thinly-sliced tomatoes. Cook 2 minutes longer. Garnish with a well-beaten egg that has been cooked on a well-oiled pan for 1 minute. Serve with rice, a garnish of green onions and soy sauce. Serves 4 to 6.

JADE GROWING OUT OF CORAL (a salad of bean sprouts and escarole) . . . Heat ½ cup vinegar, ¼ cup water, ¼ cup sugar, 2 teaspoons salt, ¼ teaspoon pepper and 2 tablespoons diced onion. Pour over 2 (1-pound) cans bean sprouts, drained. Stir, chill (in freezer if necessary to save time). Toss with ¼ cup peanut oil. Place in shallow bowl. Decorate with upright fronds of crisp escarole or romaine.

PEKIN PEACHES UNDER VELVET DUST (peaches in a meringue shell topped with cream) . . . Buy or make a meringue shell or individual meringues. Hollow and fill with partially thawed frozen peaches and cover with slightly sweetened whipped cream. Dust with finely crumbled Chinese Noodles from a can.

VIII. PETITE MARMITE M. BASILE SUPPER

On the top floor of the Plaza Athenae Hotel in Paris, there are tiny rooms that were undoubtedly servants' rooms in the days when gentlefolk traveled with maids and valets. Imaginatively decorated, the windows look out on the roofs and chimney tops of Paris. At night, the Eiffel Tower gleams close like a great jeweled scabbard in the sky. People from all over the world ask to be on this floor. Not only because of the rooms and the view, but also the courtly head floorwaiter, M. Basile Chernyzoff. A tall, white-haired and elegant White Russian, he looks as if he must have been no less than an Archduke in the Imperial court of the czars. An authority on fine foods and wine, M. Basile has helped to plan and has served some of the most distinguished meals in Paris.

But the dish that I remember most nostalgically is not rich, elaborate or exotic. On the menu it is listed as *Petite Marmite Henri IV*. But for me, it will always be . . . *Petite Marmite M. Basile.*

Petite Marmite M. Basile
Salade aux Fines Herbes
Glazed Apricot Flan

PETITE MARMITE M. BASILE . . . Billed on the Plaza menu as a soup, some might call it a stew. It is not quite either! The various ingredients are not cooked together. Vegetables and meat all retain their own identities. The broth is rich but sparkling clear—not at all thickened. Diced or julienne leftover meats may be used, but at the Plaza, lately, they have been using chicken giblets.

Cook 2 sets of chicken giblets with ¼ onion, ½ bay leaf, ½ teaspoon salt, ⅛ teaspoon pepper and 3 cups water until tender . . . 15 minutes in your pressure cooker. Remove giblets and slice. Combine with one 10-ounce can condensed consommé, one 10-ounce can condensed chicken broth, 1 cup water and the liquid from the giblets. Add 1 cup each of the following: lightly cooked green peas, carrots, cauliflowerettes. Heat and simmer 5 minutes. Serve with melba toast rounds and grated Parmesan cheese. Serves 6.

SALADE AUX FINES HERBES . . . There is "a rule" in France, that *fines herbes* must include at least 3, never more than 7 herbs. Ideally, they should be fresh, but dried may be used if you soak them at least 5 minutes in warm water, lemon juice or vinegar. Fill a china bowl half-way full of well-washed, crisp dry greens torn into tiny pieces. Dress at the table by sprinkling first with 3 tablespoons olive oil or salad oil. Toss until leaves glisten. Sprinkle with salt and pepper, then with 1 tablespoon lemon juice. Add 1 teaspoon each chopped parsley, tarragon, chives and/or basil. If herbs are dried, use half as much.

GLAZED APRICOT FLAN . . . Fill a ready-baked pie crust or crumb crust with vanilla pudding made according to package directions, but flavored with an extra teaspoonful of almond extract. Over the pudding, arrange well-drained, fresh, canned or frozen apricot halves, round side up. Add 1 tablespoon lemon juice or water to ½ cup apple jelly and melt over low heat. Spoon carefully over apricots. Chill 5 minutes in the freezer.

IX. POT AU FEU

Honored like the baked beans of New England for Saturday night supper, is *Pot au Feu*—the pot on the fire—in the French household. Tradition has undergone a revolutionary change lately. Now, an amazing number of French housewives admit that even the classic *pot au feu* is being cooked *sous pression*—in a pressure cooker.

Pot au Feu Broth in Cups
Boiled Beef with Vegetables
Coarse Salt, Mustard
Heated Tomato Sauce
Apples   Camembert Cheese

POT AU FEU BROTH AND BEEF . . . This, of course, is the French version of a boiled beef dinner, usually served in two parts. First . . . a cup of broth garnished simply with oven-dried rounds of French rolls; afterwards . . . the beef surrounded by the vegetables. For 6 persons, put into the pressure cooker 3 pounds short ribs of beef cut into serving pieces, 1 soup bone (optional), the white part of 3 leeks and 3 onions or 6 small whole onions, 1 small head of cabbage, quartered. Add 2 cups stock or water. Adjust cover, bring up pressure according to manufacturer's directions and cook at 15 pounds pressure 20 minutes. Bring down pressure, remove cover, skim. Add one 10-ounce tin consommé and 1 soup can water. Cook uncovered over medium heat about 5 minutes longer or until beef is tender.

HEATED TOMATO SAUCE . . . To 1 cup of any good prepared marina or tomato sauce, add 1 tablespoon olive oil, ¼ teaspoon marjoram or oregano, serve in heated sauce boat.

X. RAVIOLI EMBELLISHED
Embellished
Crusty Herb Bread
Greenbrier   Apples à la Mode

EMBELLISHED . . . To serve 4, put 2 jars or RAVIOLI in tomato sauce into a shallow casserole with 2 tablespoons olive oil, 1 teaspoon oregano, or 1 tablespoon fresh, and sprinkle with 2 grated cheese. Heat at 350° about 20 minutes or bubbly and brown.

GREENBRIER SALAD . . . A specialty at the Greenbrier Hotel in White Sulphur Springs, Virginia. In the bottom of a salad bowl place the leaves from a bunch of well-washed and dried watercress. Discard thick stems. Sprinkle with drained, diced canned beets. Around the edges of the bowl arrange leaves of endive. Toss with French or Italian dressing.

CRUSTY HERB BREAD . . . Brush brown 'n serve French bread with butter or olive oil. Sprinkle with any desired dried herbs and bake accordnig to directions.

BAKED APPLES À LA MODE . . . In a hurry, use canned or frozen baked apples and serve with vanilla ice cream.

XI. SIX-FOOT HERO SANDWICHES

Some years ago, a famous Italian food shop on Ninth Avenue created a major sensation in Manhattan when they introduced hero sandwiches 4 and 6 feet long. Given sufficient notice of 3 or 4 days they could be induced to deliver their prodigious creations within the city limits Mondays through Fridays. But not, of course, on Saturday or Sunday.

Once we wanted to give a party over the weekend in the country 50 miles from New York and were goaded into trying to reproduce the gigantic heroes using materials readily available in our small town. So, to produce a hero 6 feet long, we use 6 loaves of crusty Italian bread about 4 inches wide. Cut both ends off 4 loaves and leave an end apiece on 2 other loaves. Fit together end-to-end so that you seem to have one long, long loaf. Then cut what you seem to have one long, and hollow them out a crosswise all the way through much bread. From this po so that you don't have too other hero sandwich. you proceed as for any

Tomato Soup with
Six-Foot Hero Sand
Floating Island or Fresh Fruit and A

TOMATO SOUP WITH POPCORN . . . To p Cakes mato soup add ¼ teaspoon thyme or oreg with popcorn. Sprinkle with chopped chives of to-

SIX-FOOT HERO SANDWICHES . . . Soften butter and smoothly spread both sides of the bread. Cover the bottom of one section with thinly sliced salami or bologna overlapping generously. Cover the next section with sliced cheese, the next with thinly sliced ham. Garnish with sliced olives, strips of pimiento, well-drained cole slaw or vegetable antipasto or any other sliced pickles or pickled vegetables. Tomato slices and lettuce should be used only when you plan to eat the sandwich rather promptly. Press the 2 halves together and at serving time cut into sections anywhere from 2 to 4 inches wide, depending of course, upon the size of your loaf.

Since the Hero Sandwich is the main course for supper, count on about ⅛ pound cheese and/or sliced meats for each person. A 6-foot Hero to make 32 portions will require 2 pounds thinly sliced cheese, 1 pound cooked ham, 1 pound thinly sliced bologna.

FLOATING ISLAND . . . To serve 8, make up a package of lemon-flavored gelatin according to package directions. Swift-chill in freezer 7 to 10 minutes or until slightly thickened. Add 2 egg whites. Set in a pan of ice cubes and water and whip until fluffy and thick like whipped cream. Pour into a mold or pile immediately onto a chilled deep platter and serve with a custard sauce made by adding 1 egg and an extra cupful of milk to a package of instant vanilla pudding. Add a teaspoonful of almond extract.

XII. SOPA CON ALBONDIGAS

A magnificent *Sopa con Albondigas,* vegetable soup with tiny meat balls, is inspired by Spain and Puerto Rico. This soup is put together in a flash because you use canned minestrone and canned meat balls. Afterwards, a huge salad and a deep dish berry cake. With crusty bread and red wine, this meal has a rustic sophistication.

Sopa con Albondigas
Lima Bean Salad
Crusty Bread
Deep Dish Loganberry Cake

SOPA CON ALBONDIGAS . . . To a large can of ready-to-serve minestrone, add a can of meat balls in tomato sauce, 1 can condensed consommé, 1 can water. Simmer together 10 minutes. Serve in bowls or large mugs. Sprinkle with grated Parmesan cheese and chopped parsley. Serves 4.

LIMA BEAN SALAD . . . Chill and drain 1 can (about 2 cups) cooked Lima or kidney beans, or chick peas. Combine with 1 large onion chopped, ¼ cup chopped parsley, 3 tablespoons salad oil, 3 tablespoons wine vinegar, salt and freshly ground black pepper to taste. Mix thoroughly but lightly so as not to crush the beans. Serve in a bowl that has been rubbed with garlic, lined with crisp lettuce, garnished with quartered tomatoes.

DEEP DISH LOGANBERRY CAKE . . . In a 2-inch baking dish, place a quart of fresh loganberries or 2 packages of frozen loganberries (thawed). If fresh, sprinkle with sugar. Cover with cake batter made from a package of yellow cake mix. Bake according to directions. Spoon from baking dish and serve warm with cream.

XIII. WEIGHT-WATCHERS' PIZZA PARTY

There is a weight—or is it simply weight—on almost everybody's mind these days. So we plan a pizza with crust that is neither a crust nor a dough but protein-rich ground beef.

Weight-Watchers' Pizza
with Hamburger Crust
Crisp Green Salad Bowl with
Oil and Vinegar Dressing
Fresh Fruits
Margharitas

WEIGHT-WATCHERS' PIZZA WITH HAMBURGER CRUST . . . Make sauce by combining 1 (8-ounce) can tomato sauce, ¼ teaspoon garlic salt, ½ teaspoon sugar, ⅛ teaspoon each dried basil, marjoram and thyme. Simmer about 15 minutes. Meanwhile, season well 2 pounds lean hamburger meat. Press in a 12-inch pie pan or on pizza sheet, turning up the edges slightly. Cover with sauce and garnish with 1 red onion thinly sliced, ¼ pound Italian salami cut in thin slices, ¼ pound mozzarella cheese thinly sliced. Sprinkle with ½ teaspoon oregano, ¼ cup grated Romano cheese. Place immediately in oven and bake at 450° for 10 to 12 minutes.

MARGHARITAS . . . In Italy *Margharitas* are usually round, baked in tiny muffin or cupcake tins, but they can also be square. Mix together 2 eggs slightly beaten, 1 cup light brown sugar, ½ cup flour, ¼ teaspoon baking powder, ¼ teaspoon salt, 1 cup walnuts or almonds cut into small pieces. Spread mixture in a well-buttered 8-inch square pan. Bake until cake shrinks away from the pan . . . about 10 minutes at 350°. Cool slightly. Cut into 1 inch squares.

A SIT-DOWN BUFFET

THE BALANCED MEAL IS OUT. This is the biggest news in dining circles. No longer is a proper meal balanced dangerously on the knee or against your neighbor's elbow. The plate-on-the-lap phase of our nation's social history is definitely on the wane.

The catch-as-catch-can buffet has begun to pall.

No longer is it smart or *au courant* to mate a drippy green salad and a sour-cream-sauced beef stroganoff on the same plate.

At long last our Brave Young Men have taken a stand against stand-up suppers.

Because the pendulum always takes a long swing in the opposite direction some charmingly stuffy old fashioned dinner party customs are being revived. The men, as in Edwardian days, are once again allowed to enjoy their cigars and port—or more likely their coffee and Cognac—alone in masculine privacy at the dinner table whilst the ladies flutter away to repair the lipstick ravages in the hostess' bedroom.

Paper napkins are frowned upon at meals that aspire to be called a dinner party.

Tables, like women, have taken to long skirts that sweep the floor. The tablecloth is supplanting mats, which always somehow manage to make a table look cluttered.

A new era of elegance is not only on the way; it has, in fact, arrived.

This, of course, is a different source of elegance . . .

not a return nor strictly a revival, but an evolution. The new dining elegance is based on self-service and not on servants. This is an elegance which may, and then again may not, be costly.

One of the most interesting manifestations of the new trend is the comfortable dinner party served as a buffet but enjoyed by guests cosily seated at a table. We were about to say *around* a table for we note that tables are getting rounder. Round tables encourage conversation. There is as was known in King Arthur's day a certain magic about a round table promoting sociability—a sense of comradeship.

Dining chairs, we are pleased to report, are becoming more comfortable. Even the newer folding chairs so necessary to our social lives—are deeper and wider once again as in our grandmother's day; hostesses arm themselves with tape and go about measuring the distance between one setting and another. They are remembering the rules that appeared in early editions of Emily Post —there should be not more than 18 inches between plates—not less than 12.

Please Be Seated

First requisite for a proper sit-down buffet dinner party are pre-set tables with the silverware and the glasses all in place. There should be salt and pepper on the table. Bread and butter too, if you like. Generally there would be some sort of centerpiece and perhaps a pitcher of water, or a decanter of wine.

Bridge tables may be used for this type of service, but even more popular are round tables improvised with folding tops that fit over bridge tables. At these tables eight can be accommodated and the conversation can be reasonably cosy, but the party is less likely to break up into fragments as it may when the bridge table technique is used.

The guests serve themselves of course from a buffet table where, let us hope, bowls and casseroles stay fire-hot through the meal on electrically heated trays or over bevies of candle-warmers. By the same token, chilled foods stay frigidly chilly on a new type of serving tray that maintains arctic temperatures for hours without the bother and mess of ice and drip. These new cold trays hold in their middles so-called cold cells that are frozen beforehand in your freezer compartment.

On these heat or chill-maintaining trays, plates as well as foods may be kept heated or chilled as the occasion demands.

Now, praise be, it is considered a social crime to serve a salad on the same plate as drippy hot foods. Even at buffets, salads are served separately on frosty plates, unless of course the whole meal is cold.

More Sophisticated Menus

Even in small apartments and little ranch houses, company menus are getting more sophisticated. Even the teenage hostess is becoming wary of the old clichés like baked hams decorated with pineapple and maraschino cherries and the dreary casseroles of just plain old macaroni and cheese. Definitely these are passé.

There has been a lot of re-thinking of the subject of first courses. At any buffet they are difficult to manage. Even at a sit-down buffet they present some problem unless they can be placed on the table before the guests sit down. Even so, they must be cleared away before the main event.

Often the problem is solved by making the appetizer an integral part of the meal even though it is served beforehand with cocktails—alcoholic or otherwise. Soups, chilled or hot, are easier to serve before the meal in cups or mugs rather than bowls or soup plates.

Fewer Problems

Compared to the old-fashioned buffet supper party, the new sit-down variety presents fewer problems. It is no longer necessary to serve only fork food. The happily seated guests can use a knife or even a sword if need be. If you become adept at certain types of table drama, you can take the center of the stage behind the buffet table and toss your salad or flame your fruits in full view of your audience—admiring, we trust.

There is only one thing to keep in mind; everything should be utterly, completely—let us say idiotically—easy to put on your plate. Make up your mind that when it comes to putting food on their plates all guests are all thumbs. There should be nothing to cut, nothing to pry apart, nothing to dismember. If there are garnishes that are inedible (by rights there shouldn't be), these should be conspicuously segregated.

Fair Means or Foul

By fair means or foul—by a maid (you should be so lucky), by a husband (likewise!), or by your own twelve hands, the tables should be cleared before the dessert is served. A rolling table helps enormously. Forget about the old dictum against piling plates, but do try to be discreet about scraping them in full view. Not appetizing!

Once again, if you have some help—working for pay or love—the dessert may be passed at the little tables, so that the coteries can remain cosily clustered and the conversation uninterrupted.

Or you could have the dessert brought to each table and served by one of the . . . GIRLS.

Otherwise, be ruthless. Simply announce, "dessert and coffee are now on the table." Let Nature take its course.

Especially Appropriate

In addition to special occasion menus in this chapter, a great many of our Fast Gourmet dinners are blissfully appropriate for sit-down buffet dinner parties. To mention a few:

The rack of lamb *Maderia* accompanied by baby asparagus around cream, green mashed potatoes, and Alice B. Toklas chocolate *mousse,* page 126.

The breast of chicken cacciatore and spaghetti with white clam sauce, followed by Charlotte Kimmelman's slimming lemon soufflé, page 65.

Duck *à l'orange* with rice made with burdened rice broccoli and lemon butter, glazed strawberry tartlets; see page 74.

Chicken with black cherries, potato puffs, frozen ice cream roll *au chocolat,* page 66.

Skewered lamb in the Persian manner, rice with a golden eye, a Scheherazade fruit cup, page 122.

Sweetbreads Oriels on toast, accompanied by baby squashes, corn on the cob, followed by pineapple mandarin, see page 193.

SPECIAL OCCASIONS

❧❦☙

I. APRIL FOOL'S DAY

Ever since cooking began—or at least for a long, long time, cooks seem to have had a sense of humor and a taste for gastronomical foolery! So it seems no less fitting that an April Fool Dinner should have dishes that look and taste like what they are not.

We begin with "caviar" served with the traditional caviar trimmings, but made of eggplant. The meal goes on with a Mock Venison Steak—actually lamb—and a *Trompe l'Oeil*, fool-the-eye dessert, that looks like a poached egg, but turns out to be a round slice of vanilla ice cream pleasantly topped with half an apricot.

Eggplant Caviar with Sour Cream, Chopped Egg,
Chopped Chives, Melba Toast
Mock Venison Steak
Currant Jelly
Hominy Cakes
Baby Lima Beans with Butter Sauce
Celery, Radishes
Trompe l'Œil Dessert

EGGPLANT CAVIAR . . . Bake or broil peeled eggplant until soft and tender. Mash coarsely with fork; flavor to taste with lemon juice, salt, pepper, a little olive oil if desired. Pass in separate small dishes: sour cream, chopped hard-cooked egg yolk, hard-cooked egg white, chopped chives. Provide thinly-sliced rye bread or Melba toast.

MOCK VENISON STEAK . . . Even seasoned huntsmen have been known to get a dreamy look in their eyes when confronted with this make-believe venison steak, especially if it is presented with the classical accompaniments to game, such as currant jelly and crisply fried hominy.

For each person, provide 1 lamb steak, cut about ½ inch thick. To serve 6, place in a bowl 2 thinly sliced onions, 1 crushed clove garlic, 1 cup dry red table wine, 2 tablespoons vinegar, ½ cup olive oil, 2 teaspoons salt, ½ teaspoon pepper, a dash of cayenne pepper, and ¼ teaspoon marjoram, rosemary or oregano. Stir well. Add 6 steaks. Let stand several hours or overnight. Drain, and sauté quickly in butter, first on one side, then on the other. Two or 3 minutes on each side would be sufficient.

HOMINY CAKES . . . Prepare quick-cooking hominy grits according to package directions for making mush. Chill in small square pan. Cut into ½-inch slices or diamonds and brown slowly on both sides in butter until crispy.

BABY LIMA BEANS WITH BUTTER SAUCE . . . Can be purchased quick-frozen complete with sauce.

TROMPE L'ŒIL DESSERT . . . Place on flat small dessert plates, a round slice of vanilla ice cream. In center of the ice cream place ½ canned apricot, round side up. Sprinkle ice cream with a few grains of nutmeg to represent pepper; apricot with sugar, to look like salt.

II. CHRISTMAS TREE-TRIMMING PARTY

In France, a yule log is not for burning. The *Buche de Noel* is a symbolic cake sold by all confectioners at Christmas time. Essentially it is the same as our jelly rolls or our cream-filled chocolate rolls.

So we were inspired to create an instant yule log that requires no baking, no cooking—on your part, that is!

The secret: buy 2 or 3 ready-baked jelly rolls or chocolate rolls filled with whipped cream. Press them close together to make a long roll and frost with this slightly incredible rich and creamy chocolate frosting made by the simple expedient of adding sour cream to packaged semi-sweet chocolate pieces that have beeen melted over hot water.

For a tree-trimming party or a quick and easy Christmas Eve supper, the *Buche de Noel* is properly preceded by a great steaming tureen of oyster stew, a candle-lighted mountain crowned with crisp raw vegetables, pickles and relishes. There should be relays of hot rolls as well as sea biscuits and Trenton crackers. A big bowl of grapes and ripe persimmons interspersed with Christmas balls!

Tureen of Oyster Stew
Heated Sea Biscuits au Gratin
Candlelight Mountain of Raw Vegetables, Pickles
and Relishes
Relays of Hot Rolls
Buche de Noel   Grapes and Persimmons

TUREEN OF OYSTER STEW . . . To serve 4, prepare 2 cans frozen oyster stew according to directions, but add 1 cup fresh, canned or frozen oysters or clams and ½ cup white wine (optional). Float on the tureen or in each bowl, 1 tablespoon butter for each. Sprinkle with chopped chives and paprika.

HEATED SEA BISCUITS AU GRATIN . . . Brush large sea biscuits with melted butter and sprinkle with grated cheese. Set in the oven just long enough for the cheese to melt. Serve piping hot.

CANDLELIGHT MOUNTAIN . . . Set a candle in its holder in a shallow bowl or a deep platter. Around the candle make a pyramid of crushed ice. Arrange in rows on the ice, crisp raw vegetables such as radish roses, carrot and celery curls, pickles, olives (black and green), spiced crab apples. Garland the base with greenery and stubby votive candles. Light the candles.

BUCHE DE NOEL . . . To make a party-size log to serve 10 or 12, set close together on a long tray or platter, 2 jelly rolls or chocolate rolls. Cover with mocha frosting made from a packaged mix. Or use . . .

MIRACULOUS CHOCOLATE FROSTING . . . Melt over very low heat or hot water, two 6-ounce packages semisweet chocolate pieces. Stir in 1 teaspoon instant coffee, 1 teaspoon vanilla, 1 teaspoon almond extract. Add 2 cups commercial sour cream. This makes a luxuriant amount of frosting, enough to spread an inch deep over the log. Make swirls and appropriate log-like markings with a fork. Sprinkle lightly with sugar to represent snow clinging to the bark. Garnish with sprays of holly.

III. CHRISTMAS BREAKFAST

Silver-Spangled Grapefruit
Broiled Ham Slices
Baked Eggs in English Muffin Shells
More English Muffins, Plain-Toasted and Buttered
Cinnamon Candy Jelly
Large Cups of Coffee or Tea

SILVER-SPANGLED GRAPEFRUIT . . . Cut grapefruits in halves. Scoop out the fruit in sections. Sweeten with a little honey and add, for each grapefruit, a tablespoon of sherry (optional). Paint grapefruit rims with a little honey. Place each half cut-side-down on a saucer covered with ⅓ cup granulated sugar made verdant with 3 drops green coloring. Refill the shells adding orange or cubed apple sections if fruit looks skimpy. Dot the green rim with silver candies and garnish with cranberries cut to look like flowers.

BAKED EGGS IN ENGLISH MUFFIN SHELLS . . . Tear English muffins in half with a fork. Scoop out soft centers. Drop an egg into each one. Season with salt, pepper and a couple of drops of *Worcestershire*. Bake in moderate oven (350°) 6 to 8 minutes or until set.

YOUR OWN CINNAMON CANDY JELLY . . . In a large saucepan place a quart of sweet apple cider or apple juice. Add 2 tablespoons red cinnamon candies and 1 box powdered fruit pectin. Mix well. Place over high heat, stir until mixture comes to a hard boil. Then all at once, dump in 4½ cups sugar. Bring to a full rolling boil. Boil hard 1 minute stirring constantly. Remove from heat, skim off foam, pour into 8 jelly glasses. Cover with ⅛ inch melted paraffin. For gifts, decorate paraffin with silver dragées and red cinnamon candies.

IV. CHRISTMAS DINNER

Must a Fast Gourmet admit defeat—cry "auntie" when the time arrives to set a full-scale holiday dinner on the table? We say no. Especially because holiday birds (turkey and ducks as well as chickens) can now be bought even in small towns and along the highways . . . hot and brown off the turning spits.

In this menu, we glaze the festive bird with melted currant jelly. Serve it encircled by a Della Robbia wreath of lemon or huckleberry leaves studded with love apples and cranberries or tiny marzipan fruits. The joy of having a wreath rather than the usual garnishment . . . you lift it off in one piece. Carve with ease.

If you want to add the splendor of your own home baking to the menu (or bake a gift for a special person) do try Wisconsin Whiskey Wafers. Our recipe was developed from one that a pretty young schoolteacher-bride brought in her steamer trunk from Germany a hundred years ago.

Madrilene with Goldfish Croutons
Glazed Birds in a Della Robbia Wreath
Rice and Pecan Dressing
Red Cabbage with Chestnuts
Avocado and Grapefruit Salad
Orange Sherbet   Wisconsin Whiskey Wafers

MADRILENE WITH GOLDFISH CROUTONS . . . One Bright-Eyed Young Thing serves canned consommé Madrilene from a goldfish bowl . . . garnished with the new-style croutons shaped like goldfish that can now be bought in plastic bags all over the country.

GLAZED BIRD IN A DELLA ROBBIA WREATH . . . Reheat a barbecued bird in heavy foil in a hot oven (400°), 5 minutes to the pound. Meanwhile, add 2 tablespoons sherry, vermouth or orange juice to 1 cup currant jelly. Heat until melted. Brush bird with melted jelly and allow to glaze in the hot oven or *low* under the broiler 5 minutes longer.

RICE AND PECAN DRESSING . . . To 2 cups packaged pre-cooked rice, add 2 cups chicken broth, ¼ cup onion, finely chopped, 1 tablespoon dehydrated parsley, 2 tablespoons butter, 1 teaspoon salt, ¼ teaspoon pepper, a few grains of cayenne pepper. Bring to a boil. Cover and allow to stand 10 minutes. Then add 4 tablespoons heavy cream, heated, and 1 cup chopped pecans. This may be used to stuff a bird or may be served separately.

RED CABBAGE WITH CHESTNUTS . . . To 2 jars sweet and sour red cabbage, add 2 tablespoons butter, ¼ teaspoon ground cloves. Heat and serve sprinkled with cooked, canned or roasted chestnuts that have been broken into bits.

WISCONSIN WHISKEY WAFERS . . . Beat 4 tablespoons soft butter until very creamy, adding gradually 4 tablespoons sugar, then, bit by bit, ½ cup sifted or instantized flour and 2 tablespoons whiskey. Beat just long enough to blend. Drop by tiny dabs 2 inches apart on ungreased cookie sheets. Bake in a moderately hot oven (375°) 5 to 6 minutes until a thin rim of gold appears around the edges; tops will be pale. Place a pinch of cinnamon in the center of each. Allow to cool slightly. Remove with spatula. Makes 4 dozen.

V. FOURTH OF JULY

On the Fourth of July, in Chatham, Massachusetts, the annual Strawberry Festival is celebrated and strawberry shortcake reigns supreme. Needless to say, this shortcake is made with biscuits, for in Chatham cake is an outrage, a travesty, a felony.

Should the shortcake be family-size or individual, square or round, the cream plain or whipped? Answers depend on where and whom you ask.

Many will admit privately, however, that a right-honest-looking and tasting shortcake can, in this day and age, be achieved without the old bother of sifting "your flour and baking powder 4 times together." Some of the best of Chatham's shortcake mistresses use a popular packaged biscuit mix which now comes pre-measured in 1-cup packets. Even faster are ready-to-bake biscuits; fastest are quick-frozen. All should be brushed before baking or heating with soft butter or heavy cream and may also be lightly sprinkled with sugar.

This is a typical strawberry festival season supper. The shortcake is the belle of the meal, so the rest of the menu must be light.

Chatham Chowder   Sea Toast
Dill Pickles   Celery   Olives   Radishes   Spring Onions
Honest Strawberry Shortcake

CHATHAM CHOWDER . . . To a 15-ounce can New England-style condensed clam chowder, add 1 soup can milk, 2 tablespoons butter, ½ teaspoon *Worcestershire* sauce. Heat but do not boil. Place Sea Toast in the bottom of a heated bowl or very large soup plate. Ladle the chowder over the cracker and sprinkle with freshly ground black pepper or paprika and chopped chives. Serves 2 for supper.

STRAWBERRY SHORTCAKE . . . To make 1 large or 6 small shortcakes, add to 2 packets or 2 cups biscuit mix 2 tablespoons sugar, ½ cup milk, ¼ cup melted butter or salad oil. Beat 15 strokes. Knead gently 10 times. Pat out half the dough into a round or square pan, dot with bits of butter, pat out the rest of the dough and place on top. Bake 15 to 20 minutes in a hot oven (450°). Have ready a quart of strawberries, sliced or crushed and sweetened. They should be very cold. Split the hot shortcake, spread with more butter, soft but not melted. Put the crushed fruit on the bottom half. Turn the top half upside down and place it on the bottom half. Cover with more crushed berries, then with 1 cup heavy cream, whipped. Top with whole berries. Or omit whipped cream and pass heavy cream in a pitcher.

"Shortcake is never quite right unless served in a soup plate."

VI. HALLOWEEN SUPPER

A scholarly friend who loves good food and enjoys collecting lore about old food customs, has planned a Halloween supper party with more than a touch of sophistication. A simple, economical supper, easy to reproduce in a hurry and well worth copying.

She will start with an unusual pumpkin soup served from a mixing bowl, set dramatically inside a hollowed-out pumpkin shell. By placing the bowl inside the shell, you still have your pumpkin quite untouched . . . to bake in squares or make into a pie.

The main course is a modern day version of Boxty

cakes that were formerly made from one-half raw, grated potatoes and one-half cooked, mashed potatoes. But quick-frozen potato pancakes or those made from a packaged mix will do very well. And the old rhyme still goes: "Boxty on the griddle, Boxty on the pan, if you don't eat Boxty, you'll never get your man."

Pumpkin Soup in a Pumpkin Shell
Boxty Cakes
Frizzled Ham
Iceland Salad
Applesauce with Lime   Soul Cakes

PUMPKIN SOUP IN A PUMPKIN SHELL . . . For 6 servings, cover 1 package quick-frozen cooked pumpkin or squash (the same thing botanically) with 1 quart hot water. Add 1 can condensed gumbo Creole soup, 1 can condensed consommé. Heat until pumpkin is completely thawed and the soup bubbly-hot. Season with 1 teaspoon curry powder. Garnish with croutons of toasted bread brushed with garlic butter.

BOXTY CAKES . . . Reheat quick-frozen potato pancakes in ¾ inch salad oil at 370° until hot and crusty or drop batter made from a mix into ¾ inch of oil. This method makes cakes more delicate, gives a crispier crust.

FRIZZLED HAM . . . Have boiled or baked ham cut about ¼ inch thick. Heat briefly in hot butter only about 30 seconds on each side.

ICELAND SALAD . . . Combine ½ cup heavy cream or evaporated milk with 2 tablespoons lemon juice, 1 teaspoon sugar, ½ teaspoon salt, ¼ teaspoon pepper. Mix well and pour over shredded iceberg lettuce.

APPLESAUCE WITH LIME . . . To 1 can applesauce, add 3 tablespoons lime juice; sprinkle with grated lime peel.

SOUL CAKES . . . Years ago young people went a-souling—singing for soul cakes before All Soul's Day. Once they were made in the shapes of men and women; later they were round mounds with raisin eyes and noses. A quick, simple way: Make up 2 cups biscuit mix as for drop biscuits, but add 2 tablespoons sugar, 1½ teaspoons cinnamon. Bake according to directions.

VII. HOLY SATURDAY SUPPER AND EASTER SUNDAY BREAKFAST

Greek Bean Soup
Crusty Bread and Rolls
Tray of Cheeses
Tossed Fruit Salad
Creamy Mayonnaise Dressing

GREEK BEAN SOUP . . . Simmer together about 10 minutes 1 can condensed vegetable-bean soup, 1 can condensed tomato soup, 2 soup cans water, 1 to 2 cloves crushed garlic, 2 tablespoons chopped parsley. As a main course serves two.

TOSSED FRUIT SALAD . . . Add 1 package quick-frozen mixed fruits (thawed and drained) to a bowl of mixed greens. Toss at the table with mayonnaise thinned with cream.

On Easter Sunday . . . a delightfully easy repast starring a centerpiece dessert of Show Bread put together instantly from a ready-baked coffee ring and colored Easter Eggs.

Oranges on Forks, Jamaica Style
Baked Ham or Ham Steaks
Red Gravy
Big Hominy
Scrambled Eggs with Chives
Easter Show Bread
Much Coffee

ORANGES ON FORKS . . . Chill oranges and peel with a sharp knife so that fruit is exposed. Into each spear a silver fork or a skewer. Decorate with a perky ribbon bow.

RED GRAVY . . . Scrape crusty bits off pan in which ham has been baked or fried. Add a little hot water and enough cayenne pepper or *Tabasco* sauce to suit your taste. No thickening!

BIG HOMINY . . . Comes in cans looking like snowy-white, soft and tender popcorn. Heat in its own liquid. Drain and serve with butter and a sprinkle of freshly ground pepper.

EASTER SHOW BREAD . . . From the top of a large ready-baked coffee ring scoop 6 or 8 shallow egg-shaped depressions. In each one place a colored Easter Egg.

VIII. HOP-JOHN PARTY FOR NEW YEAR

It is the day after Christmas and in your mind the thought keeps stirring that you ought in some way to pay off some of your holiday social debts. So why not an old-fashioned Hop-John party on New Year's? For briefing on this interesting project, we sent an appeal to Eloise Barksdale, since Hop-John parties are a tradition in her home town of Fort Smith, Ark.

Post haste came help. Eloise went so far as to write us a poem.

> Hopping John in the Southern way
>   should be eaten for Health
> On New Year's Day
>   The recipe handed down to me
> Says this fine dish
>   Brings Prosperity
>
> Boil a fresh hog jowl
>   with some black-eyed peas
> Add rice and red pepper
>   and it's bound to please.

For those of us who might not have immediate access to the jowl of a hog; nor the time to soak and cook the black-eyed peas, we have evolved, with Eloise Barksdale's assistance, a quick and tasty version using canned black-eyed peas and what she calls instant rice. The menu is traditional and unalterable. "Turnip greens and turnips too, cole slaw, corn bread, buttermilk and egg custard pie."

Barksdale Hopping-John
Turnip Greens
Diced White Turnips, Eloise
Cole Slaw
Arkansas Corn Bread
Egg Custard Pie

BARKSDALE HOPPING-JOHN . . . Dice ¼ pound salt pork and fry out until crisp. Add 1½ cups packaged pre-cooked rice, 1 large can black-eyed peas with the liquid and 1 cup water or stock. (There should be about 2 cups of liquid altogether.) Bring to a boil uncovered. Season *quite jauntily* with red pepper or several drops of *Tabasco* sauce as well as freshly ground black pepper. Add salt if it is needed. Stir with a fork. Cover and allow to stand in a warm place about 10 minutes so that the rice will absorb all the rich flavors. Four to 6 servings.

TURNIP GREENS . . . Prepare quick-frozen turnip greens according to directions and add to each package, 2 tablespoons finely-chopped onion which has been browned in a little pork or bacon fat. For the true Southern taste there should be a sting of hot pepper.

DIICED WHITE TURNIPS, ELOISE . . . To serve 6, wash, peel or dice 2 pounds white turnips. (These are milder, cook faster than yellow.) Cook until tender (10 to 15 minutes) in salted, peppered, boiling water in a covered pan. Drain. Fold in ½ cup heavy cream which has been whipped and seasoned delicately with 1 tablespoon lemon juice or rum.

ARKANSAS CORN BREAD . . . Mix and sift together 1 cup cornmeal, 1 cup flour, 3 teaspoons baking powder, 1 teaspoon salt. Add 1 cup milk or buttermilk, 2 eggs, well beaten, 2 tablespoons melted shortening (preferably bacon, ham or sausage drippings). Bake in a shallow well-greased (8 by 8-inch) pan in a hot oven (425°) about 20 minutes and serve in squares.

EGG CUSTARD PIE . . . Follow your grandmother's rule or buy it quick-frozen or from the bake shop. Sprinkle with nutmeg and slivered almonds or coconut.

IX. JEWISH NEW YEAR

In other times and other lands, the feast of *Rosh Hashanah* might well have consumed many hours and even days of preparation. Now these menus can still retain their immemorial flavorings, but instead of being roasted slowly in a bag, the chicken often goes under the broiler. A Carrot *Tzimmes* starts with a can and is cooked speedily on top of the stove instead of slowly, slowly in the oven. Rice is garnished with pine nuts symbolic of riches, but packaged and pre-cooked.

The honeyed baked apples symbolizing fertility and giving a "foretaste of sweetness in a good year to come" ... are also out of a can.

> *Broiled Chicken Rosemary*
> *Rice with Pine Nuts*
> *Quick Carrot Tzimmes*
> *Radish, Cucumber and Scallion Salad*
> *Honeyed Apples   Sponge Cake*
> *Hot Tea in Glasses*

BROILED CHICKEN ROSEMARY . . . Heat together ¼ cup olive oil, 1 teaspoon salt, ¼ teaspoon freshly ground black pepper, 1 teaspoon fresh or ½ teaspoon dried rosemary, ½ teaspoon cumin seed (optional), ½ teaspoon paprika, 1 clove garlic, crushed. Allow to cook 1 or 2 minutes. When slightly cooled, rub the entire surface of a broiling chicken with the herbal oil. Broil slowly about 5 inches below the heat until brown and tender, flesh-side first, then turn and broil skin-side until brown, crispy and done to a turn.

RICE WITH PINE NUTS . . . Prepare 2 cups pre-cooked packaged rice, substituting for the water 2 cups boiled hot beef broth. Add 1 teaspoon curry powder. Garnish with 4 tablespoons pine nuts (often called *pignolias*) heated in 2 tablespoons of olive oil. Serves 4.

QUICK CARROT TZIMMES . . . Drain the liquid from a can of carrots. To this liquid add ¾ cup honey, 1 tablespoon lemon juice. Cook uncovered until reduced to about ½ of its original quantity. Meanwhile, melt 2 tablespoons butter. Off the heat, blend in 2 tablespoons flour. Add the flour and butter to the sauce. Put back on heat; add the carrots. Bring to a boil; simmer 2 minutes longer.

HONEYED APPLES . . . Drain syrup from a can of baked apples. (They usually come in threes.) Combine this syrup with ½ cup hot water, ½ cup honey, 1 cinnamon stick or ½ teaspoon cinnamon. Bring to a boil. Meanwhile place apples in a baking dish. Fill centers with 1 tablespoon chopped walnuts mixed with 1 tablespoon raisins. Pour hot syrup over the apples and heat in a hot oven or on top of the stove in a heavy, covered skillet about 8 minutes or until syrup is bubbly and apples are heated through. Serve warm.

X. MIDSUMMER NIGHT

In all of Sweden on June 21 nobody sleeps . . . or so it seems. Bonfires blaze on all the hillsides. In the little towns, village squares and the paved courtyards on the farms there are tall poles (Maypoles of June) surmounted with hoops of flowers, garlands of leaves.

In many ways Midsummer Night is like our New Year's Eve; except that night never falls. Only for an hour or so between midnight and one in the morning, the land is clothed in a shadowy dusk. Everywhere there is dancing and food. "From six to six!" Six in the evening until six in the morning. At any hour, almost anywhere, in the castle of a count or the house of a workman, you are almost certain to find *kottbullar*, Swedish meat balls.

Usually they are served hot with boiled potatoes and green beans. But particularly on Midsummer Night many people enjoy them cold from the icebox . . . a favorite snack before going to bed, in the blazing, bright, but cool sunshine of the early morning.

Smorgasbord of Appetizers
Swift Swedish Meat Balls
Boiled Potatoes
Frenched Green Beans
Preserved Lingonberries
Melon Fingers and Strawberries

SMORGASBORD . . . The prelude to a Midsummer Night supper (or any lunch or dinner) in Sweden is likely to be a *Smorgasbord*, a cold-cut buffet. Simple or elaborate as you please! Generally there are anchovies, sardines, herring filets set out in their own tins but prettily garnished, pickled beets, cole slaw, smoked or poached salmon, various types of salami, eggs and aspics, canapés, cheeses, several kinds of bread—rye and pumpernickel, always—Swedish "hardtack" or *knockebrod* or rye crisp.

SWIFT SWEDISH MEAT BALLS . . . Every family and every cook, not only in Sweden but all over Scandinavia, has an individual way with meat balls. Some require pork and veal as well as beef. Flavorings and techniques vary, but all have one characteristic in common. They take a lot of time. In this country you can buy very good Swedish meat balls in cans or quick-frozen with sour cream and dill sauce. You can also contrive a delectable facsimile by adding Swedish accents to canned meat balls.

Start with one 15½-ounce can of meat balls in brown gravy or spaghetti sauce. Add ¼ teaspoon allspice, ½ teaspoon *Kitchen Bouquet*, ½ teaspoon dried dill weed or ⅛ teaspoon each crumbled dried basil, marjoram, rosemary, and thyme. Allow to simmer 10 minutes. Just before serving, stir in 4 tablespoons heavy cream. Do not allow to boil after cream has been added. Serves three.

BOILED POTATOES . . . Add 1 tablespoon quick-frozen chopped onions to the water in which you cook your potatoes. Drain and shake over heat so that they are fluffy and dry.

FRENCH GREEN BEANS . . . Use quick-frozen.

PRESERVED LINGONBERRIES . . . If unavailable serve whole berry cranberry sauce or black currant jam into which you have stirred a little lemon juice.

MELON FINGERS AND STRAWBERRIES . . . Cut cantaloupe or honeydew melon into small strips and combine with sliced or whole small berries and serve with wine instead of cream.

XI. PASSOVER

Not only at the *Seder* banquets at the beginning of the Passover season, but at any time, *Charoses* is a joy. It is in fact intended traditionally to symbolize the joy of the ancient Israelites upon their deliverance from bondage. A combination of chopped apples and walnuts, sweetened with honey, livened with cinnamon, dewed with a little wine! Here we have suggested it as a first-course salad.

The meal goes on to sautéed rainbow trout although any other interesting fresh or frozen fish might be substituted. Scalloped potatoes emerge out of a package. The vegetable, in case you are bored with all the usual things, is cucumber sliced and tossed in butter in a way that we learned from Chef Henri Vieilleur at the Hotel Embajador in Santo Domingo.

Charoses Apple and Walnut Salad
Rainbow Trout
Scalloped Potatoes
Cucumbers à la Chef Vieilleur
Lemon Turnovers
Strawberry Sauce

CHAROSES . . . To serve 3 or 4, combine chopped tart, unpeeled red apple, ½ cup finely chopped or ground walnuts, ½ teaspoon cinnamon, 2 teaspoons honey, 2 tablespoons red or white table wine. Mix lightly but thoroughly with a fork. Serve on a lettuce leaf in a sherbet or champagne glass. Garnish with walnut halves. During the Passover season *Charoses* is always served with *matzos*. Egg *matzos* or poppy-seed *matzos* are particularly good. They are now available in markets all year round.

SCALLOPED POTATOES . . . Use packaged scalloped potatoes prepared according to directions. Add a little coarsely ground black pepper.

CUCUMBERS À LA CHEF VIEILLEUR . . . To serve 2 peel and slice a cucumber. Sauté slices quickly in butter —just a couple of minutes. Season with salt and pepper, cover, set aside in a warm place 10 to 15 minutes.

STRAWBERRY SAUCE . . . Heat quick-frozen strawberries that have been almost, but not entirely, thawed.

XII. FEAST OF SHEVOUTH

The Hebrew feast of *Shevouth* celebrates the giving of the Ten Commandments to Moses on Mount Sinai. Down through the ages the festival has assumed various forms. In Persia and in Afghanistan it is called the Feast of Roses and clouds of red rose petals are given to the children to scatter on the *Torah* when it is taken from the Ark. In North Africa rose water is sprinkled on the worshippers in the synagogue.

As in all the feasts of early summer, among all peoples throughout history, dairy foods play an important role. So does the number seven and a cake called Seven Heavens. Modern hostesses now achieve this seven-layer cake without any fuss—no baking either—by using a ready-baked or quick-frozen pound cake and a chocolate frosting that practically makes itself, yet tastes as if it came straight from heaven—or at least Vienna.

Fresh Fruit Cocktail in Grapefruit Baskets
Bulgarian Cheese Omelet   French Fried Potatoes
Garden Peas   Spring Onions   Carrot Sticks
Seven Heavens Cake

BULGARIAN CHEESE OMELET . . . For each person, provide 2 eggs, ¼ cup grated cheese, 1 medium-size tomato. Beat eggs, add cheese. Sauté tomato in a little butter or margarine. Add salt, pepper, a dash of rosemary. Then pour the egg-cheese mixture over the tomato. Cook until omelet is set but still shiny. Turn and cook only a minute longer. Cut into halves or quarters.

FRENCH FRIED POTATOES . . . Use quick-frozen, but ignore heating directions. To make the potatoes taste really crisp and homemade, heat vegetable oil (which should stand at least an inch deep in the pan) to 370°. Drop in the potatoes a handful at a time. Cook about 60 seconds or until crisp and browned, thoroughly hot all the way through. Drain on paper towels. Sprinkle with coarse salt, i.e., kosher salt. If they must be kept hot, do not cover in any way or they will be limp.

SEVEN HEAVENS CAKE . . . With a serrated bread knife, cut a pound cake lengthwise into seven layers if it is a long cake, or crosswise if it is round. Between layers and on top spread this rich and creamy frosting. Melt 1 (6-ounce) package semi-sweet chocolate pieces. Remove from heat. Stir in 1 cup commercial sour cream, add ½ teaspoon instant coffee, ¼ teaspoon cinnamon, 1 teaspoon vanilla or rum flavoring. This cake attains its full glory if it is allowed to stand in the refrigerator at least 12 hours before serving. Serve in very thin slices, for the cake is rich. This recipe makes about 16 servings. Do not fret, it will keep in the refrigerator for at least a week and can, of course, be stored in the freezer almost indefinitely.

XIII. ST. PATRICK'S DAY BREAKFAST

Killarney Raspberry Cocktail
White Stirabout
Irish Bacon and Eggs

Assorted Brown 'n Serve Rolls
Grilled Tomatoes
Honey, Black Currant Jam
Damson Plum Jam
Coffee in Goblets—Irish or Otherwise

KILLARNEY RASPBERRY COCKTAIL . . . Something a little different. Allow 1 package sweetened quick-frozen raspberries to thaw. Press through sieve or whir in electric blender. Serve very cold in highball glasses, adding, at the last moment, a squirt of soda water—four to six servings.

WHITE STIRABOUT . . . That is the Irish way of saying cooked cereal. Serve with dark brown sugar and heated (not boiled) milk.

IRISH BACON . . . If you cannot get Irish use Canadian bacon sliced at least ¼ inch thick. Place in a heavy skillet. Cook over low heat 3 to 5 minutes turning frequently. When done the lean part is a lovely reddish brown, the fat a pale-gold color.

COFFEE IN GOBLETS . . . For Irish Coffee heat stemmed 8-ounce goblets. Place a silver spoon in the glass. Pour in 1 jigger (1½ ounces) Irish Whiskey. Add 3 teaspoons sugar. Almost fill the goblet with strong black coffee. Stir. Top with heavy cream slightly whipped so that it stays on top. "Coffee Otherwise" omits whiskey. It is still a joy to sip the sweet, hot coffee through a little cloud of chilled whipped cream.

XIV. THANKSGIVING DINNER

"How," asked a neighbor smirking sweetly, "are you going to manage a turkey dinner and still keep the promise to your readers that nothing in your book will take more than 30 minutes to cook?"

So glad she asked that question. Had she not heard about the rotisseries on Route 7? There are several of them and poultry shops in Danbury where, with—or often without—notice, you can get turkeys ranging in size from 5 to 20 pounds already roasted and wrapped in foil. All over the country this service is available—even in some dime-store chains. You have nothing to do except set your turkey in a hot oven (400°), just about 5 minutes per pound. To give the skin an appealing crispness, the foil should be slightly opened during the entire sojourn in the oven. Five minutes before the turkey is ready to come on stage, remove the foil entirely.

So that no one need ever know of your time-saving ruses, you might stuff the cooked turkey before heating with this new version of a very old-fashioned stuffing known in our part of Connecticut as Apple Knocker Dressing.

Hot Spiced Cranberry Cup
Rotisserie Turkey
Apple Knocker Dressing
Small Onions in Cream Sauce with Walnuts
Green Peas with Celery
Tomato Aspic Salad
Sneaky Pumpkin Pie

HOT SPICED CRANBERRY CUP . . . To serve 4, heat a quart of cranberry juice with 1 teaspoon whole allspice berries, 2 sticks cinnamon, ¼ cup sugar. Simmer about 10 minutes and serve in small heated mugs.

APPLE KNOCKER DRESSING . . . For a small turkey, use 1 (8-ounce) bag herb-seasoned stuffing. Melt ¼ pound butter. Add 2 cups canned apple sauce, bring to a boil. Add 1 full bag (3 cups) stuffing. Stir over heat another minute or two. Add no other liquid. Pack loosely into the turkey or bake in a shallow buttered pan at 400°— about 8 or 10 minutes or until gently crusted.

SMALL ONIONS IN CREAM SAUCE WITH WALNUTS . . . To serve 4 to 6, use 2 (8-ounce) packages of quick-frozen prepared onions in cream sauce. Heat according to package directions and sprinkle with ¼ cup coarsely chopped walnuts.

GREEN PEAS WITH CELERY . . . These also are quick-frozen ready-to-heat. Prepare according to directions. Sprinkle liberally with chopped, green onion tops or parsley.

TOMATO ASPIC SALAD . . . Use the kind that comes jellied ready-to-slice in a tin.

SNEAKY PUMPKIN PIE . . . Sneaky, because you buy your pie ready-baked and then with a few deft touches, serve it forth redolently oven-warm and bedizened with spice.

Let your store-bought pumpkin pie share the 400-degree oven with the turkey during the last ten minutes. Immediately after removing from the oven, pour on 4 tablespoons slightly warmed rum, *Southern Comfort* liqueur or frozen concentrated orange juice—thawed but not diluted. Sprinkle pie with freshly grated nutmeg. Serve warm.

XV. THANKSGIVING NIGHT SUPPER

Appetite comes with eating. So say the French. And it is an often observed but rarely mentioned fact that your family is likely to be more, rather than less hungry in the evening after a Thanksgiving dinner.

So this is the moment to have a big bowl or tureen of turkey soup, hot bread or rolls, a tossed salad spangled with fresh fruits and, if all the holiday pies are gone, a cosy, steamed pudding, made in your own wily fashion by the simple expedient of heating over hot water a can of date-nut bread.

Perhaps this is the moment to remember that the most delicious soups are made of throw-aways such as the carcass, skin and little bits and pieces of the holiday bird. Best of all and incredibly quick and easy to do if you use a pressure cooker! Any broth you do not use this minute, you can pour into a refrigerator tray, freeze in cubes. Next day, scrape off any fat and store in plastic bags plainly marked. Such cubes of stock are the jewels of a gourmet cook.

Turkey Potage
Citrus Salad   Lakewood Dressing
Toasted Italian Bread
Steamed Date-Nut Pudding
Brown Sugar Hard Sauce

BROTH FROM BONES . . . Place in the pressure cooker the broken-up bones of a turkey (or a duck or a chicken). Add 1 large onion, sliced, 1 carrot, also sliced, a handful of celery tops. Add 3 cups water. Cook under pressure 25 minutes. Bring down pressure immediately or allow it to go down naturally. Strain and season to taste. This is richly concentrated broth.

TURKEY POTAGE . . . This soup may be made from your own concentrated turkey broth (as above), or from canned, condensed turkey noodle soup. To serve 4 heartily, add to 2 cups condensed turkey broth or one 10½-ounce can condensed turkey noodle soup, one 10¾-ounce can condensed cream of vegetable soup, 1 cup water, 1 cup tomato juice, 1 cup cooked turkey, cut into julienne strips and 2 tablespoons chopped parsley. Heat but do not boil. Serve with a spoonful of leftover dressing in each bowl or sprinkle with packaged herb-flavored stuffing.

CITRUS SALAD . . . To a bowl of crisp greens add 1 grapefruit and 2 oranges cut into sections.

LAKEWOOD DRESSING . . . Combine ¼ cup olive or salad oil, 1 tablespoon grapefruit juice, 1 teaspoon vinegar, 4 drops *Tabasco,* ⅛ teaspoon pepper, 1 teaspoon salt, 1 teaspoon celery salt, 1 teaspoon sugar. Mix thoroughly. Add 1 tablespoon finely crumbled Roquefort or blue cheese.

STEAMED DATE-NUT PUDDING . . . Remove date-nut bread from tin. Heat in the top of a double boiler or in a steamer over hot water.

BROWN SUGAR HARD SAUCE . . . Let ⅓ cup butter stand at room temperature till soft but not melted. Cream thoroughly; gradually beat in ⅔ cup light brown sugar. Beat until light as whipped cream. Then add gradually, a little at a time, 2 tablespoons heavy cream. Flavor with 2 tablespoons sherry or orange juice added only a few drops at a time. Beating is important for a perfect Hard Sauce. If by any chance the sauce should separate, add a teaspoon of boiling water, drop by drop and all will be well.

XVI. TWELFTH NIGHT

Twelfth Night (January 6) is the day of the King's Cake, whose history is intertwined with the legends and panoply of Carnival season. In Old New Orleans, a bean or a silver coin was baked into the King's Cake. Whoever found the token reigned at the great Twelfth Night Ball and all the other festivities until the gray dawn of Ash Wednesday.

The Creole King's Cake of New Orleans is a great ring of golden *brioche* . . . light, airy, egg-yellow as a sponge cake. The original recipes are endlessly long and complicated. "Fussy as puff paste, only more so!"

Hallelujah! We have unearthed a *brioche* recipe that is stirred together quick as a cake mix. True, it does take a couple of hours to rise. But requires no attention, no kneading, no rolling. Go off and bustle about your business. Afterwards it bakes almost as fast as a pan of biscuits. So call it *brioche*. Or call it King's Cake. There is nothing more beautiful to serve hot from the oven with coffee or on the Day of the Three Kings . . . with traditional Glee Wine as in St. Louis, long ago.

Salmi of Ham
Julienne Potato Strips
Golden Squash Sprinkled with Walnuts
Celery and Green Pea Salad with Sour Cream Mayonnaise
Glee Wine or Temperance Glee
King's Cake

SALMI OF HAM . . . Melt 1 tablespoon butter. Add 1 tablespoon hot water, ⅔ cup currant jelly, a few grains of cayenne pepper, ½ cup pale, dry sherry or orange juice. Heat and stir until jelly is melted and sauce is smooth. Then stir in 2 cups cold, cooked ham cut into strips. Simmer 5 minutes. Serves 4 or 5.

JULIENNE POTATO STRIPS . . . These come in a can . . . just heat!

CELERY AND GREEN PEA SALAD WITH SOUR CREAM MAYONNAISE . . . Combine 2 cups diced, fresh celery with 1 cup cooked green peas. Serve with Sour Cream Mayonnaise—equal parts mayonnaise and sour cream.

GLEE WINE OR TEMPERANCE GLEE . . . Traditional quaff for Twelfth Night. To serve 4, combine 2 cups water with the juice and slivered rind of 2 lemons, 8 whole cloves, 2 (inch-length) sticks of cinnamon, 3 tablespoons sugar. Bring slowly to a boil. Add 1 quart Claret or any other good red table wine. Heat to just below the boiling point. Serve hot in mugs. For Temperance Glee, use 6 cups cider—no water.

KING'S CAKE . . . Have all the ingredients (sugar, eggs, flour) at warm-room temperature—about 75°. Pour 3 tablespoons warm milk over 2 packages yeast and let stand 10 minutes. Meanwhile, beat 4 tablespoons sugar into 4 eggs. Combine with ½ cup soft butter, 2 cups instantized (or sifted all-purpose) flour, ½ teaspoon salt. Add the yeast mixture to the batter. Beat 3 minutes with a rotary beater. Pour into a greased 9-inch angel food cake pan or ring mold. Cover; allow to rise in a warm place until doubled, about 2 hours. Bake in a very hot oven (450°) about 15 or 20 minutes, or until it shrinks from the pan and your finger leaves no dent.

If it is King's Cake you're making, brush while warm with honey and sprinkle with silver dragées and bright candies. Cut tenderly with an angel food cake server or pull apart with two forks. A knife is deemed a sacrilege.

XVII. WHITSUNDAY WEEKEND

This is a weekend when the skies are expected to smile and it would be a glory to gather the family outdoors for a lobster supper out—here is interesting eating.

Steamed Clams   Lobsters   Deviled Crabs
Potatoes au Gratin
Cole Slaw   Dill Pickles
Indian Pudding or Melon with Lime

STEAMED CLAMS . . . Send the children out clamming or buy "steamers" from the local market; or get a can of steamed clams in the shell packed in clam broth. Each can contains 14 to 20 clams. Heat and serve according to directions.

LOBSTERS . . . If you are not entirely thrilled by the local supply you can order fresh live lobsters shipped from Damariscotta, Maine, in a barrel complete with rockweed and all appurtenances and directions.

DEVILED CRABS . . . Use quick-frozen. Heat according to directions. Just before removing from oven, brush with melted butter or oil and sprinkle with chopped parsley.

POTATOES AU GRATIN . . . Use packaged or quick-frozen according to directions.

INDIAN PUDDING . . . Comes in 1-pound tins under various brand names. Tastes most authentic if you add about ½ cup warm water and allow to heat gently. Serve with milk, plain or whipped cream, or *à la mode* with ice cream, preferably in soup plates.

WHITSUNDAY PICNIC

Barbecued, Broiled or Fried Chicken
Pickled Beets
Macaroni and Cheese Casserole
Fresh Fruits and Berries
Mint Fudge Brownies de Luxe

BARBECUED, BROILED OR FRIED CHICKEN . . . A barbecued chicken from the corner delicatessen sometimes tastes even better cold than it does warm. So does broiled chicken, especially if it has been basted with butter and sprinkled with tarragon or rosemary.

PICKLED BEETS . . . Come in jars or you can make your own.

MACARONI AND CHEESE CASSEROLE . . . Place 2 or 3 packages of quick-frozen macaroni and cheese in a well-buttered casserole. Pour on 1 cup milk. Sprinkle with paprika and heat according to directions.

MINT FUDGE BROWNIES . . . Make them from a new Mint Fudge Brownie mix. As soon as they are removed from the oven, place 16 chocolate peppermint patties on top, return to the oven to soften the patties. As they melt, spread with spatula. You can give much the same mint pattie treatment to ready-baked or frozen brownies.

INDEX

242